£2·50

1

D1621227

FOODMANSHIP

FOODMANSHIP

Robert Charles

SPRINGWOOD BOOKS

© Robert Charles 1977

First published 1977 by
Springwood Books
11 Garrick Street, London

Printed and bound in Great Britain by
REDWOOD BURN LIMITED,
Trowbridge & Esher

0 9059 4755 X

CONTENTS

DRINK

Lurking behind the facades of Meteorological Offices and Weather Bureaux, concealed by serried ranks of silently ponderous equipment, located somewhere within an inner retreat, it is rumoured, is an item of weather forecasting apparatus much used by weather forecasters to forecast weather. Its motivating principle is thought to be sea-weed or elastic bands or some other manifestation of advanced technology.

Any alert and attentive person who happened by chance to stumble upon it might receive the impression that it resembled a small model of a house, for this is what it resembles. There is a door at one end and another door at the other. From the left hand door there comes from time to time a little old husband, and when he is not putting in an appearance a matching little old wife pops out at the other end.

There is an interpretation to be put upon this activity which expert interpretors engaged in making interpretations thereof, interpret as follows: little old man out, little old wife in — set fair: little old man in, little old wife out — storms ahead.

This simple instrument and the signs by which it foretells the weather, operates in full accord with the views society at large holds as to the ideal relative positions of male and female persons occupying houses. In that view the best arrangement is for the male person or husband to be outside and the female or wife person to be inside.

'Husbands — out: wives — in: set fair. Husbands — in: wives — out: storms ahead,' just about sums up society's view.

It is a view with which I am very willing to concur, except that as a work-at-home husband, working at home, I find it difficult to fulfil the demands of that calling without working at home. If the previously mentioned society at large wishes me to operate in some other way, the said s.a.l. can have my personal assurance here and now that I am ready to comply, once it is demonstrated to me how I can carry on my work-at-home regimen without actually working at home.

Furthermore − if that is the word I want, the second third of this equation, the wife who comes out of the door while I stay in, would − it is my understanding from a long study of what she says and does − willingly stay at home if she could be shown how this was compatible with the requirement that she put in an appearance at her office on a daily basis.

The third part of the equation − the home or house − seems to have no particular preference either way.

Now, I cannot answer for the little old man in the weather fore-casting machine. What he gets up to when he is inside his house is his own affair and not mine. I can only speak of my own experience from which it becomes clear that the working-at-home arrangement is not as clearcut as would appear.

'What is work?' society at large wants to know, working round to the idea that if one does not know what the work-at-home person is working at, no alternative scheme is likely to be dreamable up.

Working at home, one discovers, involves not only that work which might ordinarily be done elsewhere, such as writing these pages, but associated work taking the forms of washing, cleaning and cooking. And society-at-large's view being what it is (see above) the idea is spread about that work-at-home husbands in their work-at-home regime are either (a) inferior work-at-home persons, or (b) bone-idle.

Work-at-home husbands who might feel these to be harsh judgments on their chosen way of life can seek to modify the view of s-a-l by demonstrating themselves to be superior work-at-home persons by the superiority of their work-at-home work, or by ceasing to work at home and thereby no longer qualifying as work-at-home husbands.

I have chosen the former course and in evidence offer this book, the central theme of which probably is, but may not be, depending on the way things turn out, that work-at-home husbands cannot be directly compared in the way they operate with work-at-home wives because husbandry and all its works is different from wifery.

To illustrate this theme, we now cut back in time some thirty years.

She was detained at the office. We had friends coming to dinner. The time was 5:30 pm (17:30 in modern parlance). I had two hours in which to get everything ready.

We were living in London. Our flat or apartment occupied the top three floors of a Victorian terrace built in the 1860s to accommodate the rising middleclass. There were 128 steps up from the front door and a further 42 steps to the kitchen, a bleak room beneath the roof. All clear so far?

Opening the living room door a stark gale stung my face. The dim light of the standard lamp revealed snow piling on the carpet round the legs of my armchair. Snow round chair legs is not a friendly, welcoming sight. It suggests the best place to be is elsewhere.

I could see at once what had happened. The window sashes were attached by cords to counter-balancing weights inside the wooden panelling. One of the cords had snapped cancelling the counter-balancing contract, allowing the window frame to drop in its casing. An easterly wind whipped spumes of snow through the opening in a manner characteristic of easterly winds. A drift two feet deep was banked round the fireside table, rising in a steep slope towards the wall.

Fortunately, the room was too cold for the snow to melt. Seeking to return the room to that temperature at which snow normally melts, I knocked the window free with a wooden mallet, pushed it back into place, wedging it with the first item to hand, to wit, one ornamental paper-knife.

I scooped the snow into bowls and dumped the mess in the bath, situated in the bathroom, 12 steps up at the back of the house.

Then I lit the fire, that simple statement being understood to have about it the same heroic ring, as if one had said: 'Then I climbed Everest' or 'Then I went to the South Pole'.

Victorian middleclass persons liked to have plenty of room for swinging cats, the cat-swingability of our living room being ensured by its thirty feet of length and twenty dittoes of width. Cat swinging could be carried on there without, as the saying is, let or hindrance. Letting and hindrancing did not get a look-in.

The fireplace to heat this frosty cavern was as big as a hip bath. It burnt a hundredweight of coal in an evening. This fuel was stored in a bunker outside on the lower terrace, 104 steps down. The only means of bringing it up was in a battered brass scuttle that held 30 lbs at a time. In an ordinary winter evening, one had to leave the blazing fireside to forage in the black wastelands below, four times.

Coal deliveries were a perennial problem. Victorian architects were the original high-risers. Twelve high-rising stone steps rose highly from the pavement to the hallway in which our front door was mounted. Behind the door, a further 24 steps rose in a similar high manner to a small glass conservatory.

Swearing and sweating through the narrow doors, the swearing and sweating coalmen forced their way out to a postage stamp of concrete on which stood the coal bunker.

At each delivery there was a ritual to be repeated.

1. The coalmen would enter the house, survey the assault course and declare the task impossible.

2. The two juniors then left, leaving their senior member a free hand to negotiate.

3. Negotiations got under way.

4. My line was to go for the sympathy vote — outlining the horrifying difficulties of trying to keep a Victorian flat or apartment even marginally warm during the winter while the occupants thereof huddled around a flickering fire that finally flickered its last flicker and went out because of a shortfall in the coal department.

5. His line was that of unfair practices, the said practices imposing on the physical wellbeing and goodwill of imposed upon coalmen already tortured by the symptoms of a recurring hernia.

6. A few coins then passed from my hand to his.

7. As if at a signal, the two juniors returned.

8. Coal deliveries began, all three scampering up and down the staircase like gazelles with the urge.

On the last occasion the coal had been delivered wet. Now it was frozen into a solid mass. In the darkness and swirling snow I chipped at it with a hammer and chisel, confirming a suspicion that hammers and chisels are not to be recommended as implements with which to chip frozen coal. Twenty minutes hard struggle yielded one scuttle load of pieces.

Halfway up the stairs, the handle of the said scuttle came adrift, spilling the said coal down a flight and a half.

Students of coal spillage will be glad to have evidence that in such a situation, replacing the coal carefully lump by lump does not avoid the staining of the stair carpet with vast black stains. They will additionally be glad to learn that applications of soap and water serve only to spread these stains further. Persons intending to take up the mass production of stains for export would be well advised to study my technique of sloshing up and down for more warm water from the heater in the bathroom. Layers of black foam roughly describes the result.

There was still the fire to light, the approved technique for which required no skill whatever. Coal was piled in the massive hearth and a gas poker thrust into it. Lighting the gas poker was achieved by turning on the gas tap and applying a lighted match to the end where the gas came out. (I am assuming you can cope with the business of lighting a match without any directions from me.) The gas poker flares and continues to flare until the coal is able to flare on its own at which point the gas poker flare can be terminated until further notice.

Time was passing in the way time has, and I had not even begun to prepare the meal. I climbed to the kitchen (a bleak room under the roof), attempting to impose on my mind that philosophical calm that should precede all cooking.

Calm comes from calmness and the notion or concept of such a condition, viz., calm, is not advanced if there are water heaters in the locality. Water heaters, one finds, exude — if that is the word — the very opposite of calmness.

Water heaters work by the application of water pressure, itself not essentially a calm thing. When the tap above the kitchen sink marked 'hot' was turned on, in theory the previously noted pressure (water) opened a gas valve which a pilot light ignited. Cold water gurgled round inside a coiled pipe against which flames from the burning gas curled. When it had gurgled its last gurgle and coiled round the last coil, the water splashed out at the nether end, theoretically hot.

Unfortunately, dishes cannot be washed in theoretically hot water. Actually hot is the stuff required.

But, at the top of the house on a winter's night, the pressure was too low. The gas valve stayed locked solidly shut and the pilot light, baffled and frustrated, had nothing to ignite.

Some work with a fork and hairpin transferred the bafflement and frustration to myself, ignition being put back to some unspecified time. I retired, defeated, to begin the trimming of the vegetables with numb hands, the sensation being of fingers operated by rusty wires. They were as nimble as petrified twigs.

In ordinary circs. when vegetable trimming is underway, the fingers send swift messages to the thumbs reporting what they are about, and thumbs, being obliging chaps, return the compliment. But, with rusty wires invading the message transmitting departments, messages go astray or are not sent because fingers have forgotten. Thumbs twitch and curl, not knowing what the fingers are about, while the fingers grasp and ungrasp without any clear idea of movements at the thumb end of things.

This lack of coordination caused a finger to ungrasp when it should have grasped, a thumb to twitch when curling would have been more in order, and before grasping and curling could be set in motion the gas stove was alight together with the fat in the frying pan.

Those who know about fat catching alight in frying pans know that the classic remedy is to smother the blaze with a wet cloth. Such a cloth was hanging on the line above the draining board. I used it. What those who know about blazing fat do not know, and which I only realised at the instant of dousing was that the cloth in question was my freshly washed shirt for that evening.

Sourness and dark cannot for ever prevail over the forces of sweetness and light. Before long, with the fire below ablaze and things in the oven, progress, it could be reported, was being made. But, the living room still had about it that iciness that one associates with tombs. Nor was I confident that the ornamental paper-knife would stay firm. The staircase was a mess, likewise the bathroom.

The door bell rang. Normally late, our guests were early. Halfway changed into a suit for the evening, I was not in that state of elegant attire that generally is the requirement for hosts when they are called upon to dash down flights of stairs and open up for guests. I went to one of the windows that was still working as windows should, shouted a greeting down through the snow-swirling night and tossed the front door key down to them. It fell with deft accuracy straight through the grill of a drain cover.

Hosts cannot leave guests to a frost-bitten fate, no matter how imperfectly dressed. I took a dressing gown — hers, as it turned out — and clattered down the 128 steps to let them in. They were crouched on their knees in the snow trying to fish the key from the drain. I went to help. The front door slammed behind me.

Just then, she arrived. And for the first time ever, she had forgotten her own front door key . . . .

Here the script decently draws a veil over the next few moments, and cuts forward to a close-up of me sucking the blood from fingers that had been gashed during the glass-breaking episode in which I had broken the front door glass to regain access to the premises, or flat (apartment).

My mind began to mull over the immediate steps to be taken to remedy the social chill generated by this chain of — what is the word I want? Disasters — that's the word. As I led the way up the 128 steps with her snow-soaked dressing gown flapping dismally about my knees like a Requiem for Nether Limbs, the front lobes of my mind chattering with desperate good cheer — if that is what front lobes do, the rest of my mental capacity began to marshall the facts. Stairs a battle field, a refrigerated living room, a chaos of clothes to be hastily concealed behind closet doors, not to mention the prospect of furtive, whispered explanations to her while so doing.

'Brumal' was the word that just about summed up the situation. To which could be added: 'Gelid'.

The guests climbing up the 128 steps behind me were not the sort of guests with whom one could pass off such a situation as a giggle. Gigglesomeness was the very last item in their life style. Nothing at their flat was ever more than a hair wisp out of place, and flies needed entry permits and seldom got them. Such persons arriving for a dinner invitation expect as a natural consequence of their arrival that a certain sequence of events will ensue. To their view, it is the natural obligation of a host to get on with the ensuing side of the contract. And, once they were settled in the icy embrace of the armchairs, there would be no more than six or seven minutes of brisk ensuing to produce item one on the dinner agenda, to wit, namely and viz., drinks.

Mentally, I pushed wifery to one side and brought husbandry up into the firing line. 'What,' I asked, 'did husbandry suggest?' Husbandry did a swift scan across the available material and came up with Professor Schiff. (You've never heard of Professor Schiff? Then, it is high time that omission was remedied.)

According to Professor Schiff — the same chap — two mental functions distinguish man from other species: his taste for games of chance, and for fermented beverages.

Pure chance may have resulted in man's discovery of booze (variation of bouse — alcoholic drink, also a carouse). Spontaneous fermentation of grapes, apples, oranges and pineapples can produce something drinkable. This is also true of coconut milk. Man — by which one means one of those early man type men — probably, or possibly one means possibly, left quantities of the said grapes, apples, oranges and pineapples lying about the place surplus to requirements and when, they having ceased to be surplus, he returned to pick up supplies, he found the juices had turned into something other than what the said juices had been before. Man, or it may even have been a woman, had a quick suck and found it was a lollapalooza. And thus was a dynasty founded.

For mankind's need of stimulating drink proved to be universal. Recognising a good thing when he saw it, man did not intend to give it up. Neither, for that matter, did woman. At all subsequent times, in all subsequent ages, whenever the going got rough, man saw things through with a quick belt of the hard stuff.

Depending where he lived man — the same chap or chaps — could produce the necessary from the fermentation of fruits or the distillation of grains. Some remote tribes, lacking both fruits and grains, had to resort to what must go down in the record as 'desperate remedies'. The women folk sat round a pot chewing sweet potatoes and spitting the resulting mash into it. The ptyalin in their saliva acted as a fermenting agent producing a rough and ready drink. The kind of drink womenfolk are going to need if their menfolk set them to sitting round pots, chewing sweet potatoes all the time.

Illumination is beginning to illumine. The basis for dealing with stage one of the domestic crisis is beginning to emerge from the mists. What is needed is something liquid, alcoholic, and for preference — warm. Here follows the first lesson in good husbandry. It is called — Crisis Punch.

There is one commodity without which no well-stocked household should ever be. Yet, w-s h's all over the place when they come to have their well-stockedness put to the test, are found, in this particular department to be lacking. The substance which they lack is cider.

Nothing you might think is more available than cider. Apples seem to yield up buckets of it. Yet several leading British cook books make no mention of it at all, despite the groaning acres (or hectares) of groaning apple trees, groaning outside their kitchen windows. One grudgingly refers to a 'cider ice' and a wishy-washy cider sauce. Another can muster no more interest than a palid cider jelly. Is this the stuff, one wishes to ask, that British cook bookers were brought up on?

The French are just as resistant to the joys of cider. Rumour has it, that it is used in Norman cooking, but those Normans are rude chaps, and the substance most often in use in their cuisine is Calvados, a cider brandy that would have put early man (with whom is coupled early woman) down the drain more rapidly than an overflow of waterfalls.

Anyone would think cider had no respectable ancestry, an upstart in the drink cabinet trying to muscle in and rub shoulders with its more venerable relations.

No one knows where and when cider began. It may have been here, maybe there, perhaps then, or even earlier. No one knows. The name derives from the Hebrew word 'shekar', meaning strong drink, which shows those Hebrews knew what was what. The Greeks and Romans certainly sloshed the stuff down. It is mentioned in the Chronicles of Charlemagne. Records show it was being brewed and guzzled in Normandy in the thirteenth century.

One possible reason for the prejudice against cider may stem from its odd habit of turning black when cooked in iron or tin-iron utensils. But w-s h's today seldom dabble in iron or tin-iron, preferring — as in my case — cast aluminium and stainless steel dittoes. Cider can be cooked in these without any blackening. Enamelled and porcelain-lined pans are also safe.

The first ingredient for our Crisis Punch, then, is cider. But, before we proceed, a word about Punch. This is a type of drink said to have originated among English sailors somewhere about 1552 (one has to say 'about', because nobody was then counting). The essential makings were cane spirit and sugar, mixed and served warm — what we might now call a rum toddy. From this humble start it grew to become the drink for the grand occasion, than which none was grander than the shindig thrown by Commander-in-Chief of the British Navy Sir Edward Kennel on October 25, 1599. The centre piece of this bust-up was a monster punch made in a marble basin the size of a swimming pool. Into this was tipped — 80 casks of brandy, 9 of water, 25000 large limes, 80 pints of lemon juice, 1300 lbs of sugar, 5 lbs of nutmeg, 300 biscuits and a large cask of Malaga — a sweet wine from Andalucia.

A canopy was constructed across the basin, or swimming pool, to protect the brew from the rain. The serving was done by a ship's boy who sailed about on this alcoholic sea in a rosewood boat. Serving the 6000 guests took time, and the fumes rising from the surface were so potent that no boy could last for more than fifteen minutes. Volunteer replacements, it is reported, were queueing up to get in on the act.

Modern punches do not have to be based on either rum or brandy. Cider is cheaper and less heady. And you can add almost anything to it — port, red or white wine, fruit juices, spices.

On that dark night I came panting up to the kitchen (still a pretty bleak room under the roof) and settled down to punch brewing. I poured two flagons of cider into my largest pot and put this to heat on the stove. The well-stocked drink cupboard yielded up the remains of a bottle of Red Cinzano. Four wine glasses of this went into the hot cider — and one glass into me, just for encouragement. (I could equally have used White Cinzano, Red or White St. Raphael, Dubonnet or White Lillet Frère — the Red Lillet, for my taste, is a little sharp.

Further rummaging brought forth an ancient jar at the bottom of which was a quantity of age-hardened black molasses. Smart work with a spoon, twirling it in the turgid glup, transferred two tablespoons of the stuff.

With punch, it is of the essence to taste as you go. I like my punches on the sweet side, ladling in treacle, the darkest brown sugar, or even honey. Ordinary white sugar will do for persons of low discrimination.

The selection in my spice rack that night was not of a range which accords with the variety of life. Punch asks for nutmeg and cinnamon. In addition I had ginger, powdered cloves, mace, thyme, rosemary, basil and chervil. Sniffing each in turn, I popped in a pinch or two of mace and a handful of dried rosemary.

From some previous culinary escapade there were four fresh limes, although how they had remained fresh escapes me. I squeezed the juice from these and then grated what in lemons is, I am told, termed the zest, but in limes may be dubbed almost anything, namely, the skins, removing just the surface and not the pith beneath.

With all the ingredients in, the punch was becoming hot, but not so hot that it could not be drained at a draught without skinning the interior organs of the drainer thereof. Punches may be pulled, but never boiled. When water boils the oxygen it contains is driven off, taking with it the freshness of its natural taste. A boiled punch is robbed of its essential sockeroo.

Guests with a passion for tidiness are apt to be put off at the sight of an untidy punch. 'An untidy punch means an untidy mind,' about sums up their view as they cross off untidy households from their visiting list. It is the obligation of even the untidiest host to do his best by tidying up his punch with some judicious work with a strainer, taking out the bits and pieces of rind and herb leaf.

Entering the living room I could tell at a glance that the ambient temperature was moving toward the level at which Eskimoes and Polar Bears turn frolicsome. Our visitors had begun to remove their sheep skin top coats, woolly mittens, ditto hats and even their ditto scarves. Serving the hot punch, I thought it safe to regale them with Benjamin Franklin's thoughts on the use of apples. 'What you have told us is all very good. It is indeed bad to eat apples. It is better to make them all into cider.'

I was able to report that much attention had been paid to this sensible advice. Cider can now be obtained almost anywhere. It is brewed in the United Kingdom, Northern France, Switzerland, Germany and Spain. In the US of A the term 'cider' is used to indicate unfermented apple juice. The alcoholic version is known as 'hard cider'.

It is a painful experience for a speaker, when his speaking is in full spate, to observe that the activity is not getting across to his audience. This now was my painful experience. So far as our guests were concerned swathes of invisible sound absorbing material were interposed between me and them, dutifully absorbing all sound. They gave the impression of Eskimoes who had abandoned all thoughts of frolicsomeness in favour of a silent squat round an ice-hole morosely contemplating the unlikely possibility of securing a bite.

Bringing Eskimoes round to look on the bright side of life is not an easy task. Sweetness and light, in their view, is pretty much in short supply. 'Show us life,' they grunt from a squatting position, 'and we'll show you something not worth bothering too much about.' So that if activities and attitudes more in the way of jumping with joy and gambolling about with reckless abandon is what you have in mind as the theme of an evening's entertainment, something more than the punch remedy will have to be contemplated. Like coffee.

'Coffee?' you ask.

Yes, coffee.

There was an Arab person (male), I told them, variously described as a Mullah or priest. When he was not Mullahing or priesting, he may have been a simple goatherd. One does not know. His name is said to have been Chadely, Scyadly or Kaldi. Finding himself overcome by sleep in the middle of his prayers, it being the stipulation that the said prayers be uttered in the dark watches of the night, he — the goatherd chap — noted that when his goats fed on the berries of a certain small shrub, they remained awake all night, chatting as is goat's wont, and — note this carefully — jumping with what seemed like joy and gambolling with something uncannily like reckless abandon.

Not too many persons would place all that value on the discrimination of goats. But this chap did. 'Show me a goat,' it was his wont to grunt between prayers, 'and I will show you a brother under the skin or hide.'

He tried a few of the said berries himself and in a pretty short while was wide awake, jumping and gambolling with the rest. It was not long before other Arab persons who enjoyed a good jump or gambol when they could get one were crowding round for supplies of berries.

Now, it is one thing to be a goat, with a goat's liking for crunching anything crunchable. Even for Arab persons a diet of munched raw coffee beans or berries was a bit hard on the stomach (Arab). And the next thing one hears is that berries of the kind indicated were being covered with boiling water and the infusion drunk. Despite this improvement not everybody was agreed that the drink was a good thing, for the Arab name for the beverage 'kahwah' or 'qahweh' means 'bitter taste'.

However, coffee caught on. In smart Arab circles it was served to guests as a symbol of welcome. Bedouins, should you happen to drop by their tents in passing, would serve just enough coffee for four sips at a time. Should they pour you a full cup, the message was: 'Drink thou and depart'.

By 1511, there were more people going to Mecca for the coffee than the mosques. The coffee house idea spread to Cairo. Then to Europe. Even, some claim, the bard Shakespeare got to hear about it and incorporated it in some of his later barding.

The bardery in question pops up in Act I, Scene 2, Line 334 of 'The Tempest', at which point Caliban announces 'I must eat my dinner' and carries on before anyone can interpolate a quick 'So what!'

> ' . . . . . . wouldst give me
> Water with berries in't; and teach me how
> To name the bigger light, and how the less,
> That burn by day and night . . . . . .'

Having informed the above Caliban that the answers to his two queries are (a) Sun, and (b) Moon, anyone wishing to construe the adjacent words into a description of the potent powers of coffee is welcome to do so. Further evidence may be gleaned from the preceding speech by Prospero, who gloats:

> 'For this, be sure, to-night thou shalt have cramps,
> Side-stitches that shall pen thy breath up; urchins
> Shall forth at vast of night that they may work
> All exercise on thee: thou shalt be pinch'd
> As thick as honeycomb, each pinch more stinging
> Than bees that made them.'

If coffee has this effect on your stomach, you may consider the case proved. And, if proved, should you be drinking the stuff? What was good enough for Kaldi's goats might not be up to scratch for persons of sensibility and breeding.

Coffee is a stimulant. It pokes a stick in the brain and whirls up the contents. If you do not wish for these effects, there is not much point in drinking coffee.

'Why do we drink coffee?' I asked.

'Why, indeed,' just about summed up their view.

It is not an aid to digestion, I went on. And man is the only creature to take in solids and liquids at the same time, this causing undue confusion in the digestive department.

'Ah, solids,' mutters the stomach as edibles of that nature come tumbling down the pipe-line. The machinery is set in motion for dealing with solids. When everything is under way sudden ominous splashings disturb the routine.

'Oh, hell,' mutters the stomach. 'Liquids. I thought it was the other stuff.'

The machinery is switched from dealing with solids to coping with liquids. Another rumble is heard.

'Why can't he make up his ruddy mind!' growls the stomach, switches off, turns over and goes back to slumber, in which horrible nightmares cause him to twitch.

The plight of the said stomach, I went on, would be bad enough if after meals consisting largely of solids he had dumped in his lap dosings of watered wine or beer. But, what it has to put up with most of the time is wishy-washy coffee, poured down on the supposition that if eating has made you sleepy and sluggish, coffee will buck you up again. Except that, as you don't want to be too much bucked up in case you get a chance for a snooze, the coffee is made as weak as practicable without preventing it being actually identified as coffee.

The point is made in a Punch cartoon of the year 1902: '. . . and if this is coffee, I want tea; but if this is tea, then I wish for coffee.'

Good husbandry persons know that the only way to take coffee is strong and full flavoured. There are four ways of doing this: by boiling, steeping, percolating or filtering. (Instant coffee was invented by a certain G. Washington — no, not *that* G. Washington — but an Englishman living in Guatemala in 1906. But, we don't talk about that!)

Boiling and steeping are the simplest, but boiling gives the coffee an unpleasantly sharp taste. This is the method by which coffee bean oil is extracted to be used in the manufacture of soap, paint, lacquer, insecticides and shoe-polish. So, if you don't want your interior washed, decorated, polished or cleared of creepy-crawlies, don't do it.

Percolating is the most economical. Filtering gives the best flavour, provided you can find ways of keeping the brew warm, but is expensive. For both these last two methods, and variations of them such as espresso coffee in which hot water is forced through ground coffee under pressure, there are many ingenious machines on sale.

Asked to choose, the good husbandry person would, I think, plump for percolation. Not only is the extraction efficiency high, but the rapid 'plop-plop-plop' of the machine in operation is very soothing. The stomach, if consulted, gives the thumbs up to the percolator.

To which the natural accompaniment is the wail of an electric coffee grinder, the said wail being modelled on that of the wilder type of dervish who sees infidels on the horizon.

Familiarity, it is said, breeds contempt, and those who seek to hold back their contempt of coffee to at least an arm's length would be well advised to cut down on the familiarity aspect. For such persons the required items are, one decent-sized jug, and one nylon strainer, not forgetting four heaped tablespoons of medium grind coffee for each pint of water (or make that seven tablespoons per litre, if you happen to be litre-minded). As soon as the water is boiling, pour it straight on the coffee and do not heat again. Let the coffee steep for three or four minutes. Then serve it directly into the cups, remembering to pour through the strainer (nylon).

Never adulterate good coffee with boiled or warm milk. A little cold ditto will do no harm. But, if you wish to preserve the flavour, use cream.

For sweetening: dark brown sugar. Or, try a teaspoon of honey.

'I don't like coffee,' said one of our guests.

'In that case,' I said, 'it might be interesting to examine why it is that we do not drink cocoa more often.'

'I can't stand . . .' one of our guests was going to say. But, I cut in. One can't allow guests to have everything their own way.

The story begins more than 3000 years ago. The Mayas, Toltecs and Aztecs of South America regularly consumed a drink made from the seed of a tree called 'xocoatl' — so named from the Nahuatl words meaning 'bitter water'. Columbus brought back specimens of these seeds to Spain in 1494, but they were not thought then to be of any value. Cutting forward some sixty years, we find Drake's sturdy sailors chucking the stuff overboard. 'Worthless,' just about summed up their view of the seeds.

Meanwhile, the Spanish, taking notes of current activities in the South American scene, had noted that at Montezuma's Court about 50 large jars of the drink were consumed each day.

'What ho!' said the Spanish note-takers, or whatever it is of an equivalent meaning that Spanish note-takers say. 'This needs looking into.'

'Stout' Cortes was one of those who got on with the looking-into side of the operation and reported that the tree was widely grown in Mexico. When, in 1519, he brought further supplies of the seeds to Spain, the grandees began to prepare a drink from them using the Aztec recipe. Its name at this time, as noted by the Spanish note-takers, was 'chocolatl' so there had not been much movement in that department during the preceding two and a half millenia.

Spanish note-takers are noted for their tendency to keep the notes they have taken close to their chest. They are not keen on non-note-takers having access thereto. So, up to this point the drink and its preparation were a closely guarded secret. But, as is the way with liquids, it leaked out, first to Italy, then it spread to the rest of Europe. By the time it spread to England in 1650, give or take, it had come to be called Chocolate. And thereby hangs a tale of which the note-takers had not taken note.

The Mexican drink 'chocolatl' was prepared from the seeds of the 'cacanatl' tree. This name came to be shortened to 'cacao'. All clear so far?

There was, and still is, another Mexican word 'cocoa' — and in one of its meanings it refers to a type of ugly mask worn to frighten children. These masks were often in the shape of a monkey's face. The base of the cacao seed husk is wrinkled and thought to resemble a monkey's face. At some time it seems to have struck somebody that it would be a pleasant wheeze to reverse the vowel order of the word 'cacao' and so tie in the seed husks with monkey-face masks. So, when you now ask for a cup of cocoa, what you are asking for is a dish of monkey-faces.

An interesting distinction needs to be made here between chocolate and the other drinks — coffee — and tea, which I have not yet talked about.

'Oh, god,' said one of our guests.

Both the latter are stimulants, I said, whereas chocolate, or cocoa, is more a liquid food with important nutritional ingredients; it contains 17% nitrogenous matter, 25.5% fats and 38% carbohydrates, the remaining 19.5% being not worth mentioning.

'Chocolate is one of the most effective restoratives' wrote Anthelme Brillat-Savarin, the French gastronomist, sipping a mug of the stuff as he wrote. 'All those who have to work when they might be sleeping, men of wit who feel temporarily deprived of their powers, those who find the weather oppressive, time dragging, the atmosphere depressing; those who are tormented by some preoccupation which deprives them of the liberty of thought; let all such men imbibe a half-litre of chocolat ambré.'

Any modern person taking such a remedy might find himself suddenly yearning for the good old days of deprived powers, oppressive weather, dragging time, depressing atmospheres, and tormenting preoccupations. For the 'ambré' to which the said Brillat-Savarin alludes is ambre gris, an intestinal secretion (if you will pardon the language) of the sperm whale.

Sperm whales, whenever they have something they feel they would like to get rid of, get rid of it in the form of ambre gris. It is to be found, if you want to look, floating on the surface of Far Eastern waters. It is wax-like, covered with yellow and black spots and has a strong smell.

The recipe for its use in chocolate is given by Brillat-Savarin – '. . . when I get one of those days when the weight of age makes itself felt – a painful thought – or when one feels oppressed by an unknown force, I add a knob of ambergris the size of a bean, pounded with sugar, to a strong cup of chocolate, and I always find my condition improving marvellously. The burden of life becomes lighter, thought flows with ease and I do not suffer from insomnia . . .'

Another remedy, one would have liked to suggest, would be to give up the practice of gastronomy, this apparently giving rise to the weight of age making itself felt, oppression by unknown forces and the burden of life.

'I thought cocoa was just for ordinary people,' said one of our guests.

'Not at all,' I said. 'The true opiate of the people is tea.'

The discovery of which, I went on, leads one into another of those ancient narratives of remarkable implausibility. Imagine yourself to be

out on a picnic, pausing by some wayside trees, lighting a pleasant little camp fire on which to cook a meal, and while you are doing this, leaves from the above noted trees drift down into your cooking pot of hot water. What do you do? Any sensible person would scoop them out, as it might be with a wooden spoon or other picnic utensil, or throw away the water and start again.

Not so the unnamed Chinese philosopher who, some 4000 years back, give or take, found himself confronted with exactly this predicament, viz., pots cooking, water boiling, leaves in.

Admittedly, allowances must be made for philosophers. Opportunities for the practice of a little philosophising on the side are thin on the ground. No chance can be allowed to pass by. Leaves in hot water may not sound like much of an opening, but philosophers cannot be choosers. They must take what comes.

This chap (still unnamed) fell to a little philosophising on the nature of leaves, the nature of falling, the nature of hot water — you know the kind of thing philosophers get up to, during the course of which he noted a delicious aroma arising from the said hot water. Contravening every health regulation ever invented — but then, if you are a philosopher you can get away with murder — he dipped in his spoon, or whatever, the details at this point lack clarity — sipped the brew and found it deliciously refreshing. Thus was invented tea.

Because of the high cost of dipping tree leaves in hot water, the English taste for the stuff has often been ruthlessly exploited, by which one means, exploited without the exercise of the least portion of ruth, as witness a report in the *Daily Telegraph and Courier* of 1855. 'Tea is subject to such a variety of insidious arts, that the only wonder is that it should ever escape unharmed. There is first the practice of substituting re-dried tea leaves for the original and virgin specimens. In 1843 there are stated to have been eight manufactures for the purpose of re-drying tea-leaves in London alone. The exhausted leaves were purchased at hotels and coffee houses, and elsewhere, at the rate of two pence or three pence per pound, taken to factories, mixed with gum and re-dried. Even this secondhand flavour of tea is not always to be obtained. Willow, horse-chestnut, and sloe-leaves are made to do duty for the Chinese article — a fact which visitors at country inns can readily testify to from bitter experience . . . substances of a most deleterious character — black lead, Prussian blue, verdigris, — are employed to give a natural appearance to the re-dried or fictitious leaves.'

Even as late as 1933 it was reported that tea coming from China for the European market was often artificially coloured with Prussian blue, or a mixture of gypsum and indigo.

Tea, as everyone knows, is that which English persons take at four o'clock each afternoon. A habit begun by the Duchess of Bedford about 1840.

And iced tea, as everyone else knows, is that which American persons take at any time when they are not taking coffee. In 1904, an English person named Richard Blechynden had a display of tea at the St. Louis World Fair — the one where Judy Garland wanted everybody to meet her, and where she went clanging about on those damned trolleys. The weather, as it sometimes is in St. Louis, was hotter than hot, and the Richard Blechynden under advisement was unable, as a result, to sell his hot tea. There came to him the bright idea of pouring the tea over ice, thus inventing the iced tea that American persons take at any time when they are not taking coffee.

Had they known better, those Fair visitors would have known that in hot countries, such as India, one drinks hot tea to keep cool.

Its hotness leads to sweatiness this bringing on coolness.

The best drink of tea that I remember was had at a roadside stall somewhere north of Calcutta. It was served scalding hot in water-thin earthenware cups. To it was added buffalo milk and cinnamon. After drinking, one threw the pottery cups on the rocky ground where they shattered into tiny fragments that vanished into the soil, demonstrating instant waste disposal.

But, you will be wanting to know how to make the best possible cup of tea. Research has uncovered useful advice proffered by Sir Kenelm Digby in about 1640, give or take. It crops up in a piece he wrote called 'Tea with Eggs' — 'The hot water is to remain upon it (the tea leaves) no longer than whiles you can say the Miserere Psalm (i.e., Pslam 51) very leisurely.'

Taking the thing at an amble, as recommended, it ticks off 3 minutes and 52 seconds — and makes a very nice dish of tea.

Guests come and go and ours were now falling into the latter category, teeter-tottering their way down the stairs avoiding the dried coal stains, to let themselves out by the front door. I was pleased with the evening. The dinner had gone down well — I never told you about the dinner, did I? Some other time, perhaps, — The wine had been agreeable, the room comfortably warm.

As I leaned against the bannister, bathed in the agreeable knowledge of a job well done, a voice from below floated up to me.

'I thought he'd never stop,' it said. 'I couldn't get a word in sideways.'

That's the trouble with the very best husbandry. It is seldom appreciated.

The problem for an average cow is that she never knows where she is. Approach her with a polite: 'Excuse me, but where are you?' and she will raise her head towards you with an expression that suggests you have touched on one of the central questions that strikes at the very paradox of life.

'Where am I?' she slowly muses, slowly chewing.

'Yes,' you repeat. 'Where are you? Or, to be more exact – where do you think you are?'

Pondering, she gives this some thought. 'I am chewing grass,' she reasons. 'And I can see grass. Therefore, I think I am in a field. Of course,' she adds, 'I may be wrong. It's not easy ever to know exactly where one is.'

'Quite right,' you tell her. 'You are not in a field. You are in my garden.'

'Garden?' she moos, blinking. 'How ever did I come to be in a garden.'

Then follows some closely reasoned argument with pointed reference to the gap that has now appeared in the hedge separating your garden from the field where the cow thought she was, and this information is conveyed to the twenty or so of her sisters and friends who have followed her.

You enquire how she proposes to remove herself, and she will slowly shake her head as if you have advanced the discourse to some complex realm far beyond her comprehension.

'All that is necessary,' you explain, 'is that you return the way you came.'

'What way is that?' she enquires.

'Back through the hole in the hedge.'

'Hedge?' She turns her head slowly to contemplate this novelty that has entered her life. 'Hole?'

So you lead her to the hole, from which she backs away in alarm, not knowing what dark dangers may lie beyond it.

'What lies beyond it,' you point out, 'is the field you have recently vacated.'

'Field?' she rumbles, nervously. 'Tell me again about this field.'

Losing patience, you give her a sharp tap on the rump and she lumbers through the gap and begins to mop up grass as if the stuff had just been invented. Her sisters and friends, not wishing to be left out, follow in her tracks, not noticing the gap in the hedge but seeing only that she has left them. 'Parting is such sweet sorrow,' they low in passing. 'If one wants to avoid such sorrows (sweet), it is best to cut out the parting bit.'

This scenario hints at some of the differences between life in towns and that bereft of towniness. Town persons tend to assume that non-town life is tranquil.

'Admit it!' they cry. 'Your life is tranquil!'

'What do you mean by tranquil?' you enquire, seeking to place the debate on a firmer footing. The matter is referred back to that Noah Webster (1758 - 1843) in whose knowing hands the meaning of words has reposed for so long.

'Quiet; calm, undisturbed; not agitated,' says Webster, briskly.

Listen, I said, cutting forward sharply into the narrative. The time is eight thirty of the clock on a typical morning. She has just left for her four hundred metre trot across the grass to her office. I have retreated to my study and slid behind my typewriter. That fickle jade I call my Muse requires, I discover, coffee and hot toast. I pad from my study to the kitchen. Yesternight's dishes block access to the coffee and toast making facilities. One thing leads to another and before I know what I am doing, what I am doing is peeling vegetables and preparing the meals for the day. The previously mentioned Muse has put in a claim for a day off, and some drastic remedies will need to be brought into play to drag her shouting and thrashing her limbs by way of registering her protest at this highhanded industrial action, back to the work bench or, as in my case, typewriter.

'Mens sana in corpore sano' as somebody once said, hinting that the proper treatment for a reluctant Muse is a brisk workout with dumb-bells and Indian clubs. These not being available, one takes a quick turn around the premises to see what is ready to hand as a replacement. That which comes the most readily to hand is the kitchen.

I must tell you about my kitchen.

The gentlefolk who built this cottage — somewhere between 1764, when it does not appear on the local drainage map (Noah Webster was six years old at the time — I toss in this information for free), and 1782 when it does — were happy souls with rollicking round-roving eyes and quavering thumbs. Doubtless there are many activities in which rollicking and quavering are ideal characteristics for the persons engaged therein. Cottage building, however, seems not to be one of them, if one is to judge from the absence of level floors, right angles and walls of equal height. The building is a complicated hybrid of styles as if each generation of rollickers and quaverers brought their rollicking and quavering skills to play by adding something, taking something away, altering something else. Rollickers and quaverers, it seems, cannot leave a thing alone. Rollicking and quavering drives them on.

All the doors have latches, and the only fitting we have ever found to guarantee privacy in the bathroom is the hook and eye fitment generally found on gardeners' huts.

Just inside the front door is the entrance to the kitchen, the floor of which is porous brick. Persons given to floor touching report that the touchable qualities of the floor under examination can be summed up in the two words, cold and damp. This coldness and dampness can be alleviated for floor-touching persons by putting down a layer of thick, cushiony, plastic floor covering, an up-to-date version of the linoleum previous generations of occupants might have used. Floor-touchers then report an improvement in the cold and damp departments, but a decline in the door-closing area. The knobbled brick floor rises up sharply to meet the bottom edge of the panelled, home-made, 18th century door. Placing an additional thickness of plastic floor covering brings all door closing to a halt.

Town persons might view such non-door closing with grave concern. Doors, they aver, have two functions in life: (a) to open, and (b) to close. Termination of (b) removes half the usefulness of the said door, they are heard to declare.

Non-town persons take the broader view. 'What is a door?' they ask, following this with the penetrating, 'Is a door really necessary?'

'Is not a kitchen, as a kitchen, a much pleasanter kitchen than it might otherwise have been, as a kitchen, with the door open (function (a)), rather than closed (function (b))?' they want to know. Pretty soon, everyone (even the floor touchers) have become so used to the non-closing condition of the door that they all forget it was ever otherwise.

Beside the non-closing door, reading from left to right, is a non-worktop worktop, immediately beneath the window from which working persons engaged in working on the worktop are able to gaze out across the village green, remaining as they do so unaware that the said worktop started life as something other than a worktop and thus qualifying for the title of non-ditto.

It — the worktop (non) started out as a marble washtable top, coming from a bedroom dresser — of the kind on which once stood, for the early morning sluice customary in the early morning, a large basin and matching ewer.

The floor-touchers who had so much to say on the subject of damp-ness and cold now wing in with fresh data to do with floor irregularities in the window area. Advance reports hint that the said floor takes a sudden dive downwards towards the skirting board. The leg on which the worktop would otherwise be resting at this juncture finds itself without what are commonly described as visible means of support, the said visible means being several millimetres lower than they should be if they are to qualify as means of support.

Non-town persons living non-town lives in such non-town dwellings discover that this type of non-town life tends to generate its own non-town solutions. Such solutions arise not from applications of the fevered brow to matters in hand, but from circumstances entirely out-side expectations.

Assume, as an instance, that you are occupied in putting a new plug on an electric appliance. A rubber washer falls to the floor, trundles under the worktop and lodges beneath the wobbly leg. The said leg recognises that its wobbly days are ended and ceases to wobble. The rubber washer is entered on the inventory as a member of the estab-lishment and care is taken in subsequent cleaning operations that it is not by accident removed from its post.

Between the worktop and the window ledge is a gap of a size that, if it had appeared anywhere in San Francisco in 1906 alert and attentive persons noticing it would have said: 'What ho!' and made preparations to leave town ahead of the next earthquake. During cookery opera-tions a steady scatter of crumbs go over the edge and down the gap. Enough food accumulates down there to feed a thriving colony of spiders. Representations at diplomatic level have led to the signing of a mutual non-intervention pact. They don't intrude into our part of the kitchen and we don't intrude into theirs. In any case, the marble work-top is too heavy for either one of us to shift alone, and it would have to be done by one person, the other being engaged in repelling outraged spiders.

Next to the worktop is a unit constructed of surplus materials by some earlier resident to support the enamel sink. The upper compartment of this contains an assortment of household necessaries. You will discover, if you care to make the experiment, that when a large number of irregularly-shaped objects are jumbled together a natural cohesion holds them firm. But – and this is the interesting bit – try to remove any one of them and it will be found that the item wanted is always right at the back. No matter how many times this is tried, even placing a required item right at the front of the jumble, the instant an attempt is made to remove the said item, it will be found to have taken itself to the rear. During its subsequent removal the natural stability of the jumble is shattered and everything cascades to the floor.

The lower half of this unit, for reasons that have long been forgotten, houses all our alcoholic drink. Bottles pile up in there as word goes round at the annual Christmas binge and the summer duty-free ritual in Europe, that this is a good place for bottles to be.

The compartment also houses the mains water cock. Whenever we go away for more than two or three days at a time and the water has to be turned off, it is required that I lie at full stretch on the floor (cold – damp, covered with plastic) where I have a nose-to-crumb confrontation with the kitchen waste collected there and the scampering spiders feeding thereon. In this cramped position upwards of forty bottles have to be removed. These cleared, the expedition can then press on towards the water cock lurking in the shadows. It is approached with a pair of workshop pinchers at the ready. Without these, the said cock is unturnable, turning being essential to the business of turning water off.

During the period we are away, the bottles remain on the floor as a useful hazard against any unsuspecting burglar who does not suspect that bottles may lie in his path.

As with the obliging rubber washer, whenever a modification to the kitchen's modus operandi is felt to be the order of the day, week, month or longer period depending on the urgency, such modification must arise from some process of the kind that Darwin described as natural selection. The word goes round: 'Let Nature Select'. And Nature does.

Any attempt to impose an arbitrary — 'Let's-get-this-thing-cleared-up-now' type of solution invariably — if that is the word, results in a worse trouble than the trouble being cleared up. Like the spaghetti/dinner plate upset.

The only place in which metre long lengths of Italian spaghetti can be stored unbroken is behind the pile of chocolate tins now used to house cakes, biscuits and cookies. These have to be tumbled out to get at the pasta. If the said tins are removed to another place — itself an impossibility since if there were another place the said tins would not be here — then, tottering columns of dinner plates mysteriously move in from wherever they were before.

The staircase to the upper floor runs up the back wall of the kitchen. Originally, it was made of roughly sawn planks so that no two treads had the same height or depth. Nailed lengthwise to support these were two halves of a tree trunk still with its 18th century bark attached. When this began to sag like a politician's face weakened by years of uncontrollable smiling, we dismantled it and put it on the village Guy Fawkes bonfire one November 5th (the staircase not the smile). Alf, our village handyman who is good at such things, built a replacement. This opened up new vistas of storage space beneath.

But, in agreement with some Parkinsonian Law ('Goods to be stored increase to more than fill any storage space available.') these new vistas were soon de-vista'd. The interior is now totally beyond reach. Several cardboard boxes can be seen at the rear of whose dark contents we now have no knowledge. However, as with the sink unit compartment, nothing stored handily at the front of this below stairs space is ever the thing required.

Also beneath the replaced staircase the refrigerator (I call it the refrigumrator, I don't know why) is stored. This, in keeping with the age and character of the cottage is an old model that needs to be defrosted every six weeks, by which time bulges of ice prevent the door closing tightly. It is axiomatic, if axiomatic is the word, that this always coincides with any major purchase of frozen goods on special offer.

'Why go on with this?' town persons will be wanting to know at this stage. 'What is the point?'

To make the point the script here cuts several thousand miles away to a remote corner of the US of A where, for the purpose of doing research, I was staying with friends (not researching the friends, you understand).

When friends in a far-flung corner offer hospitality how is it to be repaid. What is the proper far-flung response?

Far-flinging, one discovers, is as applicable to the corners thus flung as the persons visiting them. In getting onself flung far enough to arrive at the far-flung corner in question one becomes detached from the ordinary repayment facilities of one's native hearth and heath. Should one happen to be an oil-sheik, hospitality can be repaid by the gift of a spare well. A poet might scribe a few lines. A politician could offer to vote for his host should the host ever be in the position of requiring an extra vote or so. I offered to cook dinner.

What is the word I am searching for? Disaster — that's the word.

My own kitchen, as I have outlined, is a haven of confusion, a region of peaceful chaos. Nothing is eye-level this, or split-level that, by intention. If anything is to be found in my kitchen it is because somebody somewhere thought it wouldn't matter. Kitchens, one feels rather strongly, should not evolve round the principle that anything is where it can be located when wanted.

Cooking is a leisurely skill. It starts with the gathering of ingredients — a trip to the store or pottering in the garden — their preparation in a sequence that would be orderly if one could remember where we put the needed tool or ingredient just after we had it in our hands five minutes ago, the mixing, application of heat, and slowly the particular unplanned and unexpected flavour of the day emerges. That is what real cooking is all about. Don't believe what you read in books.

Alert and attentive readers will have noted that embedded in these arrangements is a safety factor to hold at bay any sources of strain or tension. Ten points to the first person who spots it!

You don't see it? Oh, dear! Let us sidle up to it slowly and take it unawares. Assume that some item is wanted, as it might be, three medium sized onions, or the plastic disc that we use to divorce egg whites from their yolks — where might one look for these? In the vegetable tray? Or, among the assorted oddments in the third drawer down on the left?

Oh foolish and beardless youth! as a poet once said. Have you not yet grasped what I feel can justifiably be termed the nub of the kitchen arrangement under discussion. There is *no* vegetable tray, and if there were one, nobody would remember where it was last seen. Certainly, if found, there would be no vegetables in it. Other things, perhaps. Like the plastic disc for sundering egg whites and yolks. Come to think of it, that might be a very good place to look.

As for those three onions, it is necessary to start from scratch, bending down to look in cupboards and drawers, lifting up old piles of newspapers to see if they have wandered beneath them, or fetching the kitchen chair with the wonky fourth leg so you can look on the top shelf in which position your head is pressed horizontally sideways against the looming ceiling, between the oak beams, and the filters in your nostrils are working overtime coping with the large intake of assorted webs and ambient dust. This is what real cookery is all about, despite what the books say. (As for that third drawer down on the left, that has been jammed shut for months. God knows what is in there!)

It is these periodic hiatuses that allow the good husbandry person's mind to be led with a soothing, natural rhythm from one kitchen activity to the next. With everything to hand, events unfold at a speed that the g.h.p's mind cannot absorb. The onions are there and the eggs sundered before the hard-pressed mind has got a clear view of what it intends to do with them. Oniony and eggy concepts get mixed up. Onionery invades eggery, or it may be vice versa.

Soups that ordinarily (under the old style management) are masterpieces of unctuous smoothness, lump — if lump is the word I want. Mayonnaise which otherwise never curdles, does so, in defiance of every precept that mayonnaisers have always believed in.

One is, as it were, immobilised by efficiency, by the dread disease of ergomania. There is no bending or stretching for mislaid items, no anxious leaping from this murky corner to that, a dish of bubbling noodles grasped in the left hand, a wooden spoon between the teeth (where else can you carry a wooden spoon?), the right hand groping for grated cheese that should be where you thought you left it on top of the cupboard where the Hoover is kept, but isn't (the cheese not the Hoover).

Without this vital flexing of limbs, the legs become heavy and dropsical, the back grows stiff.

In my kitchen, which I now see as a classical model from which the designers of kitchens should draw their inspiration, one skips with a kind of feverish lissomeness from one urgent remedy to the next, remaining as a result, lithe, alert, flexible and sensitive to all the delightfully unexpected nuances of good cooking. With no worktop at the correct height (assuming there is a correct height) and with nothing stored where logic demands (assuming that logic is capable of making such demands), the ceaseless turning and twisting does wonders for the podgy bod. 'Mens sana in corpore something' as somebody once said again. My kitchen handles the corpore side of the contract, letting the mens sana take care of itself, which it does.

It is this understanding that makes of the English such very good cooks. (Don't believe what you read in books). Kitchens are places where cookery occurs, and cookery is a process of muddling through, and it has to be admitted that in the muddling through business no race is more adept at muddlement than the English. An English cook sets out to make a soup, which, things being found in the larder unexpectedly and getting added in, turns into a stew. This stew is then left longer than intended in the oven when the cook is diverted from the kitchen to deal with a crisis, as it might be cows in the garden, and is found to be somewhat diminished in size as a result (the stew, not the cook, cows or garden!). Exploration in the refrigumrator uncovers pastry made up for some previous dish but not used because . . . you can add in your own because here.

With time running out, the cook puts the soup/stew in the pastry making up the volume with anything that comes to hand, spices, bread crumbs, cheese — the result being an original dish that the consumers thereof mightily enjoy and wish to have repeated, this flummoxing the cook who has not written any of it down and whose memory equates with the muddlement technique by which the kitchen is managed.

These basic concepts of cookery have remained pretty well unchanged since the dawn of culinary history. The first cooks had no cook books. It is not even clear how they could have had kitchens, cookery not then having been invented. What they had were fires, cooking probably starting when some careless person left meat lying near the household (or cavehold) fire and noticing, as a result, certain improvements in flavour and a reduction in toughness. Pretty soon, primitive cooks — for that is what we shall call them as they were on the whole fairly primitive — had become quite handy at roasting and broiling, meat being cooked by being buried in hot coals or burning logs, or by being impaled on sticks held over the fire. Nothing, these primitive husbandry persons felt, was more cosy than an evening by the fireside impaling slabs of meat thereover.

A good long while later they got on to boiling, the boiling technique being held up for some time until somebody had invented some kind of container to hold the hot water. Bags made of animal hide, baskets of birch bark and woven reeds and large sea shells were all tried out as pots, and were found wanting. When pottery pots came along, attempts were made to heat the water in them by dropping in hot stones. Then one day someone had the bright idea of putting the pots on top of the hot coals. Since then, boiling has never looked back.

By the time the Greeks came along, what happened in their kitchens was getting up to pretty much the same level as what happens in mine. The tv dinner originated in Ancient Greece, its development hampered by an absence of tv, this coming later. As the Greeks lounged about waiting for tv to come along, they munched their way through first courses of roast sheep (very tasty, a roast sheep), oxen or pigs together with vegetables. In the interval when the commercials should have been on but weren't because of not having been thought of, the Greeks (the same Greeks) got amongst the honeycakes and fruit. Cheese and olives were also to hand. Frying had been invented and was done in olive oil. Cooking utensils were made of bronze and earthenware − silver and gold when the boss was invited home for a meal.

Fortunately for the Romans, tv still had not been invented. What they had come up with were orgies, which fitted in nicely with the accompanying food which was lavish, complicated and ostentatious. Meat was eaten as if meat mountains had to be cleared by this time next week. The evening meal might last for several hours. A typical menu would run something like this:

Appetizers	Raw vegetables, oysters, pickles, salt fish.
1st course	Shellfish ragout, small birds and fowl.
2nd course	Boar's head, sausage, roast pig, peacock, sow's udder.
3rd course	Various elaborate pastries.
4th course	Fruit and wine.

Roman kitchens were built round a masonry cooking range, divided into many separate ovens. Beside this would be a stone worktop (with or without spiders is not reported). Somewhere in the kitchen was usually a well. Close by were storerooms with supplies of oil in earthenware pots, salt meat, honey and dried fruits.

If the Romans had put out series of weekly scrolls for Women these would have been handicapped by the length of the run-of-the-mill

Roman recipe that tends to come out as long as a novelette. Three or four good sized scrolls alone are necessary to contain the full score on the Roman way with Roast Chicken. A brief summary reads thus:

Chop small the meat of a chicken.

Mix this with chopped kid's breast (i.e., that of a small goat and not the nearest available offspring in spite of population growth).

Put these chopped meats into a saucepan together with parsley seed, dried pennyroyal (a kind of mint), dried mint, ginger, green coriander and raisins.

Add three pieces of oat bread, honey, vinegar, olive oil and wine.

Place the saucepan in the oven and cook until the meat is tender.

Remove it from the oven and add cheese, pine nuts, cucumbers and dried chopped onions.

Pour gravy over the whole.

Return to the oven and complete the cooking.

When the meat and other ingredients are fully cooked, place on a serving dish and surround it with fresh snow (fresh what? Snow. Oh, I see. Thanks.)

And, Mrs Beeton might have added, first catch your chicken, debreast your goat, gather your herbs, bake your oat bread, cultivate your honey, brew your vinegar and wine, press your oil, squeeze your cheese, pluck your nuts and do whatever it is you have to do about cucumbers.

One can quite see why the Romans were obliged to quit Britain. Their culinary habits were quite impossible. For something more within the scope of English resources you have to turn to Chaucer who, on this matter of preparing chicken, recommended that one should '. . . boille the chiknes with the marybones. Add poudra-marchant (a flavouring powder), tart and galyngale (cypress root)'. You notice the contrast? Compared with the Roman approach Chaucer's technique is brief to the point of being stark, arousing only concern in any persons whose name might happen to be Mary, and not wishing to have their bones tampered with.

Speaking of a certain skilled cook, the same author, Chaucer, notes that − 'He koude rooste and seethe and boille and frye, Maken mortreux (pork and chicken stew) and wel bake a pye, For blankmanger (mixture of white meats cooked in syrup), that made he with the beste.'

As is often the case in my own kitchen, medieval cookery was quite

messy. They had no baking tins, glasses, individual plates or forks, and often, I don't either. I have never actually placed the food I have cooked in a large bowl at the centre of the table and invited everyone to dip in their fingers, but it has sometimes been close. In three star medieval places every person had their own spoon. I, too, can usually provide spoons.

This messy habit of lowering the fingers into food prevailed in the medieval kitchen as well. Cooks were recommended to dip their hands in the soup or stew. If it felt slippery to the touch it was thought to have plenty of nourishment in it, including, doubtless, that coming from the finger-dipping, cook-person's fingers.

When guests got tired of all this finger-dipping, and pulling meat apart with bare hands, some thoughtful medieval host dished out knives, and this, added to the existing spoons and fingers advanced food-eating technology in some large measure. Knifing, spooning and fingering became the food-eating order of the day.

But, food-eating persons in Spain and Italy felt there was still something lacking. What could it be? Knives − jolly useful for cutting. Spoons − helpful for spooning. Fingers . . . here the food-eating persons in Spain and Italy paused. Were fingers good enough? Might not there be some improvement over the humble finger which had not changed its basic design for thousands of years? Might not a fork be better? So it was that during the 17th century, forks spread from the said Spain and Italy, and knifing, forking and spooning became the food-eating order of the day.

These advancements to the benefit of food-eaters caused dark ruminations to occur in the bosoms of cooks below stairs. 'If knives, forks and spoons are all right for them up there,' these dark ruminators argued, 'what about us down here? Are we not just as entitled?' And they set about the business of inventing things to which they could become entitled, it being impracticable for them to become entitled to such things before such things had been thought of.

'What are these things to which you feel you are entitled?' persons upstairs were heard to ask when apprised of these dark ruminations down below. And the dark ruminators had no answer to give.

Turning their dark ruminations to a more creative vein, they soon came up with what can be described as a galaxy of implements to which they felt entitled. By the 16th century, a modest French chateau, that of La Mothe-Chandenier possessed a kitchen supplied with the following entitlements:

One pot-hanger
Two beaten iron cookers
One big iron spit
Two smaller spits
One iron fish slice
One grid
One big cooking pot
One big cast-iron pot with perforations
One iron pot of one seillée capacity (a seillée was a medieval measure of capacity)
Two big three-seillée cauldrons
One cauldron – two seillée capacity
Two small half-seillée cauldrons
Two big round brazen pots of four seillées each
One round two-seillée pan
One wooden press for pressing capons
Two iron spoons
One small skimmer
One round bronze pan with a long handle
Two old dripping pans
One small metal mortar and pestle
Three iron frying pans with long handles
A table on two trestles
One old bench with bar back
One cupboard with two glass doors
One cupboard for plates and dishes
Six big copper candlesticks
Six medium-size candlesticks
One deep copper basin
Two deep bronze candlesticks
Barrel of Gascony wine
Pitcher with spout
Half-litre mugs
One stone mustard pot
One small pastry table

In addition there were tammies (horse-hair sieves), couloirs (strainers), rastels (iron hooks), pots and kettles of all sizes, tartières (baking tins), a whole range of pans – each with a different use, skillets, saucepans, frying pans, the féral – a large metal water container, the becdasne – a pot with a handle and a long curved spout, copper funnels, the esmieure (grater), various ladles, and knives – each with its own area of cutment.

By the time of 'haute cuisine' in France this proliferation of entitlements had got completely out of hand. No kitchen was thought to be well-equipped unless it had dozens of casseroles, sauté pans, frying pans, cocottes (round copper pans with lids) of various sizes and shapes, stew pans, stock pots, double saucepans, braising pans, fish kettles and pans. Each item was reserved exclusively for one purpose, and persons connected with that purpose might not get round to using the particular utensil more than once or twice a year.

This increase in entitlements led to a matching increase in those persons by whom these entitlements were entitled. Dubbed the 'brigade de cuisine' they were led by a Big Hat (gros bonnet). Under the B.H. served the sauce chef, the entremettier (soups, vegetables and sweet courses), rôtisseur (roasts, fried dishes and grills), and a garde-manger (larder chef) who in addition to having charge of all supplies, also made the cold dishes such as galantines, terrines, pâtés and mousses.

Commis (kitchen assistants) were attached to the chef of each section. Sections could be subdivided into sub-sections, as it might be if the sauce section were split to include a fish chef. Entremets might contain a potagiste (soup chef). A grillardin worked under the rôtisseur and took charge of the grills. There might also be a friturier (fryer).

As is typical of management structures, this elaboration results in there being nothing for the Big Hat himself to do. In the end, after wandering among the boiling pans and the bustling chefs, he takes up golf, dropping by the old kitchen every once in a while to pass a nod and a smile with the lads.

I am not like that. I am Big Hat, and all the little hats rolled into one, wreaking disorder out of order, disaster out of triumph, staleness from freshness, dryness from succulence and oceans of spillage from meals already precariously balanced on plates, just waiting to be toppled over and getting the full topple from me as I brush past. In all this I acknowledge that I am working in close accord with the most venerated – if that is the word, traditions of the cookery thing.

'What about Big Hat and all his minions?' you will ask.

One knows all about the Big Hats of this world, decent enough chaps for the most part, but human. Chaps do not become Big Hats just by wearing big hats. To see a Big Hat at his Big-Hatest best, you must comb through the steamy backwaters of the kitchen for a little hat so little that the little hat's hat hangs low about his ears.

This little hat is doing his little-hatest best with some soup or sauce, a simple assemblage of ingredients, an uncomplicated routine of treatments. But Love and all the dreams of Love have clouded little hat's mind and unnoticed among that grand culinary concourse, there arises from his work something in the Grand Order of Error, a mistake of such magnitude that all other little hats quake at the mere thought of it.

It is half-past the last moment and His Majesty and the Grand Duchess with their august entourages are awaiting the first course which this was to have been before the Grand Error cropped up. It is then that the Big Hat moves into action, improvising with every fibre of his being, tasting and basting, racing and chasing, to produce a miracle of eating from a messy mush. H.M. and the G.D. are enchanted and send down their respects to the Big Hat, and could they have some more of the same, and thus is another classic dish born.

This is the cookery world that cooks know. My early Greek counterpart crouched muttering over his hot chytra, my Roman ditto struggled with his craticula, and there am I knee-deep in spillages wondering what the hell to do next.

What the hell to do next invariably involves water, this being a region of the culinary world that qualifies in the parlance of Big Hats as ranking high among the Large Unmentionables. Among all the vast coterie of little hats serving the big chap, not even the littlest among them devotes a fraction of his time to what might be termed 'haut lavage'. When the time comes, as come it must, for all those tartières, skillets, cocottes, fish kettles and casseroles to be washed up, these items are transported to some nether region where nether persons get in amongst them up to the elbows.

'Washing-up?' little hats are heard to mutter as, having completed their little hatting they saunter away to play golf or make love or do whatever it is little hats do in their lighter moments, 'what's that?'

And the next day when they take up a sturdy little hat posture at the work bench, indicating a readiness to begin another day of hectic little hatting, the appearance of freshly scoured utensils on their little hat hooks, racks and shelves occasions no more comment than the sun rising each morning. One does not entirely understand the machinery that makes these things happen, but one knows it can be relied upon.

For we brave members of the single hat brigade, water is mentionable. We mention it, proudly and unflinchingly, all the time.

'Water!' we say. 'Good heavens! What would we do without it!'

Mostly, what we would do without it is not wash-up, this being an activity for which water is an essential requirement. And water being, as might be said, very much of the essence, single hat cooks know it to be an untamable beast in a realm of untamable beasts. Questioned on the subject of water in the kitchen, the single hat cook expresses the view that it is pretty much of a beast of the untamable kind. 'An untamable beast,' just about sums up his view.

The Romans may have had their kitchen wells, and these wells being, as it were, deep holes conveniently located in the Roman kitchen, could well – in an emergency – besides being a well, double as a waste disposal facility. But, is there any evidence that the said Romans realised, or were aware of, the untamable nature of the beast that they were bringing into the kitchen?

I learnt about wells and water at my grand-aunt's knee, or if not her knee, another joint reasonably adjacent. Her country cottage being in that part of the country to which water had not leaked, in those days, her supplies were brought up from the well in her cottage garden.

Water from a tap, one discovers from the folk lore prevailing around my grand-aunt's lower limbs, was something akin to a drug on the market. One used it just because it was there.

'You wouldn't get up in the middle of the night,' my g-a would have said if she had been able to put words together in that lucid manner, 'and walk two miles to hammer on the door of the chemist's shop to get hold of a sleeping pill because you couldn't sleep.' One had to agree that one wouldn't.

'Why wash up, then,' she would continue, 'just because there is water in the tap?'

'Sleeping pills get took,' she would go on, 'because sleeping pills is available. And washing up waits until someone feels inclined to make a trip to the well.'

People quite admired my g-a's washing up. They came from far and wide, or the other way about, to admire the elegance of her stacking. 'Thinking of doing any washing-up today?' they would call over the hedge on their way to the farm to pick up milk warm from the cow.

'Wind's in the west,' my g-a would call back. 'Not a good day for washing up.'

It was amazing the unerring skill with which my g-a was able to identify days unpropitious to the act of washing-up. Days when the wind came from the west, south, north or east were all bad days. So were sunny or cloudy days, dry or rainy days and even days when there was no noticeable weather at all.

Then, one day, it might happen that the postman would call, or the man with a replacement accumulator for her wireless, or the potter from down the road wanting to dig a bit of clay, and she would say: 'Thinking of doing some washing-up.' And they would fetch a bucket of water from the well.

From the same g-a joint as previously, I learnt another valuable adjunct to the armoury of good husbandry (or auntery) with which the g.h.p. arm themselves against the onslaughts of the day. If water intake for the purposes of the good life is anomalous to the ideas of good husbandry, then equally, water removal falls into the same category.

'I've done the washing-up,' my g-a would announce, pleased as Punch, looking forward to stacking her next stack.

'Shall I dry?' a visiting stranger would ask, being strange to her ways.

'Don't you touch'n,' she would say, indicating by these words that the person raising the question was not to touch "n". 'Kitchen's full o' dryin'' she would add.

By this simple country statement, my g-a was indicating that in her simple country way she had grasped the essence of a profound scientific principle that scientifically stated, states that washing up, having been washed up, if left to dry, will dry of its own accord.

To this day, I never wash-up more than once a day, nor dry ever. Persons come from wide and far to admire my self-restraint. While we are waiting for the stuff to dry, I sometimes point out interesting features of the washing-up that might otherwise escape their attention.

'In this baking dish or tray,' I tell them, 'I have baked a meat pie.'

'Is that a fact?' they reply.

'It is,' I tell them. 'And have you heard the parable of the meat pie?'

They never have and I go on to tell them.

A Wise Man and a Fool were contemplating a meat pie. 'My friend said the Wise Man (for being wise he knew that all Fools were his friends), 'embodied in this pie is the entire unfolding of human civilisation.

When man gave up the nomadic life of the hunter, he found that by exposing meat to the heat of the fire he made it more palatable and digestible. He could provide himself with flesh to eat by husbanding herds of animals rather than having to chase them across the plains. He could plant fields of corn and grind the seeds into a flour for making bread and pastry. He built fences to protect his crops, and houses to protect himself. Within each house he set aside a special room where food could be stored and cooked. By these means he so improved his standard of living that he had leisure to contemplate the development of the crafts of pottery, weaving and working metals. He dreamed dreams and fashioned these dreams into drawings, paintings, carvings and sculpture. And all this rich growth of human civilisation is enshrined in our humble meat pie. What do you say to that?' the Wise Man ended.

But the Fool said nothing — could say nothing — for his mouth was full, having eaten the pie while the Wise Man spoke.

Thus Fools get fat while Wise Men get wiser.

But a cook cooked the pie, giving evidence by this cookery of the sublime sanguinity of cooks to whom the foolishness of Fools and the wisdom of Wise Men is all one, knowing, as they must that the civilisation of man rests on that foundation of three square meals a day, making of the kitchen the heart and haven of man's eternal optimism. For no cook starts to cook a meal without the expectation that all will turn out for the best. That hope is expressed in a story written by Lord Dunsany, the substance of which is that a salesman for a firm of bottled sauce makers went to the grocery store in a village where the figures showed very good business was done in selling the indicated bottled sauce.

The village was in the grip of a local mystery. A woman had vanished. Circumstances conspired to narrow the possibilities. On a particular evening, neighbours heard the woman exchanging insults with her husband. The pair lived in a bungalow standing in its own garden on the edge of the village. It so happened that for reasons unconnected with the matter, the bungalow was under observation during that night and the following days. When the woman failed to put in an appearance doing her work around the house or going to the village, tongues began to wag. These waggings finally reached the village policeman who investigated and reported.

In that report he was able to say that the husband worked all day in the garden sawing up great quantities of wood which he, seemingly, burnt in the kitchen stove, for black smoke belched from that chimney despite the summer warmth. Questioned by the delivery boy from the grocery, the husband suggested his wife had gone away for a few days, but this did not seem likely as nobody had seen her leave.

The delivery boy had brought the regular order to the bungalow. In confirming a repeat order the husband added a request for a dozen bottles of sauce. This order was to be repeated every few days.

And the salesman, trying to find an explanation for the sudden increased demand for his product, argued the case this way: suppose there had been a quarrel, an explosion of violence, a sudden savage blow that had silenced the woman for ever, what could the husband do?

The house was observed. He could not remove the body. It was summer. The days were warm. Soon it would begin to moulder, mouldering being something that cannot be hushed up for long.

But, he had the kitchen fire and all the multiple resources of the kitchen, together with a bountiful supply of wood. The body could be cut into convenient pieces and brought to the fire. Cutting the wood was, in any case, healthy exercise and gave him a good appetite.

Human flesh is an acquired taste, the taste for which he had probably not had the chance to acquire before. So, to help his wife slide down more smoothly, he doused each portion of her with the bottled sauce.

Of such unquenchable optimism are good cooks made. The kitchen is their shrine.

EGG

Enlightenment is not a thing one ordinarily associates with Tounggoo, in the Salween-Sittang Valley, to the north of Rangoon in Burma. But, it was there I saw the light about eggs.

I was there on detachment from Imphal, capital of Manipur in India. Detachment was a euphemism used by the RAF, in those wartime days, to describe a disagreeable kind of existence well below the normal standards of comfort and good cheer.

We went to Tounggoo because the Japanese had built an airfield there, said airfield consisting of a cleared stretch of brown earth across which had been laid a runway made up of strips of canvas secured by layers of thick black tar that melted in the sun's heat. When in residence the detachment force was made up of three elderly Douglas C-47 Dakota transport planes, their crews, and three tents.

The planes were death traps, not having been serviced properly for some time on the grounds that they were infested with rats. At some previous time, they had been used by the Indian Government to transport ghee. This is a slightly rancid, clarified butter, much favoured in those parts. In the heat it has a tendency to ooze. Over the years it had oozed down between the metal floor panels of the Dakota's cabins into the compartment through which the controls to the rudder and elevators ran. When the squadron fitters removed the panels to service the controls they found dozens of well-nourished bellicose rats (rats like ghee), very annoyed at being suddenly exposed to the light of day. The panels were hastily replaced without any work being done and had remained in place ever since.

For food, the detachment was supplied with Australian dehydrated mutton. This commodity came in sacks and was indistinguishable from the brown earth of the airfield. Possibly its taste was indistinguishable also, but I cannot recall that we ever tasted the earth.

We engaged a gentleman from the nearby village to tend our fire and cook the meals. The recommended procedure with the mutton was to add hot water to it until it took on the texture of warm mud. One way, we found, to make it palatable was to add large numbers of eggs.

Indian and Burmese hens lay eggs that are no more than half the size of those laid by their western sisters. Consequently, very large numbers of eggs were needed every day. Our cook put us in touch with another member of his family in the village who was able to supply these, and this fellow came out every day with a basketful. Unfortunately, for some reason, he had it fixed in his mind that the egg contract was part of a package deal whereby we would acquire exclusive title rights in his sister for a sum to be mutually agreed. Each day he would arrive with his tattered female relative in tow. The day's asking price for the eggs evidenced his current strategy for finalising the sale of his sister. A low price was a kind of loss leader, a come-on to encourage a good bid sisterwise. A high price transferred the girl to the bargain department in the form of a human Green Shield Stamp.

We might have lived out all our time in Tounggoo in this atmosphere of thwarted commerce had not the entrepreneur in question, in accord with the brisk buckling of swashes adopted by those robust merchant princes of old, changed his merchandise. He went into the uncut jewel trade, and we got his sister off our hook by laying out hard rupees for quantities of blue sapphire, ruby and emerald.

But the experience taught me that one of the essential expedients in the resourceful cook's ragbag of tricks is the adding of eggs to whatever is below par.

The egg has been a regular item of human diet for a very long time, eggs of all kinds, those of many types of bird as well as the eggs of fishes and reptiles. The common hen heads the list so far as most of us are concerned. Her egg is one of the most easily digested of all foods. Its average weight is two ounces, of which weight 12% is made up of a calcareous porous substance, namely, the shell. Inside is to be found the albumen and the vitellus, or yolk. One of the lesser known problems of obtaining eggs of decent quality is the embarrassing matter of hens' diet. Be it known that those of the free range ilk, if they pick up too many insects and not enough worms, become constipated. This encourages the production of eggs which, alas, have a bad taste and are unfit for children to eat.

Eggs in the 'gros oeuf' class are those of the ostrich, turkey, goose, peacock and duck. Mini-eggs come from the pigeon, guinea-fowl, pheasant, partridge, lapwing, plover and gull.

The egg, and the hen which supplies it, has aroused the derision and praise of poets in about equal proportions. Roy Bishop comments on 'The Inefficacious Egg' in these terms:

> 'The egg is smooth and very pale;
> It has no nose, it has no tail;
> It has no ears that one can see;
> It has no wit, no repartee.'

Taking the more or less opposite view, Oliver Hereford salutes 'The Hen'.

> 'Alas! my child, where is the Pen,
> That can do justice to the Hen?
> Like Royalty she goes her way,
> Laying foundations every day,
> Though not for Public Buildings, yet
> For Custard, Cake and Omelette.
> Or if too old for such a use
> They have their fling at some abuse . . . . . .
> No wonder, Child, we prize the Hen,
> Whose Egg is mightier than the Pen.'

Almost everyone will have come across the celebrated curate's egg that first loomed in a *Punch* cartoon of 1895.

'I'm afraid you've got a bad egg, Mr Jones.'
'Oh no, my Lord, I assure you! Parts of it are excellent!'

Alphabetically speaking, the first version in the culinary recital of the egg is the boiled ditto to which the proper accompaniment, as everyone knows, is two slices of fresh brown bread and butter and a pinch of salt. Estimates of the time necessary to cook such an egg to perfection, as given in various standard cook books, are generally on the short side. My three minute eggs turn out to be nasty runny things that remind one of primeval ooze and the origin of life, not a subject to be brought up at the tea table.

Let me tell you what I do, and you can judge for yourself. The time to cook an egg depends on its size and since I like them cooked in this simple fashion, I shall be dealing with largish eggs. These I place in a pan of cold water and put on moderate heat. If the water heats up too rapidly, bubbles will bounce the egg about and crack the shell. Similarly, if you heat the water first and then slide the egg into the boiling liquid, the sudden shock to its system is also likely to crack its shell. When the water boils, turn the heat down to the lowest level at which tiny bubbles continue to rise, and start timing five full minutes. At the end of that time remove the egg, which you will find to be nicely cooked through, including the outer layer of yolk which will have a deliciously liquid centre.

The appearance of such eggs at the table has been the foundation of British civilisation and the Empire, and the decline of same can be traced directly to the decreasing frequency with which properly boiled eggs are now consumed. Further confirmation of this can be found in Denmark which has not properly developed a civilisation or an Empire. Some years back I was engaged in chatting up a film in Copenhagen with a company on whose lot stands (or used to stand) the oldest sur- viving studio, dating from 1904 and now given over largely to spiders and properties in about equal proportions. At the appropriate hour I was conducted to the canteen where there was placed before me, as a starter, a shallow dish containing a jaundiced eye of the kind that comes after a few nights of whooping it up with the lads.

This eye gave the strong impression of not liking what it saw of the world. It had a nasty, suspicious, brooding, vengeful sort of look, as one who sees usurpers and villains on every side. For my part, the feeling was mutual and I would as soon have let that eye explore my insides as I would a mess of meal worms.

Rejecting a national dish is something one does not do lightly in Denmark. The residents are very liable to draw the wrong conclusions. It suggests to them a metaphorical slapping of their nation across the face with a wet fish, and this they feel obliged to resent. In fact, I have always blamed the failure of that film contract to come to the boil on my own inability to eat a raw egg.

Yet, it happens that a raw egg is so totally digestible as to cause problems in the human stomach, which is geared to giving foodstuffs passing through a healthy hammering to reduce them to a digestible frame of mind. But the raw egg swoops through before you can say pepsin and rennet. Arriving at the intestine, the raw egg is completely absorbed, leaving behind no residue on which the waiting intestinal muscles can obtain a purchase and thus giving rise to the condition commonly known as 'egg bound'. Even with cooked eggs, the residual matter is so small as to give rise to this same condition.

Eggs are not always sought for themselves alone. Natives of Africa use the egg shells of the ostrich as water containers, the egg itself weighing, on average when full, about three pounds. The largest known egg was that of the elephant bird of Madagascar (fortunately now extinct) which had a capacity of 10 litres. One can imagine the domestic difficulties likely to arise were 10 litre eggs to arrive regularly at the breakfast table.

The word egg probably comes from the Greek, via Latin (ovum), Gaelic (ubh), Irish (ugh), German (ei), Middle English (ey), Anglo-Saxon (aeg), Swedish (ägg), which just shows how different people's minds tend to run along the same lines.

Egg production is one of the world's success stories. The average get-up-and-go hen lays about 220 eggs each year when she is in training. In 1970, hens around the globe had racked up a staggering total of 390,000,000,000 eggs. Chinese hens were the busiest with 73,000,000,000 to their credit. Next came the USA with 70,000,000,000 eggs rolling from 314,000,000 birds. Third in the production stakes is the USSR, hotly pursued by Japan.

As to consumption, the average American citizen leads the field by packing away 314 eggs per annum and thus ranking high among the leagues of the egg bound. He is followed by his co-egg eating confrère in the UK (270), Japan (269), West Germany and Austria (250), Western Europe − the rest (210), Eastern Europe (190), and the USSR trailing with a miserable 140.

Of the six ways of cooking eggs, I have already touched on the first − boiling. The others are poaching, frying, scrambling, baking and in omelettes. This may suggest that the egg is fit only for the plainest of treatment. Peruse then, this account of eggs being served at Trimalchio's feast as described for us by Petronius, being typical of the grandiose feasts of Imperial Rome. '. . . A tray was placed before us containing a basket in which there was a hen, carved out of wood, wings spread out as if she were sitting. Up stepped two slaves, and, after rummaging in the straw took out pea-fowl's eggs, distributing them among the guests. I am afraid they might have been already hatched, but let us see if they are still edible. For the purpose of eating these eggs, spoons weighing at least half a pound each were handed to us and we broke the eggs, which were made of light pastry looking exactly like the shell.

I was just about to throw away the one which was served to me,

NEW LAID
(LARGE)

as I thought it was addled and had become a chicken already, when one of the guests, who was an old hand at these tricks, stopped me: "There is something in it,' he said, "I don't know what it is, but it is excellent." I then looked in the shell and found a fine, plump, beccafico (garden warbler) in it, deliciously spiced, hidden inside the yolk . . .'

The poached egg is a subject on which one could wax loquacious, given the change. The classic method is for the egg to be broken into a cup, and poured from the cup, smoothly, into a pan of simmering, but not boiling, water. But, there is a certain lack of decorum in this simplicity which will become readily apparent. The egg white swirls in the water to form a tangled skirt to the yolk, which while no doubt giving pleasure to those artistic souls who see in this a symbol of the restless nature of the free spirit, yet looks messy on the plate.

A poached egg lacking these ethereal refinements but more suitable for reposing on a crisp slice of buttered toast can be secured by using a simple apparatus. In this, the bowl of the egg container rests on the surface of simmering water: the egg when removed from it (remember before sliding in the egg to wipe the inner surface of the bowl with butter, margarine or vegetable oil) retains the shape of the container and does not slop about. Seven or eight minutes of cooking are necessary to obtain a firm yolk with liquid centre.

There is a French device consisting of a small glass jar with a glass lid secured by a metal clip. This also can be used as a poacher, the interior having first been given an oleaginous wipe, as advised above. However, I am not very much in favour of this Gallic utensil for the reason that it results in an egg with a tallish up-and-down shape that will not rest sturdily on toast, but topples over. The more squat British model is, to my mind, more stable.

Here, the distinction between poaching and baking begins to blur. The same device can equally be used to bake eggs in the oven. Many cooks are crisply enthusiastic about these, but I do not care for them. Eggs cooked in proximity to water seem to preserve a certain moistness which is pleasant in the mouth. The difficulty with baked eggs is that they have to be exposed to heat for a much longer period to achieve my ideal of a firm yolk with aforementioned liquid centre. Just as nature abhors a runny chocolate, so this part of nature has a strong bias against eggs in the same condition. Primitive man, it would seem, was the chap conditioned by the hard times in which he lived to be obliged to creep up on the nests of innocent birds and suck the raw eggs therein. Surely, we have moved on somewhat from that.

Baked eggs, in whatever container, that remain in the oven long enough to firm up the outer rim of yolk, arrive at the table with repulsively rubbery whites. I have known slices of this substance to slide from the fork on to the plate, and bounce — not a pretty sight.

The ability to produce a decent boiled or poached egg is a valuable skill within the scope of any budding cook, and it is a creation not to be sniffed at. Eggs in that state of virtue can be considered as a universal food. Vasari, in his Lives of the Painters, describes how Piero di Cosimo, finding that eating interferred with his work, took to living exclusively on hard-boiled eggs. He cooked these a hundred at a time, and kept a basketful beside his easel, dipping in whenever the Muse escaped him for the moment.

It was Pope who declared in the Imitations of Horace: 'The vulgar boil, the learned roast an egg.' Fortunately, we know enough about Pope not to take the comment seriously. And, as if to draw the dotted line between the crudities of British culture and the refinements of France, De La Reynière crowed rather like a cock who has ambitions to get in among the hens, 'They know in France, 685 different ways of dressing eggs, without counting those which our savants invent every day.' This is like saying that one knows 685 different ways to dress ladies, not counting those which couturiers dream up every season. When you return to basics, you are left with four limbs and a torso around which there has to be draped variations on the trousers and sweater, skirt and blouse theme.

The present repository of French culinary law, the Larousse Gastronomique, lists a mere 286 ways of dealing with eggs, not counting the basic boiling, baking, poaching, etc. In addition, some 122 different titles appear under the general heading of "omelettes". Musicians would describe these as "variations on a theme".

These days it cannot be denied that the shortest and surest way to a girl's heart is via her taste buds, and this was a route that a musician friend of mine explored most thoroughly. Musicians have a problem that they share with actors and parliamentarians in that when they are professionally employed, the hours of their labour are those which customarily are reserved for light dalliance and similar pleasantries. This musician to whom I have directed your attention, solved this difficulty by requiring his current attachment to attend at least the latter half of whatever performance engaged him during which she might be decently impressed by the nimbleness of his fingering as he raced through arpeggios, or slashed a pathway to the heart of the most impenetrable obbligato.

Afterwards, they would stroll back to his apartment, this stratagem neatly guaranteeing that she stood on his doorstep late at night, happily relaxed and with a good appetite. His invitation in for a quick meal was never refused.

This was where resourcefulness and good planning paid off. For the dish he invariably elected to lay on the table was one that virtually cooked itself, allowing the first stages of the previously mentioned dalliance to be got under way elsewhere.

The meal was served in a framework of fresh French bread, chilled wine and a tossed green salad. The nub or kernel of it was egg, in this case, four eggs broken into a dish or bowl and beaten by hand with a fork.

There is a knack in beating eggs. Those who use mechanical aids will miss the heights in this department. Nothing suits the task better than an ordinary fork, which grasped firmly in the hand, is agitated rapidly

to and fro through the naked egg. To begin with, this will consist of
white and yolk separated. As the beating continues, these come together. If they are urged into a union too vigourously, they become
what smart chefs call − bruised. This condition can be readily diag-
nosed. If the liquid in your bowl is an even yellowish colour, then it
is an even bet that you have somewhat overdone the beating and
bruised your eggs. Ideally, the white and yolk should be nicely inter-
mingled, and yet still be separate enough that one can detect threads
of the one and strands of the other. In this state, the eggs are ready
for whatever use you intend to put them to.

The intention here is to pour the liquid into shallow pottery dishes
especially intended for that purpose. But, before doing so, there remain the master touches to be added. These consist of the addition of
a tablespoonful of fresh cream, and a like quantity of whatever leaf
herb takes your fancy (rosemary, chervil, thyme or marjoram are
excellent). Stir these into the egg mixture. And, do I again have to
mention that one wipes the inside of the egg dishes with either butter,
margarine, or vegetable oil?

On top of each dish is scattered chopped mushroom, or a whole
small button mushroom. Both are placed on a baking tray and put in
a medium hot oven where they can be safely left to their own devices.
Fifteen or twenty minutes later, your average girl is actively wolfing
this down (served in the dishes in which it has been cooked) and
mentally notching you pretty high on her dalliance list.

The attractive thing about this dish, and a multitude of variants, is
that it can be cooked in the most meagre of circumstances. Should
your habitation contain no more than a single gas ring, success yet lies
within your grasp. The baking and poaching processes are interchange-
able. Instead of shoving the egg dishes into the oven, place them in a
saucepan with no more than half an inch, or a little over one centi-
metre, of water. When this boils, turn the heat down to simmering
level and retire to the gay dalliance as before.

Of the long list of egg recipes recorded in Larousse, probably seventy
or eighty are variations on this theme, different herbs, other flavourings,
crumbled bacon instead of, or as well as, mushroom. It is up to every
young romantic to find his own pathway to the stars.

Continuing our survey of egg splendour, we arrive at the last of the
methods that deals with the natural, unaltered egg − namely, frying. It
has been suggested that this is one of the earliest forms of cooking

known to man, eggs or otherwise. Primitive man placed foods on rocks heated by the sun. Strong men in Australia, it is reported, break their eggs on the corrugated metal roofs in the outback and there let them sizzle in the searing sun. One would have supposed the roofs less than ideal as cooking surfaces, both on the grounds of hygiene, and also because, presumably the eggs would stick as they do in thin metal frying pans and one doesn't quite see how the eggs are to be removed after frying without breaking the yolks or otherwise damaging them as an article of food. But, presumably these are not considerations likely to daunt strong men.

The fried egg, put together with bacon or ham, is one of the classic dishes, the virtues of which are universally extolled. A.P. Herbert would not hear a word said against it:

'Bring porridge, bring sausage, bring fish for a start,
Bring kidneys and mushrooms and partridge's legs,
But let the foundation be bacon and eggs.'

In Holland, bacon and eggs, or ham and eggs, 'uitsmijter' as it is called there has achieved the status of the national dish. In effect, it seems to be available at any meals establishment at any hour of the day, on demand.

Before we consider the niceties of cooking the fried egg, you might care to consider the social implications of serving fried as compared with other forms of cooked egg.

Gertrude Stein, describing the particularities of a Parisian cook: 'Hélène had her opinions; she did not, for instance, like Matisse. She said a Frenchman should not stay unexpectedly to a meal, particularly if he asked the servant beforehand what there was for dinner. She said foreigners had a perfect right to do these things but not a Frenchman, and Matisse had once done it. So when Miss Stein said to her, "Monsieur Matisse is staying for dinner this evening," she would say, "In that case I will not make an omelette but fry the eggs. It takes the same number of eggs and the same amount of butter but it shows less respect, and he will understand."'

As to the proper frying of eggs, I revert to the formula which I have previously expounded, namely, that the ideal to be aimed at is a yolk with a firm outer layer and a squidgely liquid centre. Of course, the degree of squidginess is a matter of personal taste. In addition, it is my experience that few people relish eggs on which large globules of runny white slide about the upper surface like remnants of pond spawn.

The most suitable instrument in which to fry eggs is a heavy, vitreous-enamelled, cast-iron pan. Into this should be placed a knob of butter or margarine large enough to cover the surface to accommodate the egg, which should be broken into a cup and poured carefully into the pan when the fat is hot but not smoking.* As soon as the white is firm enough, slide a spatula under the egg to make sure that it is not adhering to any part of the metal. During the remainder of the cooking, the pan should be gently agitated so that the egg slides about. In addition to giving the wrists valuable exercise, this will ensure that the egg is evenly cooked, and that there is no burnt outer fringe. At the last moment, carefully slide a serving slice under the egg, making sure that the lower edge of the yolk is not nipped and ruptured, and turn the egg over, cooking it in the inverted position for no more than twenty seconds. This will get rid of the runny white, but preserve the liquidity of the yolk.

During all these cooking operations it should never be overlooked, or omitted, that the flavour of egg is enhanced by the introduction, during the cooking, of a few grains of salt and the lightest dusting of ground pepper.

These days it happens rarely that eggs bought in shops or supermarkets have deteriorated to the condition in which the celebrated curate discovered his to be. But, just to keep store managers on their toes it is worth describing here a quick and handy check on the status quo of any egg currently under consideration for the next menu. As Charles Dana, who as a busy New York newspaper man was well acquainted with every variety of egg from the sandwiched, through the hard-boiled to the bacon-and-egged, once pointed out: 'All the goodness of a good egg cannot make up for the badness of a bad one.'

---

*If it should happen that when you break the egg in a cup, you find the yolk is ruptured, do not despair. All is not lost. There is a simple tool to remedy the situation. It consists of a plain metal ring, about one and a half centimetres deep, which rests in the hot fat at the bottom of the frying pan. The damaged egg is poured into this. The ring holds the egg firm until the white has solidified. Slide then your spatula under the ring, and run a knife around its inner edge. The ring can then be removed and the egg will be stable enough to continue cooking as normally.

Inside the egg is a membrane that contains the white and yolk ensemble. At the larger end of the egg this comes away from the shell to form an air chamber so that the infant chick, if and when it ever gets to the hatching stage, can breathe. The shell of the egg is porous, and as the egg languishes on the supermarket shelf, moisture leaks through it, causing the air chamber inside to grow larger. The older the egg, the more voluminous the chamber.

It likely happens that you will have somewhere about your kitchen a pan of some kind holding a weak saline solution, such a one, for example in which you are about to cook vegetables. Pop the egg under consideration into this. If the egg is so fresh that it is still warm from the hen, it will sink like a stone to the bottom, the air chamber in it being singularly small. The average so-called fresh egg from the store will just about keep its shell above water, floating sluggishly. If the egg bounces merrily on the surface of the water, showing no inclination whatever to sink, it should be instantly proclaimed bad and declined with thanks.

There remains but two of the basic ways of cooking eggs yet to be described. Of these, scrambling is the simpler. (For some reason, this is often incorrectly called 'shirred eggs' in America. These, in fact, are cooked unbroken in an oven, and in France are known as 'looking-glass eggs').

This is a method of cooking that demands a certain level of smart attention on the part of the practioner concerned. There is no lee-way here for the quiet gossip with neighbours, or the hectic pursuit of trespassing flies, and similar activities that ordinarily fill out the domestic day. For my own part, this is one operation where I find it necessary to wear my spectacles so that I can peer closely at the eggs. The moisture rising from the pan steams up the glasses so that I cannot see, and I am awaiting the introduction of steam-resistant lenses for use in the kitchen.

Two eggs are sufficient, in this instance, to satisfy the normal appetite, and these are lightly beaten in a bowl so that they are unbruised.

We here come to a matter of serious consideration for those cooks who clean up their own messes, in this case, saucepans in which scrambled eggs have been cooked. Those portions of the egg directly in contact with the hot surface of the pan will stick most tenaciously to it. Subsequent soaking will do little to reduce the amount of laborious scraping necessary to remove it. The remedy, I have found, is to melt a small knob of margarine in the pan before cooking commences. Soaking then allows the egg to be lifted away without too much distraction from higher thoughts.

The pan to be used, in any case, must be a cast metal one and not a thin-skinned steel ditto. Melt the precautionary marge, pour the beaten eggs in, place on a moderate heat, and stir continuously. After a short while you will notice solid flakes of egg forming at the bottom of the pan. Your stirring here should be designed to bring these to the surface, allowing more liquid egg to flow to the bottom and become solidified. Watching ever more closely, you will discover a magic moment at which all the egg is solid and yet with still a liquid patina or sheen. The time to remove the egg and serve it on hot toast is ten seconds before this happens!

Success here requires of the cook a certain divination for which the only preparation are age and experience. But, as you would expect, there is a way round.

At this point purists will avert the head, savants mutter in their beards and students of the cordon bleuisme churn their gastric juices in impotent rage, for good husbandryman that I am, I cannot turn aside from my clear obligation.

Those not favoured with sublime anticipation should add what I call a slosh, and which in real terms turns out to be two tablespoons of milk to each scrambled egg, or half that quantity of cream. This preserves the liquid state of the cooked egg for a much longer period of time, and its removal from the stove becomes less critical. However, its character is changed also. The undiluted egg solidifies into tall, towering craggy yellow cliff faces, like ice bergs, while the milked eggs cook into a less dramatic mass of creamy yellow foam, which is yet palatable and delicious to eat.

France, which has the gourmet reputation as a nation, is a top-and-tailer in the meals department. At the top the results are so supreme you could not reasonably expect to better them anywhere else. At the bottom, she produces meals that are so abysmal a Chicago sewer rat would sniff with disgust and scamper away. These deplorable offerings tend to run along wherever tourists and travellers go, as if the French would not dare to do anything so awful to their own kin, but do not care too much what happens to those just passing through. Two of the most stomach-curdling horrors that I ever remember coming face to face with across a plate were both French. One was at the Paris Motor Show; the other at Mont-Saint-Michel.

There was a time when, as one bowled along quiet provincial roads in France, for a quick meal almost any cafe would whip up some kind of an omelette at the drop of a few francs: au nature, au fine herbes, au fromage or au jambon. Together with a cluster of pommes frites, fresh bread (you used to be sure of fresh bread in France even on a Sunday morning when people collected, and still do in many parts, their hot loaves from the bakery on the way home from early morning Mass) and a carafe of wine. It is ironical, therefore, that one of the historical havens of the French omelette was at the previously mentioned Mont-Saint-Michel where now, to my taste, only a bowdlerised version of the original article is now generally available. There lived in those parts at the end of the 19th century a certain Madame Poulard who, taking over a mediocre establishment called the Auberge de St-Michel Tete d'Or, converted it into the Hotel Poulard and laid the foundations of a world-wide reputation with a simple recipe for an omelette.

There are two schools of thought about omelettes: one says that they should puff up, the other that they should lie flat. I am a flat omelette man, and in this I find myself in total accord with the celebrated Madame Poulard. In 1922, she committed the secret of her omelette to paper, and this, in translation, is what she wrote: 'I break fresh eggs into a terrine (earthenware bowl), I beat these well, I put a large knob of butter in the frying pan (poêle), I pour in the eggs and I stir constantly.' This splendid lady died in 1931 at the age of eighty, but she had retired from the hotel trade many years before.

Even today, it is the practice of small local French restaurants to serve their meals 'en famille'. There is no choice either as to meal, or time of eating. At 12 noon for lunch, or 7 o'clock in the evening for dinner, everyone who is going to eat is there, ready. If they are locals, they have their own customary chair, their own napkin in its ring. The meal is served all at one time. Any passing stranger either has to wait, perhaps an hour or more, until the serving is finished. Or is met by that characteristic Gallic shrugging of the shoulder which says more clearly than any words: 'Because I do not want to see you, friend, you are not there.'

This was the tradition to which Madame Poulard conformed. In the years before 1914, her menu cost 2.50 francs, and never varied. The price included fresh, locally brewed Normandy cider and fresh butter on the table. The meal began with the celebrated omelette and was followed by ham, fried sole, pré-salé lamb cutlets with potatoes (pré-salé strictly speaking, means young lambs fattened in meadows bordering the sea, rich in aromatic pasture that gives a delicate flavour to the flesh), a roast chicken, salad and dessert.

The origin of the name omelette is interesting and unexpected. It derives from the Latin lamella meaning a thin plate, properly of metal. This, in Old French became la lemelle which was corrupted into l'alemelle which by then had come to refer to the thin blade of a knife. Another form, alumelle, was a word for the sheathing of a ship. Alemelle became alemette when used to describe the thin skin formed by the eggs in the bottom of the cooking pan: this changed to aume-lette, and then to its modern spelling omelette.

Having brought you (I hope) patiently through the ground work, the time has now come to expose you to what may be termed the husbandarial aspects of the egg. For it is a potent force, a ready butt-ress to prop up the tottering reputation as a cook, ready to redeem the situation when all the world seems about to crumble in upon the beleaguered kitchen.

Let me write a brief scenario, which goes something like this: the Muse who ordinarily beams fitfully upon your typewriting labours has emigrated to the South of France. She, meanwhile has impressed upon you that the evening meal cannot be a second past 6 o'clock because she has a committee meeting at 7:30, and has to rush some-where else to collect vital documents beforehand. Deviscerated by the hard grind of producing the day's quota of five pages, rewritten, it seems, ninety-eight times, you come to the kitchen later than you had planned with a mind empty of any illumination as to what the menu might be. Gloomily, you grope about the interior of the refrigerator. Your fingers stub against the gelatinous remains of the Sunday roast. In the absence of other inspiration, the dreary carcase is withdrawn, its meat dragged from its bones by a kitchen knife you have not the spirit to sharpen. These dreadful fragments, as one in a dream who follows a dreaded course of action, or a winding path that leads to nowhere else but the edge of a vertiginous abyss, you press through the mincer. Other remaindered morsels emerge from dark corners: some jellified gravy, a few crumbs of a pre-packed savoury herb stuffing, half a can of soup, a scattering of dried old raisins whose packet had burst from which rending they had found their way into the flour, the sugar and the desiccated coconut. All these bric-a-braceries you mix together into some kind of patty that hangs in your hand like a leaden weight as you realise its neat profile will fall apart into an ooze, as shapeless as an extra-territorial life force once it is exposed to heat. It is here that inspiration strikes. You break two eggs upon the mass. These, under heat, combine the ingredients into something of good order and succulence. 'What's this?' she asks, fifteen minutes later, having wolfed through your creation with every evidence of relish. 'Just a little thing I put together,' you reply modestly.

There is another expedient that I do not know how to spell correctly for I have never seen it written down. It came to me by word of mouth, and for whatever you think it is worth, I know it as Kartoffel-puffer. This is another of those 'when-all-else-fails' last resorts.

Its central ingredient is grated potato, which may not sound remarkably exciting. But then, have you ever really grated a potato? This is not an expedient normally to be found in the modus operandi of English, or even American, cooks who tend to confine themselves to the pots-mashed, pots-chipped and the pots-roast variety and not to bother their heads about any naughty foreign activity in the humble tuber department. They don't know what they are missing. When the chips are down in the hopper of the mincing/grating machine and a shower of white shreds comes with a powerful surge from the front end of same you feel that the culinary life is being lived to the full and all aims, ends and expectations thereof, wholely realised.

The next stage in this noteworthy dish requires the use of a large garden. If yours happens to be of the patio or roof style, then your neighbours must be prepared for the impression that the cataclysmic end of civilisation that all the newspapers have been talking about for as long as I can remember, is about to come to the boil. For, during the grating operation outlined above you will discover that the potato contains a considerable quantity of water which now has to be removed. And this is how to do it.

Take a clean towel and wrap the potato gratings up in it. Retire to your garden, take a firm stance with legs wide apart, and whirl the towel wildly round your head. A torrent of potato water will cascade from you, while, at the heart of it, you will remain quite dry. After a minute or so, the gratings will be quite dry also. The potato flavoured water from them, containing useful nutrients, you will find is good for any crops, flowers or lawn that you may have in hand.

Back in the kitchen, the towel-dried potato gratings are placed in a bowl and an egg broken on them, the whole stirred so that the egg is well distributed. I am being deliberately vague about quantities here because they are not critical. One egg is sufficient for any amount up to about a pound of peeled potatoes, and I do not think, ordinarily, you will be wanting to cook more than that. But, if your table is gargantuan and the number of persons sitting down to the trough legion, then add another egg.

The egg coated potato is lightly dusted with pepper and salt and hand moulded into burger or rissole size mounds which are then placed in a medium hot frying pan, the bottom of which is well-covered with fat — meat dripping will impart the best flavour.

Cook the kartoffel-puffers slowly — the heat has to penetrate the interior and break it down to a soft mouthwatering mass and this takes a little time. A long-pronged fork pushed in now and then will let you know how affairs are progressing. When all seems nice and soft within, bring up the heat to crisp the outside, turning the puffers regularly so that they cook on both sides.

This dish is good enough to eat on its own. With it, you can drink a refreshing glass of chilled lager — on a hot day, there is nothing better.

One other great offspring of the egg is mayonnaise, of which there is no certainty about its origin. For the past three hundred years or so we have had chaps like Pepys and Aubrey busily scribbling away, putting down on paper this, that and the other and anything else that happened to be brought to their attention. You would have thought that with something as fundamentally useful as mayonnaise somebody would have made a note as to how it started. But, no — nothing but empty dross and idle tongue-wagging.

There is a tale that one of Napoleon's chefs wished to create a special dish for his esteemed commander on the occasion of that worthy's birthday. But, being in Iberia and cut off by Wellington from essential supplies of butter and cream he had to make do with what local supplies he could muster which proved to be eggs and olive oil. Alas, this story will not emulsify — the sauce was in use before then.

Another fiction is that the word mayonnaise derives from Port Mahon in Minorca, and that it was invented by a cook of the Duke of Richelieu who was laying siege to the British there in 1756. Sadly for the romantic among us, this too has to be discarded. The sauce is even older than that.

In the opinion of the French gastronomic historian, Carême, the name comes from the verb manier — to stir. Another view is that it is a derivation of a very old French word moyeu — the yolk of an egg.

The sages tell us that the making of a mayonnaise is one of the trickiest of all culinary tasks. Anything is likely to bring on the dreaded curdle. You might judge the whole hand of nature to be against you. Never, it is said, start a mayonnaise if the wind is in the west, nor yet in the east, the south or the north. Never start one if the tide is going out or coming in, if the glass is rising, falling and especially not when it is standing still. Failure will dog your efforts if birds are in song, or silent, butterflies on the wing or notable by their absence, bees in honey or deprived thereof, rain approaching, receding, or if there is a drought.

Persons of the cookery persuasion, in my experience, do not ordinarily work in their kitchens in sub-arctic conditions, nor at temperatures comparable with those prevailing in the Sahara or the tropical rain forest.

Those of us who deal with ordinary ingredients in ordinary states of preservation have little to fear. Mayonnaises, by and large, are too courteous to curdle and are all too willing to see the thing is done right.

Only the electric mixer proves to be a thorn in the sauce, bedecking itself with glibly optimistic instructions intended to snare, delude and lull into a false sense of mayonnaisical propriety. Yet, these pitfalls are readily avoided, by clearing the brain, the brow and the voice, and asking firmly the simple question: what is a mayonnaise? Back comes the answer, straight from the oracle: it is an emulsion of egg yolk and oil. How is it to be achieved? you ask again. By allowing droplets of oil to fall upon the yolk in the presence of a rapidly twirling whisk.

Consider then the mixer, an excellent thing in its way and generally with hardly a word to be said against it, but definitely defective in the egg yolk department. Your average yolk, once inside, slides smoothly to the base of the container where it rests comfortably awaiting further developments. The "on" switch is alertly applied. The blades whirr like the swords of dervishes in a Cairo nightclub. The egg yolk looks on, interested but not involved, for the blades are whirling above its head and will continue to do so unless you are prepared to invest in sufficient eggs to bring the level up to those of the sweeping blades.

Otherwise not a shadow will disturb the eggy meniscus and the oil, no matter how delicately dropped, will be given a poor reception and the inevitable outcome will be the sinister curdle.

Yet, there is a way whereby all cooks can do their mayonnaise thing with suave nonchalance and aplomb. Having separated the yolk from the white with one of those ingenious plastic devices designed for that purpose, all that is necessary is to take up a position beside a broad basin with a container of oil (olive, corn or plain vegetable) in the left hand and an electric hand mixer in the right. Should you happen to be left-handed, these positions can be reversed.

Do you have the general picture clear in your mind? Basin, oil, hand mixer, and so forth? Right, then I will continue.

Flick on the mixer with your thumb or other convenient digit. Insert the blades into the yolk. There will be an initial scatter of yellow, but then everything will settle down into a steady flow. Rotate the left wrist so that the merest dribble of oil falls on the yolk.

By this agitation, you are trying to persuade the yolk to absorb the oil, not just to mix with it. It is like racial harmony, the egg and oil must join hands in the one community, and not just rub shoulders.

You can quickly tell if it is happening. Success is signalled by the forming of a thick, smooth cream which continues to grow as you add more oil. The evil curdle makes itself known by a thin, pale-yellow fluid, which falls apart the instant you stop the whirring blades.

But egg yolks are decent enough fellows, willing to get along with any immigrations of oil. Come one come oil, they say, and bend themselves to the task of making a good mayonnaise. You can aid them in this by adding small quantities — a table spoonful or so, of either vinegar of lemon-juice. For something powerfully interesting, try lime juice. Two egg yolks and half a pint of oil will make a firm mayonnaise that can be stored in the refrigerator.

By these recitals, I have hoped to make you aware of the valuable resourcefulness of the egg. If you have a soup that lacks body, beat an egg into a little cream and pour it in. If your white sauce looks as weak as a wet Wednesday, work an egg into it. Should your cheese rarebit turn sloppy, stiffen its backbone with an egg. Indeed, whenever in doubt . . . . . .

I have always been fonder of the egg than the chicken that laid it. I ascribe to Samuel Butler's view that: 'The hen is an egg's way of producing another egg'. But, credit must go where credit is due, as this anonymous verse suggests:

> 'The codfish lays ten thousand eggs,
> The homely hen lays one.
> The codfish never cackles,
> To tell you what she's done.
> And so we scorn the codfish.
> While the humble hen we prize.
> Which only goes to show you,
> That it pays to advertise.'

VEGETABLES

There came a heavy hammering at the door suggestive of big boots, large bodies and hard, horny hands that in their demands for attention from us of the indigenous population would not be denied. I did not deny them, and opened up. Their thick, dark-blue woollen coats, cloth caps and official issue, black wellington boots filled my kitchen.

They were not unexpected. Missionaries from the Gas Board had been besieging the village for a week, converting us all from the heathenish coal gas to the puritan North Sea stuff.

'Time for coffee?' I asked, this being the first of the good husbandry ploys in such a situation. Once, I might have mumbled something about tea, but they can adapt their ways too, and have learnt not to expect tea from the likes of me.

Their work on my stove would require the removal of the ingredients cooking thereon. 'Got some spuds on the go, then,' said the cheerful one, removing same, thus ending for the time being, any hopes I had about getting ahead with the preparations for my celebrated Creamed Cheese Potatoes.

'Had you realised,' I began, now that there were to be long empty hours to fill, during which time it was my clear obligation as a good husbandman to divert their attention, so far as I was able, from their tasks in hand, 'Had you realised that the humble potato is a mere infant among vegetables?'

'Oh ah,' said the mournful one, chewing what might have been one of yesterday's meals, regurgitated. His very inertia spurred me to my task, as one who sees a six-barred gate ahead when only the five-barred variety is expected, and knowing that the steed on whom one is mounted has a rooted antipathy to anything over three bars.

Imagine, I began, a busy day in 1539 — you know how busy those 16th century days could be — and one of the Spanish crowd (not stout Cortes's mob, but one of the other lot — Pizarro's group) were bundling up some things to be shipped back to the old country. A quantity of plants had come in from Peru and it seemed a good idea to bung a few in to see what the jolly farmers back in Spain might make of them.

On receipt, said aristocratic farmers read the brief and somewhat obscure instructions, which said something to the effect that the communities of mountain Indians found these a usefully nourishing food. There was, as a matter of fact, a curious technique they had evolved for preserving the crop. It was harvested and left lying out overnight, exposed to the nipping frost at those altitudes — something over 3000 metres. The next day, all the chaps, gals and kids got together and began tramping up and down on the crop until it was thoroughly crushed and all the moisture driven off. This marching up and down rigmarole was repeated for the following four or five days, after which the crop was stored in its dried state. When required for food, the chunu, as it was called, could be mixed with water and eaten. Thus was the freeze-dried method of food preservation invented.

The Spanish farmers, as who would not, read all this with their eyebrows raised in the way that high-born people from those parts do when they feel that everything about you is too upsetting for words and the best thing is to put you to the sword and save everybody a good deal of trouble later on. 'Eat this!' they hissed in their high-born Spanish manner, and turned from the prospect with every evidence of disfavour. Yet, they planted the small brown globes anyway, and when these came up, they congratulated themselves on having grown such an attractive display of flowers whose proper place was to grace the interiors of the elegant haciendas in which the aforesaid high-born Spanish persons lived.

And, so it was that the potato came to Europe, serving as a table decoration and an ornamental plant. From Spain, high-born gentry all across the Continent picked up the idea and put potato flowers in their window-boxes. Of course, the British, being an insular island people would have nothing to do with these European follies. Hardly a single potato plant managed to make the crossing from Calais to Dover. It remained for an English high-born person, one Sir John Hawkins, to bring in a few tubers in 1563, but the British were not impressed, and the idea died out.

Then, Sir Francis Drake, who had an inbuilt dislike of high-born Spanish persons, and especially those out and about on the high seas, had been cruising in the region of Cartagena on the Columbian coast,

which is on the deluxe Caribbean side of South America, when he
picked up a few seed spuds. As it turned out, he was returning to the
UK via Virginia, and as usual, the newsmen got it wrong and spread it
about that this was where these tubers came from.

British poor people, like poor people in most places then, were
having a pretty thin time of it, foodwise. Breakfast — if you could call
it that — was hardly worth creeping out of the blankets for. All you
might expect to find on the table would be a few hunks of the poorest
quality rye bread, or maslin (a coarse mixture of rye and wheat) and a
jug of ale. The mid-day meal was generally pottage — a mess of peas and
beans sometimes flavoured with a few scraps of bacon but usually not,
together with some cheese and more bread. The evening meal could
consist of oat-cake, bread, cheese, ale and eggs if things were on the up
and up. It would seem that at the lowest estimate, a few potatoes
would have been a welcome addition to such a basic diet.

But, these poor people were not entirely out of their tiny tubers.
The potatoes of those days were not the round, well-furbished specimens of the present age. Thinnish and a touch on the scrawny side, the
original potato was part cousin to the nightshade and contained
noxious substances which, unless carefully cooked out, could cause
stomach disturbances of the order, a little more than somewhat.

And so the potato trade grew slowly, with people being undecided
whether they were best used in flower or cooking pots. Some years
chips were up — other years, the chips were down. The Hospice de la
Sangre at Seville included potatoes in its order for supplies in 1573.
Twenty years later, a certain Gaspar Bauhon commissioned a number
of French farmers in the neighbourhood of Lyons to pop in a few rows.
Jules de L'Ecluse reported that by 1601 potatoes had become so
common in Italy that the peasants cooked them with mutton just as
they did ordinary vegetables, like turnips and carrots.

But, the spud was far from home and dry. It was banned in Burgundy in 1619 on the grounds that it caused leprosy. This may have
been a genteel cover-up for another opinion, widely bandied about at
the time, that the potato was an aphrodisiac ('They increase seed and
provoke lust, causing fruitfulness in both sexes'). Again, at Besancon in
1630, potato growing was forbidden — and indeed, the French continued in their Gallic way to be suspicious of the potato until 1771
when, in a thesis by the economist and agronomist, Antoine-Auguste
Parmentier, it was listed among the vegetables that could be consumed

in times of food shortage (the others were horse-chestnuts, acorns, the roots of bryony, irises, gladioli and couch-grass, so even Parmentier thought you would have to be pretty desperate to resort to the potato.)

In 1787, when food was short, Parmentier as a practical demonstration of his academic theme, took over 50 acres of land near Paris and grew potatoes. He was a cunning Frenchman and knew how to attract the attention of his bucolic neighbours. During the daytime, he arranged for soldiers of the Garde Francais to patrol his fields and guard the crop.   At night, the soldiers were withdrawn. The locals, being persuaded by these stratagems that something of value was to be found in the fields, crept in and did some neat work with spades. Pretty soon all adjacent village cook pots were bubbling with potatoes. To commemorate this ingenuity, items on French menus containing potatoes are often given the name Parmentier. This is not entirely merited, for it seems Antoine-Auguste had not quite the open face and simple heart that he professed. He had, in two words, been got at, or nobbled. Certain interested parties were pressing for the legalised use of potato flour in the making of bread and had diverted quantities of silver coin of the realm into the 'poche' of the aforesaid economist/ agronomist person with this end in mind.

At this point in the story the ordinary Hollywood film director would bring up a swell of violins and there would be a slow fade to a flashback when it all began. The camera would come zooming in over the miserable hutments of early man, and because the ordinary Hollywood film director of the classic mould will spare no expense to get the details right, there will be laid on what is generally termed a cast of thousands, standing by in case of need. Instructions to the props man would be something to the effect: 'Lay on the pulses, Sam.' And, Sam would duly oblige.

For pulses were just about the first vegetables that man cultivated – and we are speaking here of early man from the sixth or seventh millenium vintage.

'Oh ah,' said the melancholy one, whose conversational range was not of the most expansive. The essential elements of my stove had been reduced to their component parts, and the cheerful one was giving out those self-evident signs that indicate that packing it in for lunch is the next order of business on the agenda, with a subsequent adjournment to the pub clearly discernable from my kitchen window, straight across the Green.

'Care for a spot of lunch, here?' I asked brightly.

'What you going to cook it on?' asked cheerful chops.

'I've got some beer,' I said, some instinct informing me that this might indeed be the primary ingredient of the mid-day meal.

The mournful one laid down his cloth cap with a firmness of purpose that made clear his belief there was no point in expending money on beer in pubs when the same article was freely available on the premises now under conversion.

These pulses, I went on, deftly pouring, consisted for the most part of beans, lentils and peas, which makes the frozen ditto of the latter species residing in the freezer compartment of my refrigerator something respectable like antiques. Peas and beans were grown by the Hittites, also by the Assyrians and were also included in the lists of vegetables under cultivation in the garden of King Merodach-Baladan of Babylon who, as every Hollywood film research person knows, is of the 8th century BC. Peas were found in Twelfth-Dynasty tombs of Egypt together with quantities of beans and lentils. The same commodities have come to light at Swiss prehistoric lake-sites, and in England, at the Glastonbury 'lake-dwellings' of the Iron Age.

The Greeks were very partial to beans — they even had a God of Beans, and held 'bean feasts' in honour of Apollo, which is where the modern term comes from. Their relationship with it was of the common or garden love-hate variety. Pythagoras, when he was not brooding over the sums of squares on the sides of triangles, was inclined to give the bean the thumbs down. Later scholars argued that this verdict was cast against democracy on the basis that an early Greek voting system was to have all eligible males file past pots, each one casting his bean into the pot of his choice — the beans when toted up gave the score. Later studies have re-affirmed that the geometrical master's interests were purely dietary. Richard Taverner made the point for all time in 1539: 'Abstain from beans. There be sundry interpretations of this symbol. But Plutarch and Cicero think beans to be forbidden of Pythagorus because they be windy and do engender impure humours and for that cause provoke bodily lust.'

There can hardly be an item of food that at one time or another has not been accused of arousing lust — a factor which the average Hollywood director is happy to take into consideration. But it is, on the whole, the Pythagorean aspect of beans that has tended to be preserved in verse. A couplet much in vogue when I was a stripling was:

'Beans, beans, the musical fruit.
The more you eat, the more you toot!'

There are older versions, for example:

'Shake a Leicestershire yeoman by the collar
And you shall hear the beans rattle in his belly.
Shake a Leicestershire woman by the petticoat
And the beans will rattle in her throat.'

Persons in Hollywoodian high spirits are said to be 'full of beans', while those same persons, being possessed of the kind of sagacity that can wheedle an extra two per cent of the gross out of a film producer of that mythical town is said to know 'how many beans make five.' And before sister Susie started sewing her interminable shirts for soldiers she was apparently engaged packing 'Three blue beans in a blue bladder.'

Beans being of respectable antiquity, it is proper that they should be commemorated in the socio-culinary annals of such an up-market metropolis as Boston (not that of Lincolnshire in the Old Country, but of Massachusetts in the New). In the words of J.C. Bossidy:

'And this is good old Boston,
The home of the bean and the cod,
Where the Lowells talk to the Cabots,
And the Cabots talk only to God.'

Quick as a stanza, R.C. Bruce Lockhart comes back with:

'I've never seen a Lowell walk,
Nor heard a Cabot speak with God.
But, I enjoy good Boston talk
And Boston beans and Boston cod.'

One of the oldest of the prolific bean tribe is the soya of that ilk, which is not only consumed as a vegetable, and is the basis of the noted Oriental sauce, but having a high oil content, types of butter and cheese can be made from it. Soya beans, crushed in water, were drunk by Chinese peasants as a cheap and nourishing substitute for milk. In Japan, the beans were salted in oil and called 'sho-yu'. The Dutch thought this was the name of the bean itself and on the long voyage home muddled up the sounds and reported the name on arrival back at base, as 'soya'.

But, we have not finished with the little fellow. For here, the script demands a cut forward in time, with long tracking shots from a helicopter across vast regions of busily growing soya plants, while a Hollywood style voice-over reminds us that food of the ordinary kind such as steaks, chops and roasts, is now either in short supply or at a price that causes ordinary persons like you or me to turn away from the freezer compartments of our friendly neighbourhood superstore with the type of hollow laugh and cynical shrug of the shoulder previously reserved exclusively for persons crossed in love.

'Yes, folks,' the narration will state at this point. 'From the days of Ancient China, the soya bean has supported man for almost 5000 years. And like the celebrated Flanders and Swann Wom Pom, there is almost nothing you cannot do with it.'

Here, there is heard the distant fanfare of bugles, and the soya bean, like the US Cavalry of the Hollywood yore, comes storming to the rescue with the prospect of textured meat substitute and similar treats.

Next in line for our consideration is the second of the great pulse triumvirate — the lentil. The Bible, as every Hollywood film producer knows, abounds with dramatic episodes that can be used to enrich the feeblest script, by which attention the resulting film is doubly blessed in that the material introduced is entirely free of any copyright payment. Thus, the script which we have presently under observation can hurry forward into a tightening up of the action without the slightest risk of a veto from the front office and turn to the confrontation between the twins Jacob and Esau in which the former desires to secure the birthright of the latter (unspecified) for a sum to be agreed, which in the event turns out to be a small quantity of red pottage. 'Then Jacob gave Esau bread and pottage of lentils; and he did eat and drink, and rose up, and went his way: thus Esau despised his birthright.'

Later on, we find another of our heros, David, who may lay claim on the evidence here to be produced, of being the first of the great vegetarians. Being taken up by the governing power, the prison rules required him to consume a daily intake of meat and wine, and this to a man of his sensitivities and weak digestion was something up with which, as the phrase is, he could not put. Negotiations were opened with the object of having these unwelcome items replaced by pulse and water. With a keen eye for the Health and Happiness vote, Daniel specified 'Then let our countenance be looked upon before thee, and the countenance of the children that eat of the portion of the king's meat . . .'

After ten days of the pulse and water diet, a further check was made, as laid down in the terms previously agreed, and '. . . their countenances appeared fairer and fatter in flesh than all the children which did eat the portion of the king's meat.' In the required Hollywood tradition, this, naturally led to the inevitable happy ending. When those of the pulse and water diet eventually stood before Nebuchadnezzar — he was the king in question, you will recall — this same worthy found them to be 'ten times better than all the magicians and astrologers that were in his realm.' And, as they say in the testimonials that grace advertisements: 'You can't say fairer than that.'

Oddly, and, as one might say when reaching out for the most suitable phrase, by the greatest contrast, Mrs Isabella Beeton has hardly a good word to say for the lentil in her celebrated cook book, now back in the copyright stakes as a result of having been republished in recent years. Writing, as she was, in 1861, it was her information, that: 'The lentil is a variety of the bean tribe, but in England is not used as human food, although considered the best of all kinds for pigeons.' And she goes on to suggest that the reason for this rejection of the lentil — it is mentioned in just one recipe in all the 1112 pages of her book — is because it 'renders men indolent — a prejudice that may have been inherited from the Romans.'

Luckily, the French do not share this prejudice. In the Louvre there is, or there used to be — one cannot check up on every fact every single day of the week — three uncooked lentils taken from Egyptian tombs of the Twelfth Dynasty (2400 to 2200 BC). Scientists have examined these lentils with great care and have been able to give it as their confirmed opinion that they do not differ in any material particular from those currently being offered for sale in Egyptian or French open air markets.

If Mrs Beeton had taken the same trouble as we have done in these pages to give every vegetable the fairest benefit of the doubt she would have been in duty bound to report that in addition to lentils, other sources of alleged Roman indolence may have been the quantities of lupin seeds, vetches and chick peas citizens of that empire tucked into at every opportunity.

Peas may have secured the triumph of the Norman Invasion, for doubtless William's undercover gentry would hardly have failed to report to him the widespread distribution of peas among the Anglo-Saxons thus inducing in them indolence of endemic proportions.

Perhaps, as make-weight information to justify the large salaries he was secretly paying them, they might also have told him that to dream of a pea is to foretell a coming marriage. Such would not seem to be the stuff of which romances are made, but then if you happen to be no more than an indolent Anglo-Saxon, perhaps pea dreams are all you can manage.

While we are on the subject, it will not have struck you that the word pea is incorrect and arises from a curious error. The correct word is 'pease', and this generic term applies equally to the singular and the plural, as also in the word 'sheep'. But, in the translation from Old to Middle English, persons unknown decided that as there was an "s" ending, this should be dropped in the singular. So pease became pea.

The word pease, or pea — if you prefer, has a meaning in that it refers to a small thing. Students of word meanings will be captivated to hear that the same root word and meaning can be traced to India in the Hindi language in which the word 'pai' also means something small and of little value. This term eventually became absorbed into the Indian monetary system, in that an anna (a sixteenth part of a rupee) subdivides into four pice, and in turn, each pice divides into three pies.

'That's fixed it,' said the cheerful one, getting up off his knees upon which his labours had rested during the long afternoon.

'Oh ah,' said the mournful one, making a bee-line for the door.

On my stove there is an arrangement for illuminating the grill and oven at the touch of a button. It was after they had gone that I found this no longer worked.

A part of the universal experience of which philosophers are wont to wax eloquent, is the conviction time bestows on us that it is the ultimate destiny of all things not to work. This belief is at variance with the precepts of good husbandry here being advanced, and must be shrugged off with a gladsome laugh and cheerful countenance as one who would throw down a challenge to the Gods on the matter of working or non-working stoves. She was equally of this opinion and stiffened my resolve — if that is the phrase I am looking for — with a variety of forceful injunctions of the 'I'll be very interested to see how you've got on when I come home for lunch' variety.

At the crack of nine o'clock the next morning, therefore, I hastened across the Green to where the Gas men were assembled for their morning period of tranquility and contemplation, and made my way towards the smallest, most fretful, insubstantial wraith of a man, by whose air of having an inner vision of the Tartar hordes advancing across the steppes towards him with the undisguised intention of removing by the most effective means his essential organs, I recognised the fore, or boss, man.

'I can't see to everything myself,' he said before I had spoken.

I explained that everything was far from what I had in mind, that anything might come closer to it, and that to be precise to the point of pedantry, the item I hoped would soon appear at the top of his agenda under the heading 'matters in hand' concerned definite shortcomings in the stove-starting department.

He came, and stood over the lifeless form of my stove with his head held low in despondent contemplation of his professional runes.

'What you need,' I said, 'are a few onions. There are those who hold onions in high esteen as a means of generating instant pep.'

'Onions!' he said, backing away and coming to terms with fresh visions suggesting those of his organs remaining unsullied by the Tartars were about to be impaled upon red hot skewers. To ease his mind, I set out to put him in the picture.

The most ancient of the roots and tubers, I began, are the onion, leek and garlic. Root vegetables may have become useful to man because, being protected by the soil, they stood up to the worst ravages of the weather. Onions placed on a flat stone beside a fire and turned regularly, could be baked nicely.

The Turks have a story that pinpoints the onion, and cousin garlic, as early starters in the vegetable race. The Devil left Paradise to set foot on earth, and where he placed his right foot there grew an onion, and in the imprint of his left foot arose the garlic.

Onions were popular in Egypt, indeed bread, beer and onions were probably the staples of diet for those who built the pyramids making of that region a place always to keep upwind of. Roman food snobbery kept onions down the bottom of the comestibles scale as fit only for peasants. There, the leek reigned supreme — Nero thought it was good for his voice.

By contrast, modern medicine considers that too many onions can cause anaemia. But then, in the view of modern medicine there is hardly a single food that is not positively lethal once it is free to roam the highways and byways of the digestive track. Salt, as an instance, can shorten the life of any man by up to thirty years should he consume as much as an ounce a day of the stuff. Caffeine, the essential ingredient

of tea and coffee is fatal at a dose of one third of an ounce. Nutmeg can
kill, as can avocado pears. Liquorice brings on high blood pressure.
Spinach and rhubarb cause kidney stones. Carotene, which gives egg
yolks, sweet potatoes, mangoes and carrots that attractive yellowy-
orange colour can bring the same bloom to your cheeks in the shape of
jaundice. Cabbage encourages goitre. Or, you can be poisoned by green
potatoes, bitter almonds and lima beans.

But to return to our onions, when the Jews left Egypt, these were
among the commodities they felt the lack of most. 'We remember the
fish, which we did eat in Egypt freely; the cucumbers, and the melons,
and the leeks, and the onions, and the garlick.' All they had at the time
was manna, a substance not very much favoured by them.

Researchers into the mores of by-gone times among whom I number
myself, must inevitably bow to the conclusion that in all matters of
ordinary life the knee must be bent to the word of the common peasant, in the matter of onions and related vegetables just as surely as in
higher issues of the heart. 'Onions,' says the peasant voice, 'make a man
wink, drink and stink.' Which unsalubrious prospect is modified by the
view that 'Lovers live by love as larks live by leeks.' Yet, lovers who
carry the ardour of their passions into ripe old age are commonly put
down by the soubriquet 'dirty old' and this the peasant voice captures
in his unrelenting way 'Like a leek, a dirty old man has a white head
and a green tail.'

Leek, one discovers is the word that links all these vegetable varieties. Garleac is Old English for garlic: Holleac (hollow leek) stands for
chives, and Hwitleac (white leek) is what the Old Englanders called the
onion.

Garlic, possibly the most ancient member of this small clan, comes
from such distant times that in China it has its own ideogram. The
Greeks and Romans had hardly a bad word to say for it. Aristophanes
said it was good for athletic prowess. Virgil believed it gave strength to
peasant workers. Pliny maintained it was a cure for consumption.
Celsius claimed it was a cure for fever. Hippocrates said that it was
'hot, laxative and diuretic, but bad for the eyes.' Greek criminals were
given garlic to purify them of their crimes. Even the prophet Moham-
med pitched in with a testimonial.

'In cases of stings and bites by poisonous animals,' he wrote. 'Garlic
acts as an antidote. Applied to the place bitten by a viper, or to the
sting of a scorpion, it produces successful results.'

Coming to more modern times, Bernardin de Saint-Pierre reported that the smell of the vegetable — '. . . which is so dreaded by our mistresses, is perhaps the most powerful remedy in existence against the faintings and nervous maladies to which they are subject'. Alfred Franklin said of sixteenth century Parisians, that they did not neglect — 'to eat garlic with fresh butter during the month of May.' This, it was thought, set them up, healthwise, for the rest of the year. And, as is wellknown, doctors of that era carried cloves of garlic in their trousers pockets as a protection against the attacks of infectious air and epidemic diseases.

Indeed, only one serious thumbs-down verdict on garlic turns up in the annals of classic literature thus far scanned by this scribe. It comes in Horace's Third Epode — 'If ever any man with impious hand strangled an aged parent, May he eat garlic, deadlier than hemlock.'

'Can't stand the stuff, myself,' said the stunted fore-person, his head deep in that part of the stove normally reserved for foods awaiting the application of some hours of heat.

A popular dish with the Roman peasantry, I told him, not wishing his attention to be diverted from the task in hand, was composed of onions, garlic, wild celery and cheese all pounded together with rue in a mortar.

'Pretty powerful,' said a voice from somewhere among the pipes.

Not at all, I said. Mrs Beeton, whose name as an authority on culinary matters has possibly come your way before, has in her publication of 1861 to which I have referred more than once, a recipe for what she calls — 'Bengal Recipe for Making Mango Chetney' which lists in the following order, a ¼lb of garlic, a ¼lb of onions, ¾lb of powdered ginger, a ¼lb of dried chilies, ¾lb of mustard seed, 2 bottles of best vinegar, and 30 large unripe sour apples.

'Need a gas mask to live with that lot,' he said.

Madame Beeton is not a person to be without a remedy for every situation, no matter how extreme and should she have happened to be available for employment in these ruffled times might usefully have occupied herself running the United Nations or some similar administrative body. In this instance, she recommends the chewing of parsley as a means of removing from the breath any lingering traces of onion or other odours.

'Won't work,' he said emerging. 'Have to get new parts.'

'How long will that take?' I asked.

'Your guess,' he said, 'may be as good as mine. Better, if it happens you are a pessimist. Myself, I'm always optimistic and invariably wrong.'

His estimate, for what it was worth, ran to two weeks. Two months later, the parts arrived accompanied by a standard Gas person issue of large boots, cloth cap and thick blue overcoat.

'Could do with a coffee,' he said, shedding the official coat like a cocoon and emerging from it a brighter, younger person. 'Not myself today,' he added.

Not wishing to embroil myself in enquiries as to who he had become for the purpose of reinstating my stove to normal operational efficiency, I directed his hand and eye towards a dish of radishes in preparation for the lunch which in due course of Gas persons time, I hoped to consume.

Herodotus records, I told him, that he saw an inscription in Egypt which said that the builders of the Great Pyramid ate enormous quantities of radishes, together with onion and garlic.

'They told me about you,' he said, bending to his task with a stern gleam in his eye that suggested that if he was above nothing else, he was certainly above small talk.

But, when once one has established a reputation there is nothing for it, but to leap to its defence at every opportunity.

Did they also tell you? I asked him, that radishes are not mentioned in English cookery books before the 16th century. And that the Anglo-Saxons used a concoction of them to cure shingles, madness, demonic temptations and possession? That a poultice and drink of the radish was useful in curing pains in the right side? That radish salves were a specific remedy for headache, pains in the joints, eye-ache, warts and weakness in all limbs?

'They've sent the wrong parts,' he said, rising like a Neptune from a turbulence of pipes. 'I'll have to re-order.'

'How long will that take?'

'It shouldn't take long,' he said. 'But it will.'

And it did. Three months later, his boots were back again, upended beneath what had become a desolate region of my kitchen, being not so much used as in former times.

'What is it today?' his voice asked from an inverted position.

Almost absent-mindedly, I remarked that turnips had also been called bargeman's cabbage, kalewort and summer rape.

'Rape?' he queried.

Rape, comes from the Sanskrit 'rap', meaning a swelling or bigness. It is associated with the Latin 'rapa' – a root. The Irish form is 'raib' – in Old High German the word is 'raba', which in the modern language turns into 'rübe'. An Old Slavic word 'repa' becomes the Russian 'rjepa'.

'Funny word – rape,' he said.

It has long had romantic connotations, I went on. Young girls used to signify the termination of the soft-words-and-sweet-music arrangement by handing the boy friend a turnip. Said b.f. then slouched off to girl friends new. In the language of flowers, the turnip blossom signifies dreams of love. La Beeton, not overly given to romantic excesses in her work, limits the turnip to boiled and mashed versions of same, followed by the German Mode of Cooking Turnips, Turnips in White Sauce, Boiled Turnip Greens and Turnip Soup.

'They've sent the wrong parts again,' he said.

Over the months our relationship became one of mutual challenge. He would attempt to find some new way of saying: 'the wrong parts'. This is a challenging task, for the words in question illuminate a corner of the English tongue where variety is lacking and the introduction of new terms something to be heralded with lutes, virginals and sackbuts. For my part, while the vegetable panoply is extensive, running to hordes and multitudes, the conversational gambits by which these can be introduced so as to sustain the listener's interest are not so extensive as not ultimately to result in a limp flapping of the inventive muscles.

Carrots were once used in beer instead of malt, I told him. And, the colouring matter therefrom made a handy way of giving butter a hearty yellow bloom.

'They've sent the wrong parts,' he said, in the tone of voice that suggests the owner is about to turn in his boots for general stiffening and toning up all round.

Common names for parsnips used to be humpy-scrumples, limper-scrimp, rumpet-scrumps and wippulsquips.

'The wrong parts,' he echoed.

Visit followed visit: sometimes he came with a smile, at others, a frown. His air of gentle apology gradually slid away into one of derision at the inadequacies, if that is the word, of those who work at office desks in high places. 'I told them,' he murmured once or twice, as if the burden on his shoulders was of such a weight that it had to be shifted for comfort and easement.

There was one day when he came with a smile of a magnitude as of one who has seen the waters of the Red Sea recede at just the moment that his dearest enemy has expended a vast sum in buying the necessary equipment to take up the sport of water skiing. 'They've come,' he said, presenting a small box for my inspection, as if they should contain the Crown Jewels or some similar valuables.

Withdrawing from his van for the first time in my presence that hallowed bag of tools without which no Gas person is to be considered properly dressed, he applied himself to the task in hand, to whit, the revival of the grill and oven push-button lighting apparatus as previously described. A few moments deft work with the tools of his trade served to confirm a dark suspicion that had loomed on his brow almost before the work began that events were rapidly falling out in the pattern generally categorised under the heading — too good to be true.

'They don't work,' he said.

No attempt on my part to restore his good spirits had any effect. I gave him a quick belt of beets.

The beet has been known from the most ancient times, I began. On English farms it used to be known as the mangel-wurzle. This is a garbled translation from the German, viz — if you will pardon the expression — mangold (beet) and wurzel (root).

On his next abortive trip, I had prepared and ready for him, a broadside of cabbage. Originating possibly in the Balearic Isles, Greece and Sardinia, it was introduced to the UK — of course, it wasn't called that then — by the Romans. Symbolising gain and profit, it is the emblem of the self-willed. Ambrose Bierce said of it: 'Cabbage — a familiar kitchen-garden vegetable about as large and wise as a man's head.'

'I don't know how you put up with it,' he said as he left.

Bringing to me the regulation small cardboard packages of wrong parts became for him a kind of hobby, a welcome interval of relaxation in an otherwise taxing life that obliged him to rub shoulders with Medes and Persians, on the one hand, and Huns, Goths and Visigoths, on the other.

Did you realise, I said at one of our regular sessions, speaking across the kind of cup of tea that I had learned was the kind he liked, that Captain Cook's sailors chewed celery to prevent scurvy? Or that the Jews of ancient times, having been cast out of Egypt, made their way to Palestine, whereupon among the topmost of their priorities was to lay about with a hoe and other like implements, to scatter seed and do

everything necessary to ensure that therefrom they could rely upon a
good supply of cucumbers. Likewise the lettuce, I continued. The Cos
variety of which is named from that Greek island upon which the celebrated Doctor Hippocrates first saw the light of day and set about his
life's work of putting together in a form capable of being understood
by all other doctors – the hypocritical oath.

Not to mention the tomato, which being brought to Europe by
others of those active Spanish fellows from Mexico and parts thereabout, in 1550, or years thereabout, was greeted on arrival by nothing
but hostily and harsh words, these being directed to its bright colour
on the grounds that anything of that colour is bound to be indelible,
if not worse. Only the footloose and feckless Italians clasped the
tomato to their bosom, naming it the love apple or pomi d'oro, a title
which it still bears in that country today, or something thereabouts.

Once give a veg a bad name and it takes years to live it down. Three
hundred of the same later, Mrs Beeton, wrote of it: 'The fruit of the
love-apple is the only part used as an esculent (a Beeton-type word
meaning something edible or eatable), and it has been found to contain a particular acid, a volatile oil, a brown, very fragrant extracto-
resinous matter, a vegeto-mineral matter, muco-saccharine, some salts
and, in all probability, an alkaloid. The whole plant has a disagreeable
odour, and its juice subjected to the action of the fire, emits a vapour
so powerful as to cause vertigo and vomiting.' Which makes one wonder
why tomatoes are not now marketed with one of those neat, govern-
mental labels on each one, proclaiming it a health hazard.

But, we live in enlightened times, I told him at his next arrival (he
had given up even mentioning the parts as he clumped through the
door). A scribe writing of the mid-sixteenth century states that: 'At
the commencement of the reign of Henry VIII neither salad, nor
carrots, nor cabbages, nor radishes, nor any other comestibles of a like
nature were grown in any part of the kingdom; they came from Holland
and Flanders.'

'I wish I could cook,' he said and then, continuing in the tone of a
member of the electorate who forsees a forthcoming election in which
he is committed to placing his X in a certain box regardless of conviction, 'I'm getting married.'

My gift to you, I said, shall be one of some magnificence in that it
condenses years of horny-handed experience hardwon at a cost that
defies description. You shall have from me not a single recipe, nor yet

a dozen, but something that runs to hundreds or even thousands. For it is a recipe that is as numberless as there are vegetables in the soil of the earth.

At this, he drew up a chair and sat down, being of the opinion that the matter in hand would take some time to unfold. But, in that, he was wrong.

The recipe I have in mind, I said, is so simple that children could describe it. Nothing more is required than a largish, heavy saucepan (something of the 3½ pint or 2 litre capacity), and a quantity of boiling, lightly salted water to occupy same. Into this can be tossed almost any vegetable, be it a pulse, root, tuber or green leafed. The only other equipment needed is a long-pronged fork of the kind that comes 'au pair' with carving knives. The vegetables under consideration are cut, or otherwise trimmed to whatever seems a convenient size or arrangement in the eyes of the practitioner. As the water (once boiling, reduced to a simmer) works its will on the veg, the degree of softness induced can be tested by inserting the fork at regular intervals. This is a branch of the culinary art, the skill of which can be gained by any man.

'Boiled vegetables,' he said, his enthusiasm being no greater than had he just then discovered beetles with their spindly legs hard at work at the to and fro motion and making steady progress across the upper surface of his beer.

'There is more,' I said. For, if by this intelligence you gain the knowledge of a thousand recipes, then shall that gift be doubled by yet one further insight.

I am speaking, I said, of the roux.

'Who's roux?' he asked.

The roux, I answered, is the basis of all sauces. Much has been written of the craft necessary to accomplish its making in accord with the precepts of the master chefs, but a plain wooden spoon and an active stirring of the hand will take you a long way towards that objective.

Take an ounce of margarine, or an eighth part of a half pound block which can be arrived at by dividing the block into half, then halve the halves, and halve again. Drop this final ounce into a heavy saucepan and place on a low-to-moderate heat. If you value your reputation as a follower in the footsteps of the grand masters, do not attempt to speed up the process or alter the setting of the heat once you have begun.

When the margarine is nicely melted and bubbling pleasantly add to it one ounce (a heaped tablespoon will do) of flour. As you stir, this will quickly combine with the marge to form a substance not unlike the stuffing to be found in cheap upholstery. Pour in a modicum of milk, i.e., a slurp or splish of same, and continue to stir with a steady rhythm, which is necessary not so much for the purposes of the task in hand, but because you are going to have to keep it up for a little while yet. After the first splish, the milk will become absorbed to form a material like the stuffing of cheap upholstery after four years hard wear. Splish or slurp again and continue to stir. After each dribble of milk has been absorbed you will see the beginnings of a smooth sauce. (It is important not to re-slurp until the slurp before has been taken up.) Here, you are entirely free to add or not add further milky liquid at your own discretion depending on what viscosity of sauce you had in mind, thick or thin.

Here, your choice of flavourings is as wide as the Dutch sky. (It was Rembrandt, or Van Eyck, or one of those other Dutch painting chaps who mentioned that the sky in Holland is wider than anywhere else. Subsequent commentators have attributed this characteristic to the flatness of Dutch terrain.)

'What's that got to do with it?' he asked, his brow as furrowed as a field under the plough.

'Nothing,' I said, for it is self-evident that the talent for good, plain husbandry does not necessarily co-exist with that of literary appreciation.

Let us consider the carrot, I went on, a vegetable not noted for its ability to lend sparkle and zest to the domestic occasion. Allow us to surmise that the fevered face of the hard-pressed husbandryman peers in at the half-stocked shelves of his refrigumrator (well, that's what I always call it.) to find only, it being the end of the week, two commercially made meat pies bought two weeks back because of the alarmingly low price at which they were being auctioned off, and a bunch of sad and weary carrots, they in whom long periods of reflection on the inequities of life have left nothing but a profound mood of disillusionment.

Bring the life back to their cheeks with a brief spell in simmering salted water as previously advised. Meanwhile, bend the elbows to the making of a white sauce in full accordance with the instructions to be found printed in the body of this chapter. When made to the thickness that pleases you, add to it a mini-modicum or half-teaspoon of mustard, either powdered or made-up. Pop in the cooked carrots, whirr or whirl your spoon like a dervish, and arrange with due decorum on plates, placing at the summit the said meat pies which have, meanwhile, been heating in the oven.

When the thingummies were in the wilderness they ate manna with everything. A more recent authority recommends chips on the same basis. In my advancement of the white sauce routine I can, and do, claim the additional benefit that whereas manna is always manna, and chips chips, white sauce is pretty much whatever you care to make it, and I dare say that you could indulge in the stuff at every meal for a thousand days and not repeat yourself once, at a conservative estimate.

Almost any edible can serve as a flavouring, even the cider mentioned in chapter one, bringing to the taste buds a regular touch of the 'well-well-what-do-we-have-here' reaction. All the herbs and spices qualify, as do essences and liquors of many kinds. It remains only for you to experiment, as someone might once have said to Dr. Frankenstein, he having just then stumbled across a miscellaneous collection of assorted limbs and other body components.

This putting together, I added finally, for I could see by his regular shifting back and forth on his chair, and the way his eye scanned the four quarters of the room as one who, in an emergency seeks the exit, that my lengthy description was running him into overtime thus calling up in his spirit an urgent desire for the active life and the open air, this putting together of the world's vegetables straight from the boiling pot, and all the world's flavourings opens the door on an untold richness of culinary splendours the like of which your ordinary hamburger person, or meat-and-two-veg merchant could not, even in the most troubled of their nighttime visions brought on by a certain digestive effervescence and interior rumblings, conceive.

'Also, on the writing of long sentences,' he muttered, rising to his feet and reaching for his cap. 'Pity about your stove.'

Not at all, I reassured him. It is one of the tenets of good husbandry that there is an answer to every problem. And I took from the cupboard where I had been storing them the box of tapers I had discovered in the local ironmongery. With these, I can light the grill and oven just as readily as if push-buttons had never been invented.

I never saw him again. But shortly thereafter, I saw the announcement of his wedding.

A gift seemed in order, and I arranged for there to be delivered to the reception, a small beribboned package. Some matters are too personal for public disclosure, and I shall make no statement as to what was contained therein.

But, the packet was identified by a large label on which I had written in large letters so that everyone present could read them, an inscription that was in every way most suitable, in the rather raw traditions of the ceremony, for a young man to receive on the day of his nuptials.

On the label were the three words — 'The wrong parts'.

I do not know if his marriage was blessed or not. But if it should have turned out that his gas appliances do not rattle to the ticketty-tack of tiny fingers, I know exactly how he feels. My push buttons still don't work either. But then, I can always fall back on tapers. Husbandry triumphs over all things.

SOUP

'Did I ever tell you' I asked, 'how the restaurant came to get its name?'

I was speaking to Mr Clutch who was, as we say, 'at it' again.

Mr Clutch is our local handyman and he has been 'at it', so far as we are concerned, for the better part of fourteen years.

The event that I wish to recall began perhaps ten or twelve years ago, when Mr Clutch arrived to install a modern, solid fuel stove, accompanied by a back boiler, in what was then a blank wall in the front room of the cottage. In those days Mr Clutch was otherwise engaged during the daytime, and so his sessions with us began in the evening.

He would arrive, as he did on that occasion, and there would be a good deal of sleeve rolling up, overall putting on, and I have even known the decorous changing of trousers.

The blank wall in question proved to be as false as the flimsy fibreboard of which it was composed. Lurking behind it, like a blot on the escutcheon over which a thickish layer of paint has been worked, was a nasty, narrow Victorian grate into which, with patience, three modest lumps of coal might have been introduced, but no more. With our full approval, Mr Clutch cut it out.

Behind it was another of slightly more generous dimensions, reminding one of the skin-flintery rubbing of hands while installing a more economical grate in front of a generous one.

'Cut it out,' we said, and Mr Clutch did just that. Behind it was another grate, yet larger still. And another behind that, tempting one to issue the declaration that one was definitely going a bundle in grates.

A loose brick at the base of these excavations suggested the possibility, when removed, of some vast cavern behind it. Mr Clutch squatted comfortably in a ruminative position and communicated silently with that vast storehouse of inner knowledge that tells him all there is to know about such things as fireplaces. Rising again, he spanned his arms across the wall, and at the furthest extremity of his left hand began to chip away at the soft plaster, uncovering at a depth of half an inch, a wall of bricks curving inwards. Doing a double straddle with both legs and arms combined, he moved rightwards about eight feet, and chipped again, cutting down to, at the same depth, another sector of the same brick wall, curving back from where the other had gone.

By now, midnight had struck, and the time had come for even handymen to down tools and hurry away to seek the comfort of that which somebody once said (I can't remember who) 'knits up the ravelled sleeve of care', or some such phrase.

Not that there was not — if you will excuse the double negative, a good deal of unravelling going on in all departments that night. Issues of great moment had to be weighed finely in the balance. Mr Clutch would be returning on the morrow requiring an answer one way or the other: namely, to close or open up. Should one take the prudently cost-paring course of averting the gaze from the works of the past, and return to the previous task in hand, to wit, the installing of the previously purchased stove? Or, should one toss prudence together with associated budgetary considerations, out of the window, or up the chimney, or wherever it is that one does toss such matters on these occasions?

As early as his other preoccupations would allow, Mr Clutch hot-footed it to our front door the following evening, his face showing evidence, by paleness of colour and deepness of wrinkle, of that inner torment that urged him to preach caution on the one hand, and reckless abandon on the other. There, in the kitchen, we pledged ourselves to abandonment and operations began anew, chipping and cutting with ready hands and light hearts, caring not one jot for the desert of rubble accumulating in what was once our feet-up-on-the-stool and head-nodding-on-the-cushion front parlour.

Soon, other village talents had to be called in to the work, one such calling made in the general direction of Mr Backhand, who has a truck, led to the utterance of the immortal phrase that what was required was the removal of 'two tons of 18th century dirt.'

Those who had originally closed the fireplace, sought to confine the draught by packing the cavity behind the brick wall with mounds of earth from the garden. During the removal operations conducted by Mr Backhand and his large black dog who never left his master's side, clearly bearing the opinion that those who would uncover old fireplaces must be persons of evil intent and not to be trusted, gardeners came from miles around to run through their hands and marvel at, soil that had not felt the touch of a human spade for two centuries.

Once the handyman strip-tease was completed, there was nakedly revealed for all to see, a handsome brick archway spanning the fire-place and supporting the upper floor. Behind this there protruded downwards a screen of bricks like a vast pink, buck-tooth. To one side was a bread oven.

Through all these operations Mr Clutch bore the air of a missionary who, tramping through uncharted territory and expecting to find only a handful of sinners waiting to hear what he has to say, discovers a great gathering of heathens all as anxious as hot pie to get on with the hymn singing and passing the hat round for the collection.

And we came to recognise, over the years, that whenever he came to get 'at it' again, while the ultimate results would be superb and the cost much less than might reasonably have been expected, the time taken would be longer than that period originally estimated by a matter of four or five times.

Now, it may be reasonably asked, what all this has to do with restaurants, and that explanation shall not be held back from you for a paragraph longer.

It is the responsibility of the good husbandryman, not only to make weighty decisions as to the closure or otherwise of discovered fire-places, but also to ensure that those therein engaged, in this case one handy person and one wifely ditto, are suitably nourished during the period of their activities. When the air is thick with floating grime, and all available horizontal surfaces are occupied by tools, and debris, or have been removed to make way for more tools and debris, the conclu-sion as to what is the most suitable nourishment to offer is not an easy one to come to.

Mr Clutch is a large man with large needs. But, the large knees that go with the rest of his equipment make it virtually impossible to balance plates thereupon. Meals of the ham-and-eggs variety, coupled with those involving steak-and-kidney pudding with gravy or sausage and chips are debarred on the grounds that, there being nowhere to rest the plates with any degree of stability, no deft flourishing of knives and forks is possible.

Thus, one is led to the making of great buckets of thick soup, and hence the remark with which this chapter began, made at a moment of pause when Mr Clutch was making inroads to his third plate of the brew, and getting himself set up for the fourth. At such moments, his digestion requires the addition of some light conversational matter for its proper functioning. It seems, I said, he having indicated by a twist of his head that he was ready to receive information on the subject of restaurants and the naming thereof, that in the 18th century should one happen to feel the need for a quick snack, or something more substantial, that the only establishments to which one could resort were cookshops or inns. But in France there was a man named Boulanger who made and sold soups and as part of the promotional puffery for getting these products into the stomachs of cash-paying customers, he called them restaurants, that is, substances, which when imbibed, had restorative powers. They must have been quite good soups because friend Boulanger's enterprise prospered. More and more of the French citizenry clamoured for same. And to Boulanger's way of thinking, the time had come to expand on the grand scale.

But, there was a snag. He was not a member of the Corporation of Eating-House Keepers, and was therefore restricted to humble soups and nothing of a more complex composition, like stews and roasts and other dishes of that kind.

The question arose, what exactly is a soup? How is it to be defined? Where is the line to be drawn between a thin stew and a thick broth? A tricky question, as it turned out.

To test the ground, as it were, Boulanger began to serve his clients with sheep's feet in a white sauce, no doubt listing this on his bill of fare as 'Sheep's feet soup'.

The Eating-House chaps took him to court, and after a good deal of this-ing and that-ing, with everyone getting hotter under the waistcoat, the matter reached the attention of the French Parliament which passed a special bill to declare, officially, that sheep's feet in white sauce was not a stew, and by implication therefore, to be considered as a soup. As a result, said sheep's feet became famous all over Paris. People crammed into Boulanger's establishments where the best sheep's feet were reputed to be sold, and this public interest put his establishments on the eating map. The name "restaurant" which he had originally applied to his products, became in the common usage of the time, attached to the places where they were served. Thus, the restaurant, properly speaking can now be considered to be a place where one goes to have one's vital forces restored.

There are in these days, alas, many places of business going under this name of "restaurant" where no such restorative process is readily discernible. For that matter, often the reverse occurs, and one requires a day or so of light activity to recover from the disagreeable experience.

This is, one regrets to say, particularly the case in both England and American and one wonders whether places calling themselves "restaurants" should not, in the former case, have actions taken against them under the terms of the Trades' Description Act, or, in the latter case, their operations should not be brought to the attention of the eagle-eyed gentlemen of the Federal Trade Commission in Washington.

It would be pleasant at this juncture to be able to recount the tale of how soup came to be first thought of. It would be beguiling to hear how this ancient Chinese philosopher, making his way on foot, set up his meagre camp by the roadside, gathering twigs with which to light a fire under his pot of water. And as he sat meditating in the way elderly Chinese philosophers have, an activity which when you or I do it is called falling into a doze, there came a sheep which stood in his pot. Nudging the sheep politely to one side, the old philosopher remarked what an interesting aroma came from the heated water, and plunging in his spoon, in that abandoned way philosophers have, without the slightest regard for the most simple concepts of hygiene, he tasted the brew and found it good, thus giving name for the first time to Sheep's Foot Soup.

Regretfully, no such story has come down to us. It can only be remarked that the Chinese certainly consumed soup from ancient times; for the rich, according to a third century BC poem, there was sour and bitter blended in the soup of Wu – if you wish to know more about this gentleman you should look him up in Who's Wu – and for the poor, bean curd soup with rice. Fish soups also were very much in vogue.

Soup was also served in India where dietary theory took a complicated form. The rule of table there was that each meal should consist of thirty-two mouthfuls. The stomach, it was said, is divided into four compartments. The knack of good eating, according to these Indian theorists, was to fill two compartments with solid food, one with liquid, leaving the fourth empty to allow for the free circulation of what was, with a lack of decorum, called wind. As a candidate for the liquid intake, soup filled the bill nicely, although one conjectures whether a good deal of turning and twisting was involved to make sure

that it went where it was supposed to go, and not mistakenly get mixed up with the solids or the gases.

The Romans served soup of a thick, gruelly kind, what in modern parlance would be known as 'rib-sticking'.

At these words, Mr Clutch leaned forward and took unto himself a fourth helping, his spoon cleaving a path through the turgid liquid like the pressing back of the Red Sea for the passage of the Israelites from Egypt.

The so-called convenience soups, I continued, which have their modern form in packets of dried powder and compressed cubes, had their origin in the 18th century in a preparation much enjoyed by travellers. A stock made from veal, meat trimmings and pig's trotters was boiled until all the water had been driven off. When cold, this mixture set like a solid glue and could be carried about in the pocket or handcase for years. A piece of it dissolved in hot water supplied an acceptable soup.

Although literary tributes to the qualities of soup are comparatively rare, those that are to be found have a certain fulsomeness that suggests the enthusiasm of the writer is far from half-hearted.

Saki (H. H. Munro) once declared: 'I believe I once considerably scandalized her by declaring that clear soup was a more important factor in life than a clear conscience.' While, Thackeray — William Makepiece, once unbuttoned his thoughts in this fashion: 'This Bouilla-baisse, a noble dish is a sort of soup, or broth, or brew.' Not quite up to what one expects of the unrestrained Thackerarian style in full flow, but nonetheless showing us where the chap's true feelings lay.

Molière, who preceded the Parisian "restaurant affair" previously detailed, by some hundred years or so, had one of his characters say: 'I live by good soup and not by fine language.' And another fellow whose reliability can be depended on in the matter of foodstuffs, Jean Anthelme Brillat-Savarin, who was ten years old when the Sheep's Foot Soup balloon first went up, gave it as his firm opinion later in life that: 'A rich soup, a small turbot, a saddle of vension, an apricot tart: this is a dinner fit for a king.'

There is a proverb of unknown origin that circulates in French military circles to the effect that 'Soup makes the soldier', and having experienced, on one occasion, a French military soup of unrivalled oleaginousness — if that is the word — one knows exactly what is meant.

In fact, the only literary bad notice that has come to hand thus far, is from the pen of Heinrich Hoffman:

> Augustus was a chubby lad,
> For ruddy cheeks Augustus had:
> And everybody saw with joy
> The plump and hearty, healthy boy.
>
> He ate and drank as he was told,
> And never let his soup get cold.
> But one day, one cold winter's day,
> He screamed out, 'Take the soup away!
> I won't have any soup today.'

To search for the origins of words is very much like the harvesting of truffles as practised in the nether parts of France in which dogs and pigs are put to the task of locating the smell of these fungi from their growing places underground. The animals in question apply themselves to the task with what can only be described as pongers joy. They sniff.

They snort. Their nostrils distend, opening to the delight of the in-coming odours, like the tent flaps of the fortune-telling lady's establish-ment at a fair ground drawing open to welcome willing clients.

It is much the same with us who have some passing interest in the origins of words. We peer. We pry. We poke around in old tomes, testing the ground, inventing connections and enjoying our fancies just as does the truffle-sniffing sleuth.

The word soup provides just such an opportunity, I said.

Mr Clutch lifted a curiously shaped metal hook, thrust it into the plaster ceiling, applied his weight to it, and brought down a crashing mound of crumbling ruin held loosely together by limp wooden lathes.

Readers will, no doubt, be puzzled by this development. At the last report, the said Clutch was squatting uncomfortably in front of the newly opened fireplace. So let us explain that the action has moved forward in time a couple of years or so. During the interval of this script cut the discovered fireplace has settled down to routine oper-ations, taking in anthracite grades of coal — and therefore smokeless — and sending out quantities of heat to which the cottage, in its two hun-dred years of existence has not been previously accustomed. Certain of the sinewy, rough-hewn wooden components have begun to exhibit signs of excessive dryness and to give up their supporting roles in order to move on to better and higher things. One such component whose* inclination to move on has reached alarming proportions is the stair-case. This, in total defiance of the modern trend for neatly cut timbers and treads of equal height, is made from what appears to be an original tree. None of the steps up shares a common dimension with any other, and the support to this ancient structure consists of two half-trunks nailed along the underside, still with the original bark intact. Mean-while, Mr Clutch, in pursuance of his handymanery has become a regular visitor to the cottage, and is here now, in this instance, to demolish the staircase prior to its being given star-billing on the village's annual November Five Guy Fawkes Bonfire. Concomitant with this enterprise is the removal of the adjacent and surrounding kitchen ceiling to expose the old oak beams thereof. That concludes the summary of the action thus far. Readers may now read on.

There is in my collection, I continued, a work by the excellent Rev. Wal-ter W. Skeat in which the view is expressed that the word soup derives from the Low German "supen" — to drink, through the French "souper" — to sup.

*(See page 25)

About the associated word sup, Skeat has more to add, tracing its development from the Old High German "sufan", the German "saufen", Swedish "supa", Dutch "zuipen", Anglo-Saxon "supan" to the Middle English "soupen", all of which having the meaning to imbibe, lap up, sup or drink in.

Again, moving to the word sop, Skeat onfolds another lengthy skein from the German "suppe", the Low German "soppe", Middle Swedish "soppa", Middle Dutch "zoppe", Dutch "sop", right through to the Middle English "soppe" meaning both something to be supped and the act itself. All clear thus far?

It takes no great intellect to infer from all this that the essential quality of soup is that it is a commodity to be imbibed in liquid form. It is no hindrance to this understanding that there may be solids floating in the said liquid. Indeed, in earlier times it was the custom to have lumps of bread floating in the soup to give it body and these were called "sops".

Now let us move on to another absorbing word — supper. According to Skeat, whose diligence and industry in these matters cannot be too highly praised, this also can be connected to the Swedish "supa", Icelandic "supa", Low German "supen", Old French "soper", French "souper", to the Middle English "soper". In these forms it has the meaning also "to sup".

From this, I concluded, any reasonable person would understand that supper is the meal at which one takes in liquid refreshment. Or, to be absolutely conclusive and comprehensive in the matter, one takes soup at suppertime.

'Its too big,' said Mr Clutch who for some time during my conversation at him had been distractingly fiddling about with a metal ruler, running it alongside pieces of wood in the way handy-person-carpenters do.

On a previous occasion he had run the same instrument over the baulks of timber doing duty as our access to the upper floor and had in the meantime of his spare moments run up a replacement which, the morning after the tearing down of the old structure he proposed to move into position. Now, it was his sorrowful contention that the replacement was too long by several whiskers for the space about to be vacated for it.

We moved back into the room where the fire blazed. There is a camera technique whereby some natural event taking several weeks to occur is run through on film in a matter of seconds. This now happened to Mr Clutch, who could instantly have secured star billing in any film dealing with the life history of the prune. The process might be termed "instant shrinkage".

As he sat beside the fire, the lines on his face deepened as one watched, the skin shrank and a generally pruneful aura settled about his person as the full enormity of his error took a hold on his mind.

It was clearly a problem for Super-Soup. While I plied him with a freshly brewed broth she leapt about the kitchen with tape measure in hand, she being good at such, and worked up a theory that he, Mr Clutch, had taken as his reference point the second knot hole to the left rather than the third, this accounting for the imagined discrepancy.

There was a chap named Harvey who, in the seventeenth century came up with the idea that human blood did not just slosh around inside the skin but had some organised flow from one point to another, and it would be far from my intention to argue against such well documented ideas. Yet, there are factors that one wonders whether Harvey and the others have taken into consideration. Such a factor was visible in the visible presence of Mr Clutch who, a moment before, you might have thought had developed a serious leak in the system from which all the aforementioned blood had drained away. Now, just as in the television commercial where the happy motorist is filling his sump/radiator/battery with the new secret ingredient for smoother/swifter/more reliable running, the Clutch blood level could be seen to be rising back to normal levels. Starting at some point well below the shirt collar, it came up, lapping the chin and eddying about the cheek bones like a tidal run in full spate.

'Good stuff,' he said, and I was not clear whether his reference was to the soup in his bowl, or her deft foot-rulery. Absolute fairness demanded that the credit be equally divided.

She was right, of course. She always is. Mr Clutch was back the next morning at 6:30, having stayed up most of the night checking his figures. We, having climbed to bed by step-ladder, climbed down again — at least, I did — she has other views about the proper hour at which sleeping persons should be roused from their slumbers. But, before the morning was ended and the noon day sun, beloved of lyricists, had risen to what persons of refined speech refer to as the apogee, somewhere above the clouds, the staircase had slid smoothly into position, leaving barely a ripple on Mr Clutch's serene face.

Now a further cut forward in time occurs in the script, and the instruction to the production crew is: Mr Clutch is 'at it' again, this time continuing his theme of beams. In the view of Mr Clutch, like the sins of the exalted, wherever beams exist, they should be exposed. Encamped in the room with the fireplace, exposure was in hand.

If here I return to my soup theme, it should not be inferred by the attentive reader that the only sustenance Mr Clutch receives, or has ever received on these premises, is the previously mentioned liquid form of nourishment. But in work of that kind it is to be understood that time is of the essence, and crises abound. So that, while I make no mention here of the pies, sausages, eggs, bacon, puddings, stews and grills with which Mr Clutch's digestive arrangements have been geared to high speed operation in pursuit of his craft, the picture that must be retained in the mind is of self hovering uncertainly in the kitchen, pressing ahead with culinary activities, expecting at any moment to hear that particular comingling of sounds — the human voice against a background of collapsing whatever — that signals an instant dilemma to the solving of which one is immediately summoned. ('Could you hold this?' Mr Clutch's voice is heard to say from somewhere within a fog of rising dust.)

In these circumstances, soup is the only sure answer to the cry, when it comes, for hot food.

There is a philosophy of soup making that begins with the concept of stock. The good husbandry man has learnt from his years of hard grind that stock is a commodity on the manufacture of which the best culinary economy is based. Almost anything can be converted to stock: a statement that is even more true than the other one frequently made that almost anything can be converted to alcohol — I have never come across a beef bone beer, nor yet chicken giblet wine. But, beef bones and chicken giblets both make very good stock, the doing of which has the additional advantage that something is being made from nothing. Beef bones and chicken giblets, unless enstockulated — if you will pardon the word — are commonly consigned to the garbage can or dustbin. Yet, arranged in a large saucepan, covered with water to which a little salt has been added, placed on the stove and allowed to bubble merrily for an hour, or so, these will produce a liquid that is the foundation of many a fine stock.

Now, the average good husbandry man sets out to be all things to all persons, allowing no distinction to be drawn between beef bone and chicken giblet addicts and those of a more vegetable persuasion.

Vegetable stock is also good. It can be made by the same method as previously described, using as ingredients any old vegetable scraps of what-have-you that happen to be lying about the place. Indeed, in France — as I shall describe in a later chapter, if you will pardon the insertion of a trailer for a forthcoming attraction right in the middle of the main feature — ladies of gentle birth are given to hovering about the extremities of open air markets towards the close of business, gathering up such scraps of vegetable remains that are left behind by the busy stall-holders after they have quit the scene of commerce, later to pop them into the stock pot for the generation of that universally useful commodity — vegetable stock.

Students of the soup scene will be dazzled, once they get to grips with their subject, by the wealth of recipes for same. They abound. They flourish. They pop up on every page. Whole books have been published containing nothing else but ideas for soups. A standard work lays down seven main categories of soups. Under such headings as Clear Soups, Consommés, Thick Soups, Velouté and Purée Soups, Classical, Regional and International Soups, it deals with some 306 mixtures, and one begins to realise that the surface is only being lightly scratched.

Here a vision springs to the script of the young lad, the scion of the house, pride of his parents' eye — or to be exact, they being absolutely normal parents in every regard, pride of his parents' four eyes, caught redhanded in the act of tossing bricks through the greenhouse of M'sieur Le Maire and of removing therefrom for immediate consumption prime strawberries of matchless quality.

'My son,' says the stern father. 'You are wasting your life, throwing to one side with a careless laugh the great opportunities that good fortune has laid at your feet. Will you not repent and give up your idle and unsocial habits? Is there nothing in the world to which you would be prepared to dedicate your industry, nothing that you might take up as your life's work?'

'Father,' says the aforementioned scion, standing up straight and looking as stern as his parent. 'I cannot tell a lie. I wish to make soup.'

So, away he goes with the blessings of his family and a handful of francs in his pocket to become a potagiste or potager in one of the great kitchens in which skill he becomes so renowned that when the King of France falls into a chronic melancholy his doctors send him to receive libations of the miraculous soup, as a result of which, at about reel six or seven, our hero becomes the Duke of Burgundy, marries the prettiest high born daughter for kilometres around, and returns to the ancestral home to bail his old Dad out of Debtor's Prison, he having taken to drink.

'I owe it all to my soups,' sighs our hero to his heroine as she melts in his arms at the close-out.

How was it done? you will want to ask. 'How was it done?' echoed Mr Clutch's voice from his head up among the timber beams, now exposed.

Read on, or in Mr Clutch's case, listen on.

The purpose of stock is to provide a foundation to soup on which a towering edifice of tasteful delight can be built. It imparts to the soup a flavour, and adds to it nutricious ingredients that I will not spell out on the grounds that technical names in cold print always seem so remarkably inedible.

This said, the good husbandry chap can avoid a good deal of complication and confusion by sensibly simplifying that which has been laid down soupwise in the classic mould.

The main stream themes of the soup world are the Thin and the Thick. This can be otherwise stated as the Without and the With. Having put down clearly what the Without is without, the various forms of the With can be filled in with little or no trouble to one and all. Clear so far?

Take something of utter simplicity as Carrot Soup. Into a stock — either vegetable or meat — a quantity of the orange coloured vegetable cut small, sliced or grated is placed — and arrangements put in hand for simmering on the stove to commence. No quantities are specified because good husbandry fellows find their own way through that maze. Nor is any firm line taken on the adding of a pinch of salt or other flavouring substances. Taste for yourself and you shall be answered, as someone once said, somewhere, I forget where.

But, whatever you do, do it with confidence and style. Approach the simmering pot with a jaunty swagger. "Look here, soup," you murmur. "Let us have no disagreeable nonsense here. Let there be no bad mannered boiling over, boiling dry, no spluttering, spitting, frothing, foaming or other manifestations of ill humour. So long as this is clearly understood, there is no reason why we should not get along together splendidly."

Having murmured which, you light heartedly toss in a handful of herbs, a scattering of sugar, a touch of mustard — whatever comes to your mental taste band. And, having by these means come across original associations of taste sensation, if that is what it is now called, you can beguile all your friends, win yourself a dazzling reputation, publish a Beetonly book, be interviewed on the television, make lecture tours to America, and retire handsomely on the proceeds to a remote island where obliging turtles will crawl to your modest abode on the beach and more or less beg to be converted by your masterly touch into further award winning soups. As you can see, there is a lot at stake, here.

But, the stock theme has not yet been entirely exhausted. Further words are called for before the master soupmaker's hat fits you like a glove.

In addition to the sovereign remedies recommended, other sources of acceptable stock are available. These come in the form of cubes or tablets that dissolve in hot water. Other varieties can be found as powders, concentrates and jellies, but what the Scotland Yard chaps call the modus operandi, remains unchanged, viz., one brings hot water to same, stands back and allows the good work to commence.

Here it will be seen that the carrot soup under advisement shares something in common with that celebrated soup recipe to be found in Act IV, Scene 1 of Mr Shakespeare's "Macbeth". For starters, it requires a few poisoned entrails, a toad that has rested beneath a cold stone for thirty-one days and nights, and a quantity of sweltered venom, somewhat difficult to obtain now-a-days. The recipe continues:

> 'Fillet of a fenny snake,
> In the cauldron boil and bake;
> Eye of newt and toe of frog,
> Wool of bat and tongue of dog,
> Adder's fork and blind-worm's sting,
> Lizard's leg and howlet's wing . . . .'

it being required that said ingredients be then boiled and bubbled. Add to it:

> 'Scale of dragon, tooth of wolf,
> Witches' mummy, maw and gulf
> Of the ravin'd salt-sea shark,
> Root of hemlock digg'd i' the dark,

> Liver of blaspheming Jew,
> Gall of goat and slips of yew
> Sliver'd in the moon's eclipse,
> Nose of Turk and Tartar's lips,
> Finger of birth-strangled babe
> Ditch-deliver'd by a drab . . . .'

This, and the carrot recipe can be seen, at this stage, to belong to the Thin or Broth family of soups, and we can understand what it is such soups are without. They are without thickening, an omission which Mr Shakespeare makes haste to remedy in his next line:

> Make the gruel thick and slab . . . .'

although he gives no indication how this is to be done. This defect we shall remedy at once.

There are several schools of thought as to the thickening of soups. Somewhere earlier in this work I have made reference to the making of 'roux', a piece of work I should like to re-invoke here, for it is an indisputable fact that one person's roux is another's thickening. All that changes is the quantity of liquid added to the original butter/margarine and flour amalgam, and the fact that, instead of milk, one makes the roux with stock.

So that there is no subsequent pointing of the finger of scorn, opening up accusations of errors and omissions, as in the case of Mr Shakespeare, who as a playwright is doubtless pretty strong stuff, but as a cook lacked attention to some of the finer points of detail, let us repeat the sequence of events as required by the script.

We fade into an opening wide-angle shot of sliced, diced, grated or cut whatevers — or, if you prefer, carrots — simmering in stock. Cut to a close-up of a fork being inserted therein to demonstrate tenderness. Cut to another saucepan of the heavy style in which the margarine/flour business has just begun to get under way. The camera pans to show the aforementioned stock being drained from the carrots and poured in short bursts into the marge/flour at which a good deal of bubbling and sizzling takes place. Here, a wooden spoon comes into shot from right of frame and goes into vigorous stirring action as per requirements. As each slosh of stock is absorbed, further slurps are added. From being thickly creamy, the goo becomes thinly creamy as the liquid input is continued. At this point, the script-writer has to exercise a fine point of judgment as to the precise degree of sloshiness required; one chap will prefer something more on the lines of the Shakespearian gruel, another will go for the dribble variety. 'Chacun à son goo' as the French neatly put it.

Now the action hots up, leading to the cliff-hanging climax. Cut-away to the soup-cooker's face, showing the noble brow ridged with the effort of concentration and creative thought. Shall a herb be added here? A spice, perhaps? A touch of mustard, or whatever comes to mind and hand? The spoon stirs faster.

Meanwhile, back at the other saucepan, the cooked whatsits — in this case, carrots — lie waiting. Has our hero forgotten them? But no! There is a clatter of spoons across the worktop, a flash of stainless steel gleams from beyond the stove. The carrots are saved from oblivion, scooped up by the deft hand of the cook in the nick of time and carried safely across the wasteland of the sink and draining board to the haven of the cream sauce wherein a federal benevolence deposits them. Simmer, simmer, simmer.

But, what is this? A final twist to the plot! The script cuts forward in time. The carrots have simmered for several moments and are well integrated with the liquid. Should integration go further? Some prefer lumpiness in their soup as giving some clue to the identity of the in-gredients. Some like a kind of semi-lumpiness which can be achieved by draining off the liquid, attacking the soft vegetable matter — carrots, remember? — with a potato masher or some similar instrument of compaction and then re-uniting them. But, there is another, more refined, sophisticated apparatus.

The camera cuts to a low medium shot of the tall, elegantly shaped body of a mixer-blender rising above the surrounding terrain like the Pharos lighthouse. A tracking shot shows the saucepan containing the cream/carrot mix being brought across to it: close up, the mixture is poured in. A hand turns on the electric switch while the other hand holds down the lid else the initial surge of the liquid within will blow it off. The blades whirr wildly, the soup surges and swirls. After a few minutes, the mixer is closed down.

From it is poured an exotic carrot coloured fluid that the potagiste now tastes. His face registers ecstasy. He has arrived at the pinnacle of soup creation. Bring up a great swell of violins and brass. Close-out.

That is the basic soup scenario of the Thick or With type. But, there are variations on the theme. For some, the mere thought of roux smacks of carbohydrates and sin. It results in flab. Others blue-pencil it as being of low and worthless origins. For them, methods and ingredients of a more aristocratic description are called for. High on this list are cream and egg yolks, either singly or in combination.

To use them involves no great change in the soup script. Stock is brewed as before and the whatnots – still carrots – cooled therein, leading on to the mushing of same, or the dumping of the entire soup caboodle in the mixer. Now the practised hand brings forward a half pint, or thereabouts, depending on how close to the end of the week/ month it is and how much of the stuff the household budget will bear, for each two or three pints of soup. Divorce a yolk from its mate the white, and beat the former into the cream, and shoot the mixture into the soup and give the mixer a final whirl of the blades, or the spoon a final twirl of its bowl. Return the soup briefly to the heat and, as master soup cooks all across the world are prone to cry out at this moment: 'Eh, voila!'

There are other ways of adding the With to the soup without. Rice is one, and crumbled bread is another, both expedients well out of the aristocratic class and well into the sinful carbohydrate area. However, most soup cooks tend to fall into that social order that we keen classifiers of the social scene tend to call, when we are on form, as middle-class. And in the matter of soup-thickening, there is a middle way.

Despite shortages of other foodstuffs, the peasantry of Europe – a recalcitrant lot, and still are, if the truth of the European Common Market Agricultural Policy were ever to come out – were as stubborn as geese when you want to get along a pathway that they happen to be blocking. Geese don't budge and neither did the peasants. When edibles were on the down-and-out, you would have thought ordinary chaps would have leapt at the chance of a few heart-warming potatoes. But, not a bit of it. They spurned the spud. They rejected it, and cast it aside. In 1774 the hungry residents of Kolberg refused to eat loads of same sent to ease the situation by Fred the Great of Prussia. Twenty-one years later, an American fellow, Benjamin Thompson, who happened also on the reverse side of his visiting card to carry the name Count Rumford had much the same experience in Munich. The local lads, peckish though they were, expressed themselves as being entirely against the idea of potatoes in their soup.

All of which was a great pity, when one considers the delicacy and restorative powers of that brew. A modicum of stock, a cluster of nicely peeled spuds, a little salt, a splash of milk, a hint of pepper and you have something that will bring joy to any digestive system. In addition, and here is the vital wrinkle in this culinary fabric, the potato mash in its more solid form can be used as a thickener. The same applies to other root veg. And here, our soupy visions begin to open out into a potage panorama of limitless combinations.

Here the camera cuts back to the carrot lying naked on the work top, its elegant slimness reminding one so much of well-turned female legs that in earlier times carrots were banned because of their power to arouse libidinous imaginings in the minds of innocent cooks. But, we are made of stronger stuff than that. It takes more than a few roots to arouse lust in us. What counts with us is what the stuff tastes like, and in this we must stand up and be counted, in the view of post office administrators, with those who are beguiled and won over, not by the possibility that the lustful letters that they place trustingly into the hands of postmen will ever reach the persons of their affections to whom they are addressed, but by the particular raspberry or strawberry flavour of the gum on the back of the stamp which is released when licked.

A carrot as a carrot is all right. In my view, as a soup it is even better. But, consider the carrot as the basis of a With soup. Enstock it, cook it, season it, mash it and add to it chopped tomatoes – not fresh ones which are messy to handle, but tinned plum toms that are cheaper, easier and have a stronger flavour and better colour. If there is also added to this a glob of cream, the whole being then whizzed in the mixer, you have a soup that will unleash any potential lasciviousness in those who drink it.

Similarly, and likewise, potatoes treated in the same way, e.g., stocked, cooked, seasoned, mashed, and so forth can have their entrinsic mystery enhanced by the addition of a few leeks. And so on, and so on, and so on – said words representing the addition of several chapters of recipes which do not need here to be written down, remaining as they do for your discovery.

As with vegetables, so with soups, the world is your onion. But, as a hint of the triumphs to which a voyage of discovery across the oceans can lead, it behoves me to sketch in one such soup upon whose attractions of taste and so forth I have long relied for the unravelling of many a tricky social knot. (Be it known that even the publisher of this work has succumbed to its appeal, and no one comes higher up the resistance-to-appeal index than any known publisher.)

'Is that so,' said Mr Clutch, his face spattered with grave-like creosote stains with which he was then daubing exposed beams.

'Sitting at the very table,' I confirmed, 'that would be standing here had we not been obliged to remove it to a safer place during beam-uncovering operations.'

'How does it go, then?' he asked.

'I will tell you,' I told him. And I did.

A largish knob of butter, I began, is tossed in a frying or heavy sauce, pan, and an onion is chopped and cooked in it slowly, so that no hasty frizzling or browning occurs. When tender — remember the fork — blend in by rapid stirring one or two teaspoons of curry powder. And, as a thickener an ingredient not mentioned before, but useful if you happen to have it — cornflour. Otherwise, ordinary flour will do. As this cooks slowly with the onion on a low heat, toss in the results of peeling, coring and chopping two good sized apples of any variety, and on top of this a pint of whatever stock you happen to have about the premises, of meat, veg or stock cube origin. In course of time this will come to the boil. When it does so, lower to the simmering level, stirring regularly.

Here, we begin the tasting process, without which no successful soup-making enterprise reaches a satisfactory conclusion — if you will pardon the tautology. As the simmer-simmer-simmer carries on gradually thickening the brew by driving off the moisture from it in the form of vapour, add a little sugar, graduating the quantity by taste. Follow this with a similar quantity of salt.

Meanwhile, you will have secured a lemon, squeezed the juice from same, and by applying the empty lemon shells to the abrasive surface of a grater you have removed the outer yellow rind. This, together with the juice, you tumble into the soup.

At this point, the exhausted soup cook can put the feet up for thirty minutes or thereabouts while the magic therapy of warmth does its work.

When the time to return to the task in hand comes up, the first job is to blend an egg yolk in thick cream and add this to the hot soup. Courage, for now the job is nearly done, as King Charles said to Nell Gwyn when unloading oranges from her pannier.

All that remains is to give the soup the electric blender treatment, or the masher attack, if you prefer, remove it to the refrigumrator — that is what I call it — and chill. There it may remain until required, to be served hot on a cool day, or cold on a sweltering one. For it is one of the charms of this soup that it is just as agreeable at either temperature.

'I'll try that,' said Mr Clutch.

And he did, serving it to certain persons coming to his house, who — I do not say as a result, but the facts speak for themselves — promptly offered him a remarkably good price for it.

Mr Clutch now lives more than a hundred miles away in a converted 18th century bakery that he found going for a remarkably low price by the simple expedient of sitting in village pubs, swilling ale and plugging in his lines of communication to the local gossip. Now, he is busily exposing his own beams as assiduously as a leader writer on a left wing newspaper exposing the foibles of Big Business.

Any beams that we feel need exposing, we shall have to expose ourselves. But, at least there will be a considerable saving in our soup budget.

CHEESE

'Sometimes it happens,' I said, 'that what we think is poor husbandry turns out later on to be good. Take the matter of cheese.'

'Oh yes,' they said, grouped on the lawn, their 'oh-what's-he-on-about-now' faces turned toward me, waiting for the lunch which it was my turn to cook.

Or, for that matter, take this garden, I went on. This very stretch of velveteen grass where you are sitting comfortably was once a wilderness of weeds and rubbish.

I don't suppose, I asked them, that any of you have had to tackle a wasp nest in its natural state? None of them had.

The nest in question, occupied by wasps of an advanced choleric disposition, was situated just to the east of where that elegant cluster of rose bushes now stands.

Evidence of the presence of a wasp nest is largely provided by the presence of wasps. The nest, or residence, itself, being as it is an entirely underground installation, betrays itself only by a small hole at ground level through which the wasps flit for purposes of ingress and egress, if those are the words I want.

Books giving helpful advice on the subject of wasp nests, the removal thereof, are prone to advance such remedies as the pouring of paraffin (kerosene) therein, lighting same and standing back to watch the wasps depart with all haste.

What such students of the wasp nest removal situation seem to have overlooked is that the entry hole being of fine dimensions the penetration of the inflamatory fluid is limited. Droplets of it percolate no further than the entrance hall, causing wasps on duty there to come smartly to attention, asking themselves as they do so what the hell is going on here? or words to that effect. Emerging from the self-same entrance hole, they flutter their wings free of the thin mineral oil otherwise used for burning in lamps and produced by distillation, sometimes from oil shale, and looking about them to see who has perpetrated this liquid intrusion to their premises they espy the person thus engaged and move in for the attack. In this, they are not inhibited in the way bees are, namely, their sting is not a one-shot instrument causing as much damage in the wielder as in the victim. Wasp stings are suitable for multi-usage. They work more than once, and the paraffin pouring person, unless he is quick on his feet is likely to have rapid confirmation of that fact.

Experience, that mother of all knowledge, wisdom and invention, as somebody once said, teaches that there is only one reliable way of dealing with nests (wasp). For this the person undertaking the task needs to be draped in butter muslin, not tightly wrapped as Egyptian mummies are, but in loose hanging folds. Gloves and a hat should be worn, and a space in the drapes left for the spade to protrude.

The digging activity needs to be carried on at a brisk pace, for the longer it continues, the longer is the digger at risk.

Wasp nests are not jerry-built. When wasps put down roots, they put them down to stay, making their domicile of the best available materials, putting them together in a sturdy, long-lasting manner.

The nest shape the most liked by wasps is that commonly known as being of the pear profile, not the narrow-necked Conference pear, but the fuller bodied William variety. And the building material the most in favour with them at the time of which I speak, was old newspapers, which they reworked into a honeycomb without the honey, in which one had the impression of being almost able to read the original text.

This is the installation facing, or confronting the would-be wasp nest demolition person. It needs to be dealt with promptly from within the protective muslin, by brisk thrusts of the spade, tumbling the wasp bedrooms, lounges and nurseries out into the bright light of day, whereupon said wasps, after a certain amount of initial to-ing and fro-ing, surveying the position and getting to grips with the problem, pass the word round that the time has come to move on to wasp nests new, picking up on the way a few of the latest copies of the local newspaper.

One final act is required to complete the demolition. Wasps are busy, conservative creatures, and if the remains of their nests are left lying about, this attracts them as would a jig-saw puzzle retired military persons. They buzz back and forth over it with puzzled expressions on their faces, nudging a piece here, and rolling a piece there, just to see

if it can't be fitted together again. The would-be wasp nest demolisher, if he does not wish to have to repeat the performance all over again next week, has no option but to set fire to the scattered remains.

'What has all this to do with cheese?' they asked.

'I'm coming to that,' I told them.

The scene of a wasp nest removal can be instantly recognised by knowledgeable persons. It has about it a good deal of untidiness. Lumps of soil are scattered hither and yon, as the saying is. There are hillocks and hollows where h. and h. were not to be found before, and a good deal of returning to the status quo has to take place before the basis of a happy garden can be secured.

The opportunity for doing this is not likely to arise, if, as in this case, the wasp nest remover becomes aware of the presence of bindweed. This is a growth of which Flanders and Swann have written about, and sung about, with great charm. Yet, one feels that some of the colour might have gone out of their cheeks when compiling their verses had they ever been challenged by a growth of bindweed about their premises. It is not enough to shove a trowel into the soil and lift the offender therefrom. Bindweed roots grow long and deep. Any attempt to trace them to their source will oblige the previously mentioned bindweed operative to dig equally long and deep, forming great trenches across the terrain. As his patience and temper, in that order, reach breaking point, he will put out his hand to remove what seems to be the last inch of root which will, thereupon, break off, leaving many undiscovered yards below ground, to regrow and retrace the path back to the surface. This is the common destiny of bindweed operatives and is one of which the Greek tragedians of old might well have whipped up a poignant box-office success provoking the tears of strong men to gush down the aisles.

'What has all this to do with cheese?' they asked again.

'I'm still coming to that,' I told them.

A fact of life, I continued, of which the bindweed afflicted person rapidly becomes aware is that where the bindweed goes, there goes also the nettle, in itself a splendid plant for testing the grasping powers of resolute persons and in its day the main ingredient of many a nourishing soup, but not, in the opinion of latter-day garden retreat makers, a plant with which one can live comfortably cheek by jowl. In a word, a weed.

The removal of the nettle, root and crop − if that is the expression, is one attended by dangers against which precautions must be taken. The busy nettle operative, plying his spade, cannot at the same time be casting about him to grasp nettles. The grasping of nettles is an activity that requires single-minded concentration. The hand must be pushed forward to within a millimetre of the leaf or leaves about to be grasped; a careful judgment must be made of the movement of the leaves under consideration as brought about by neighbourhood breezes. At the appropriate instant, the hand darts forward, grasping the nettle leaves firmly, in the manner laid down by aeons of nettle graspers. Not a matter to be grasped lightly.

The nettle operative must, therefore, eschew nettle grasping as a way of life, and concentrate on nettle root removal the essence of which is the old 'follow-through'. Nettle roots are an evil yellow-orange in colour reminding one of the colour of a high born Mandarin's skin after exposure to the Chinese sun. This removal necessitates a good deal of the heave and shove activity by which quantities of soil are removed from here to there, or even somewhere else.

'Has this anything at all to do with cheese?' they asked, not very patiently.

'I think so,' I said.

The digging down and casting around that is so much an intrinsic part of the bindweed and nettle scene leads on to the discovery, if you can call it that — more like the gradual awareness of an awful omen, that that in which the bindweed and nettle roots under removal exist and have their being, as the saying is, has ceased to be solid and has become clay.

Clay is a substance of which potters make pots and as such is, no doubt, useful. Lurking a couple of feet down in the sub-stratum of one's garden retreat it has about it all the welcome qualities of a Final Demand for the payment of Income Tax.

The thing about clay is that it is impervious. It is not sensitive to comment or criticism. You may raise your voice in justifiable complaint and berate it in whatever terms of abuse come to tongue, it is unlikely that your verbal flow will make much of an impact on clay. It is, as I said, impervious. When rain falls upon it the moisture does not pass through. The net result then of the bindweed, nettle and clay operations is an area of garden retreat that is not so much a retreat as an illustration of what the site of the Battle of the Somme might have looked like somewhere about the fourth or fifth week.

It is a region characterised, as I have already mentioned, by hillocks and hollows, to which is added, after a quick fall of rain, puddles.

If one happens to be a Capability Brown, or another of those land-scape making chappies, it is possible in such a poor situation as this to stand back and take what is known as the long view, envisaging in the mind's eye graceful eruptions of gazebos and grottoes, trees shifted a couple of feet to the right, and a nice expanse of water fully equipped with ducks and other kinds of floating bird. But, if one is neither a Brown, nor even a Capability, ruder remedies must be resorted to.

As in the laying out of golf courses, the h. and h. of life must be accepted as natural hazards, not forgetting the after-rain puddles that go along with them. The poor husbandry man, in his garden, accepts the slings and arrows of outrageous horticulture, scatters his seed where he can and plies his spade about the clay in a fruitless attempt at drainage.

Cast your eyes about you, I told them. Consider the gentle rise and fall of the lawn on which you now sit, suggestive of subtle hillocks and hollows. Enjoy the irregular profile of the pond beside which you laze and marvel at the teeming multitude of natural life which has chosen to inhabit it in preference to other ponds to be found in the district.

'Yes?' they said, casting, considering, enjoying and then turning to look at me with wondering eyes. 'So what?' they asked.

'Could good husbandry have done any better?' I wanted to know. They thought that possibly good husbandry could not.

'But what?' they wanted to know, 'has any of this got to do with cheese?'

'I'm just coming to that,' I said.

I have already remarked how the casual leaving about of gathered fruits which, in the fullness of time — if that is the right expression, went a bit on the turn led to the discovery of alcoholic beverages.

'Many times,' they sighed.

The story is told, I continued, ignoring them, how man the hunter turned into man the farmer, growing crops to feed his animals, or grazing animals to eat his crops, or whatever it was that those early farmers did. Noticing that the infant animals got themselves a piece of alright from the milk of their mothers, early farmers wondered if they might not enjoy the same facility. Some experimentation was, doubtless, necessary — tugging at this and pulling at that, before they mastered the knack of squirting the white beverage from the previously mentioned mothers under consideration.

Eventually beakers of the stuff were to be found in every early farmer kitchen, available to supply nourishment and refreshment to anyone who fancied that kind of thing. As in all walks of life, there were good early farmers and poor ones, and it is suggested that one of the latter variety, having gathered in his pitchers of milk, left same lying about the premises for several days, they being surplus to requirements, he having just brought to the boil his latest batch of fermented fruits, or whatever.

But, there came the time when, having exhausted his other supplies, this self-same early farmer came to his milk to find that in the meanwhile a change had come upon it. The liquid part of the milk had lost much of its substance. Floating in it were largish white lumps of something he did not very much like the look of. His first instinct was to throw the lot away and get a fresh batch from the nearest obliging mother, as described above.

His second instinct was to remember that if he did so, his early farmer's wife would get to hear about it and have a few words to say on the subject. Much better, if he made some attempt to put matters right.

Stirring briskly did no good, the white lumps would not dissolve back into the fluid. So, he fished them all out, hoping that the remaining liquid, although now somewhat on the thinnish side, might still be usable. Just then, his early farmer's wife returned, and seeking to conceal the evidence of his guilt — this is how the script goes, anyway — he placed the congealed mass of white stuff under a largish flat stone that happened to be lying about — you know how things tend to just lie about doing nothing — in his early farmer type kitchen. Just for good measure he sat on same, chatting up his e. f. w. about the weather, state of crops, etc., and other attendant topics that came into his mind.

Then, being the kind of absent-minded person that e. f's. tended to be, his wife not having discovered the guilty secret as described, he forgot about it, and went, as they say, his ways, tending his flock and getting high on basins of left about fruit.

Several days later, it says in the script, he happens to be passing the stone in the kitchen, lifts it and sees that what has been going on beneath it is nothing less than a miracle. He tastes it tentatively — we move in for a close-up here — his face fills with the wonder and delight of it all. He has invented cheese!

Cheese then is the seed of poor husbandry and some pretty nice things have been said about it over the years. Of course, unpleasant things have been said also, but I always like to get to the good news first, as witness Clifton Fadiman, in whose opinion cheese is 'milk's leap toward immortality', than which you cannot say fairer. The French gourmet fellow, Brillat-Savarin, much given to equating sex and food, put the issue thusly: 'A desert without cheese is like a beautiful woman with only one eye.' The attention of the reader here, should be drawn to the point that the desert in question might more properly be that with a double s which follows the main courses of meals, rather than that of the single s variety to be found in the regions of the Gobi and Sahara. With a chap like B-S, one never quite knows. British authors have a more direct way of expressing themselves that leaves no doubt about their meaning. Swift states the cheese case simply and to the point, pithy perhaps is the word one is looking for. 'Bachelor's fare,' he writes, is 'bread and cheese, and kisses.'

And while we are on the subject of bread and cheese, I don't know whether or not it has come to your attention, but on the day when young David of slingshot fame found himself obliged to confront, if that is the word I want, the giant Goliath of Gath 'whose height was six cubits and a span' which in translation I calculate comes out to

9 feet 9 inches, the aforesaid David was actually in the process of making
a delivery of bread and cheese. I quote 1 Samuel, Chapter 17, Verses 17
and 18 — 'And Jesse said unto David his son, Take now for thy brethren
an ephah (somewhat more than a bushel, eg., 4 pecks or 32 quarts)
of this parched corn, and these ten loaves, and run to the camp of thy
brethren; And carry these ten cheeses unto the captain of their thousand,
and look how thy brethren fare, and take their pledge.' With a load like
that under his arm, one imagines the young David was quite glad to put
it down for a spell and get in some brisk practice with his sling.

Continuing on the credit side, Ben Gunn, the marooned sailor in
Treasure Island was heard to mention that 'Many's the long night I've
dreamed of cheese —toasted, mostly.'

When it comes to the big guns of the food world, and you cannot
get a bigger gun than Epicurus (342?–270 BC according to my Webster),
the cheese case is confirmed in terms that, as the phrase is, brook no
disagreement. 'Send me some preserved cheese,' said that gentleman,
'that when I like I may have a feast.'

Presumably also on the credit side, a curious use of cheese comes
from certain country regions of England in a version known as The
Groaning Cheese. Ladies about to launch a new young life into the
world were given a slice from a large cheese made especially for the
event. ('Have you seen young Mrs so-and-so,' the gossip tongues would
wag. 'I hear she's making cheese again!') It was supposed that this
would help to guarantee a safe and speedy delivery for the aforesaid
n. y. l. When the self-same new person had, in the correct sequence
of events, arrived, portions of the large cheese were handed out to the
mid-wife, together with any friends or neighbours who happened to
drop by for a chat. These portions were cut from the centre of the
cheese, leaving the rind as a ring, through which, on the day of its
christening, the child would be passed before it was taken to church,
a ritual which, presumably, would lend a certain atmosphere, if that is
the word I want, to the subsequent ceremony.

At the head of the debit side of the cheese ledger one might place
George Eliot — 'A maggot must be born i' the rotten cheese to like it.'
Which reminds one rather of the celebrated cheesy bit in Reade's
Cloister and the Hearth.

'The feast ended with a dish of raw animalcula in a wicker cage. A
cheese had been surrounded with little twigs and strings; then a hole
made in it and a little sour wine poured in. This speedily bred a small

but numerous vermin. When the cheese was so rotten with them that only the twigs and string kept it from tumbling to pieces and walking off quadrivious, it came to table. By a malicious caprice of fate, cage and menagerie were put right under the Dutchman's organ of self-torture. He recoiled with a loud ejaculation, and hung to the bench by the calves of his legs.

'What is the matter?' said a traveller, disdainfully. 'Does the good cheese scare ye? Then put it hither, in the name of all saints!'

'Cheese!' cried Gerard, 'I see none. These nauseous reptiles have made away with every bit of it.'

'Well,' replied another, 'it is not far gone. By eating of the mites we eat the cheese to boot.'

'Nay, not so,' said Gerard. 'These reptiles are made like us, and digest their food and turn it to foul flesh even as we do ours to sweet: as well might you think to chew grass by eating of grass-fed beeves, as to eat cheese by swallowing these uncleanly insects.'

It is worth recording that Tusser in his 'Five Hundred Points of Good Husbandry' (1573), which we have already introduced to these pages, gives as the criteria for a perfect cheese, the following:

It should not be like —
1. Gehazi, ie., dead white like a leper;
2. Lot's Wife, all salt;
3. Argus, full of eyes;
4. Tom Piper, 'hoven and puffed', like the cheeks of a piper;
5. Crispin, leathery;
6. Lazarus, poor;
7. Esau, hairy;
8. Mary Magdalene, full of whey or maudlin;
9. Gentiles, full of maggots or gentils;
10. A Bishop, made of burnt milk (this last is a reference to the old phrase, 'the bishop hath put his foot in it'. This is said of milk or porridge that is burnt. 'If the porage be burned to, or the meate ouer rosted, we saye the bishop hath put his fote in the potte, because bishops burn who they lust.)

Madame Beeton of cook book fame, being a sharp-eyed woman with a keen attention to detail had not failed to notice that some cheese eaters preferred to consume that commodity in what can only be described as a well ripened state. 'It is well known' she wrote, 'that some persons like cheese in a state of decay, and even 'alive'. There is no accounting for tastes, and it may be hard to show why mould, which is vegetation, should not be eaten as well as salad, or maggots as well as eels. But, generally speaking, decomposing bodies are not wholesome eating, and the line must be drawn somewhere.' (One can see the newspaper headlines being cast in ninety-six point type — 'BEETON DECLARES DECOMPOSING BODIES NOT WHOLESOME EATING' — and many a corpse turns quietly in its grave, confident that it will not be disturbed by those seeking a quick snack.)

La Beeton lists as the principal English cheeses, Cheshire, Gloucester, Stilton, Sage, Cheddar, Brickbat and Dunlop — thereby calling forth the wrath of all Scottish persons, that last being of Scottish extraction and now sold under the more confusing name of Scottish Cheddar. All of these survive, with the exception of Brickbat.

In this matter of cheese and all that therein goes, I have come upon a cheesy matter penned by Chesterton

'The righteous minds of innkeepers
Induce them now and then
To crack a bottle with a friend
Or treat unmoneyed men.

But who hath seen the Grocer
Treat housemaids to his teas
Or crack a bottle of fish-sauce
Or stand a man a cheese?'

Quite so, we echo, reflecting that it is this sort of thing that has given cheese a bad name among the populace at large, as indicated by the term 'cheese-paring', viz., a person unlikely to stand another person a cheese should the circumstances arise when this would be the decent and natural thing to do.

But, reverting to the early farmer scene, the impression may have been conveyed, it occurs to me, that poor husbandry was all the rage. It goes without saying that one wishes to be fair as well as accurate. Let those of the p. h. brigade be pointed out, by all means. But let it also be said that among others of the e. f's, there was a good deal of sturdy rolling up of sleeves and getting down to cases so far as cheesery was concerned.

Early farmers having, as it were, stumbled upon cheese by what we call happenstance, quickly cottoned on to the fact that it was a Good Thing, and not something to be sniffed at — unless, that is, you happen to be wedded to cheese sniffing. Once cheese had got off the ground as a comestible, it never looked back. Citizens of the Neolithic and Bronze Ages developed a passion for the stuff, as evidenced by pottery cheese strainers that have turned up in secondhand and junk shops in both Crete and Greece. That reliable reporter of Greek affairs, Homer, in his works dealing with those matters, makes several mentions of goat's milk ditto. Equally, the Mesopotamians went a bundle on cheese, and the Hittites, those mighty warrior persons, never went into battle without a few mighty cheeses to urge them on to victory. The Egyptians, too, were strong runners in the cheese stakes, little pots of same having been found in such handy hideaways as the Second Dynasty Tomb at Saqqara.

What all these persons discovered was that cheese, apart from being a tasty thing to nibble with one's daily bread, which, by then, had also been invented, was additionally a useful way of using up any milk that should prove to be surplus to requirements.

From these humble beginnings cheese went on from strength to strength. The Romans had a taste for smoked cheese. Charlemagne fancied it. The Normans couldn't put it down.

By the medieval era milk, as milk, was thought to be too much of a good thing, and was separated out into curds, for making cheese and butter, and the thinner whey which was thought to be alright for ordinary drinking. These curds and whey are celebrated in the poem wherein they feature, being given star billing alongside a Miss Muffet.

It is thought that this young luminary was none other than Miss Patience Muffet, daughter of Dr. Thomas Muffet (1553–1604) the noted entomologist with what is described as a peculiar passion for spiders. Among the many books that he produced were *Silke-Wormes and their Flies* and the much more famous *Health's Improvement* in which he wrote with much penetration, if that is the word I want, that 'Bread and cheese be two targets against death'. Elsewhere in the same tome, laying down the law as to which foods are best suited to what persons, he goes on to say: 'Other (foods) are more gross, tough, and hard, agreeing chiefly to country persons and hard labourers: but secondarily to all that be strong of nature, given by trade or use to much exercise, and accustomed to feed upon them: as poudred beife, bacon, goose, swan, saltfish, ling, tunnis, salt salmon, cucumbers, turneps, beans, hard peaze, hard cheese, brown and rye bread, etc.

This points up the fact that cheese, like life, had been getting harder since the times of the early farmers. That some of this hardening of the cheeseries accounted for the breaking out of rude humours and a general spirit of get-up-and-go can be supported by the Goths, Vandals, Gepids, Alemanni, Franks — and for all I know, the Visigoths as well. These chaps were not the sort of chaps to hang about muttering in an embarrassed kind of way that they would like a bit of a share in the Roman Empire if nobody minded terribly much. Being of the get-up-and-go kind, they got up and went, taking with them frugal supplies of meat, milk and cheese, which same supplied the necessary urges for getting-up-and-going.

The main milk suppliers at this time, it should be noted, were sheep, who in addition to keeping up a regular supply of mutton, milk and cheese (at least, the sheep didn't actually themselves produce the cheese, but you see what I mean) were also well into wool. A 13th century agricultural expert Walter of Henley declared that 20 ewes produced enough milk in a week to make 400 Imperial (500 American) pints of butter and 25 pounds of cheese. There were about 8 million sheep type creatures roaming the pastures and prairies at that time, working out at something in the region of 4 sheep per human type creature. Cheese was very popular, which was handy. If it hadn't been, large heaps of the stuff would have begun to pile up everywhere leading to traffic congestion and the blocking out of natural light.

If sheep are so good, the question has to be asked, why are they no longer in general favour as providers of mutton, milk, cheese etc., to the exclusion of other less well-favoured beasts.? The answer lays a considerable blame at the door of the muddle-headed English peasant of those days. When the question of re-negotiating grazing rights cropped up, said peasantry claimed that they needed enough land to keep a cow per person, despite being knee-deep in sheep at the time. Bright-eyed P. R. type persons were engaged to advance the case that only the cow could provide 'butter, cheese, whey, curds, cream, sod (boiled) milk, raw milk, sour milk, sweet milk and buttermilk' all of which is a calumny, if that is the word I want, against the decent sheep.

As a result, sheep were out and cows in, this change leading to radicle changes in cheese styles.

If, as has been suggested by various authorities quoted here, cheese supplies the entry to the Good Life — an opinion not shared by friend Shakespeare, who said of it 'I love not the humour of bread and cheese' — then some index as to the degree of Goodlifery enjoyed by the citizens of any country can be gauged by the quantities of cheese they produce. Cheese, the world knows, is to be found beaming a welcome on the bar counter of every English pub, and the term 'Ploughman's lunch' is universally recognised as being one enshrining the concept of bread, cheese and pickled onions. That being the case, it would be a natural assumption on the part of any sensible person to assume that England stood well up in the ranks of the cheese-makers. But, this is not so, according to figures published in 1969, which are the most recent available to me. In these listings England comes a miserable ninth behind such doughty cheese providers as Switzerland, Canada, Argentina, Holland, Italy, West Germany, France and the USA which tops the bill. Of this last nation, five States dominate the cheese scene, producing between them 43% of the national total of 909 thousand tons: these are Wisconsin, New York, Missouri, Minnesota and Iowa. England stands ahead of Denmark, New Zealand, Australia, Sweden, Norway, Belgium and Eire.

No two cheese kings agree as to what is the correct way to deal with the curds, once supplied by the obliging cows. One chap will have it this way, another that, others reject the cows' milk concept, preferring to stick to that of sheep, and even goats.

The net result of this galaxy of cheese talent is that hundreds or perhaps thousands of cheese varieties jostle and push their way down past the world's taste buds. France alone is said to account for well over four hundred of these, although some cheese experts, than which no other word on the subject is so sacrosanct — have ventured the declaration that in all the world there are no more than eighteen or twenty categories of cheese.

England being such a modest performer in the cheese race — ninth, I believe I said — that one hesitates even to mention the few better known traditional cheeses, amounting, one must add with one's honest hand on one's honest heart, to no more than two categories, at the most, the Blue and the Hard.

There is, for example, Blue Dorset or Vinney Cheese, which is a hard cheese made from skimmed milk with blue veins running through it. Caerphilly strictly speaking is a Welsh hard cheese although it is made also in Devon, Dorset, Somerset and Wiltshire. Cheshire is the oldest of the English cheeses, and as is appropriate to one of such antiquity, comes in three patriotic varieties, red, white and blue. The true flavour of it derives — so my note book says — from the saline composition of the milk of Cheshire cows, who feed in fields whose soil is rich in salt, which seems to wrap up the Cheshire cheese situation. Double Gloucester cheese — from Gloucestershire, of course — is the shape of a grindstone with rounded edges. The other Gloucester cheese — the Single, is much less well known these days. Probably inflation, or a response to that most anciently sage advice: when in doubt, double everything. Dunlop isn't an English cheese either, taking its name from the village of that name in Ayrshire, and is regarded as the national cheese of Scotland. When sold in England it is often known as Scottish Cheddar, which devious piece of English chauvinism has given rise to the separatist movement north of the border, the blood of true Scotsmen having risen to the boil, and frothed over the top. Lancashire cheese, as you might suspect, comes from the county of that name, the best of it coming from Fylde. Lancashire is also noted for Black Pudding, Braggot, Brawn, Eccles Cakes, Jannock, Parkins, Tripe and Hot Pot, but that is another story. Stilton is a village in Huntingdonshire where this cheese was first made at the Bell Inn at the end of the 18th century by a relative of the inventor, Mrs Paulet, which is the kind of family loyalty that cannot be bettered, added to which, it keeps the profits under one roof, assuming the relative in question, lives in. A statement appears in the reference books that makes one feel like running to consult the stern-faced gentles of the Department of Trade or the Federal Trade Commission. It says: 'Most of the genuine Stilton today comes from Leicestershire and Rutland.' (Rutland, of course, has been got rid of in an English tidying up of the shires, but that is yet another story). A little known cheese these days is that of Suffolk — a very hard cheese, it says, with which goes the saying: 'Hunger will break stone walls and anything except a Suffolk cheese' from which you will gather that it is pretty much on the adamantine side. One final cheese category is worthy of mention, namely Trucklets or Truckles. It comes from Wiltshire or somewhere else in the west of England. It is a blue vinny cheese, or a full cream cheddar cheese. Trucklets (or Truckles) as you can see, is the cheese that sets out to be all things to all persons.

'Isn't it about time you went and had a look at lunch,' they said.

'I'm coming to that,' I told them, and meant it.

Returning for the nonce, I continued, to Gloucestershire, there is a pub dish to be found or was to be found, in that county, going under the name of Cheese-and-Ale. The recommended procedure for getting it on a plate in front of the cash-paying customer, was to cut Gloucester cheese into thin flakes and scatter them in a fire-proof dish. On this some mustard is layered, the mixture being thinly covered with ale. The dish is placed in a hot oven and left until the cheese is dissolved, giving the cook just time to reward his efforts thus far with a further libation of the aforementioned ale. Then, returning to the culinary nub, toast is made with thick slices of brown bread and same moistened with hot ale, or the chef's breath whichever proves to be the stronger. The melted cheese mix is poured over the toast and served to the waiting c-p. p. whose tongue by now should be hanging well out. In theory, that is.

One does not like to carp, but the problem with so many of these notable dishes is that, sounding well in the theoretical pages of a cook book, they fall down in practice. Like the tourist-trapping French Onion Soup . . . .

'What about French Onion Soup?' they wanted to know. 'Haven't you already done soup?'

I speak, I said, not so much of the soup, as a soup, but of the use of cheese therein. According to the recommended procedures laid down by Escoffier and Tante Marie and other French cook-minded persons, the result in print is described as a rich, crisp crust with a cheesy flavour which lends an aroma of enchantment to the dish. In practice, and by experience of many degraded establishments along the Boulevard Sebastopol touching the 1st., 2nd and 3rd districts of Paris, the dish as it is served up has covering it a thick, rubbery skin which elongates into elastic strings when the spoon is inserted.

The Cheese-and-Ale theory falls down in a like manner, the ingredients resulting in a mess of soggy toast, covered with a thin runny liquid with a distant flavour of cheese.

'Ugh!' they said.

Exactly, I agreed with them. This leads me to that other well known cheese preparation, the secret of which should not be hidden from any self-respecting cook. I refer, I said, to the Welsh Rare-bit, commonly written as Rabbit.

My early researches into the mysteries of the rare-bit uncovered grave inadequacies in the dish as laid down by classical authority. Step by step, these have been ironed out, and I would now like to take you through this process to make the point I am trying to make.

I well remember my first Welsh rarebit, I said. It came up on a day of some strain. The domestic lute was deeply rifted, as Wodehouse might have put it, a situation characterised by the statement that words had been had, resulting in total breakdown of communication. She found she had no desire to speak to me. I had no reason to speak to her. It was the kind of day when nought but ashes and aloe flavour the sensitive tongue. Persons involved are inclined to believe that the sun has set on their fondest hopes and shows no sign of ever rising again. Woe, worry and weary wrinkles crease the face. To cap everything, my ingrowing toe-nail began to play me up again, as the phrase is, something fierce. At this rough moment in life a person requires nothing else but gentle zephyrs and the soft-skinned fingers of gently-nurtured maidens to caress the brow. On second thoughts, with a view to the subsequent resumption of diplomatic relations, said gently-nurtured maidens might get in the way. So keep the zephyrs and scrub the maidens.

To open up those ordinary channels of domestic commerce by which the coming and going of life is carried on, I made enquiry as to what she would like for lunch.

'Welsh Rarebit,' she said. And so, Welsh rarebit it was.

At this juncture, flipping through the pages of such ready-reference books as were available at short notice, it came to me with all the force of a weight-lifter, previously restricted to modest loads, who suddenly finds himself facing the big one, the full two hundred and fifty kilos, for the first time. I had never done a w. r. before.

At such moments, the chef gathers his strength, rolls up his sleeves, and sets to work in the manner of an engineer of Ancient Egypt organising his forces for the rolling into place of stone number one of a Pyramid. Casting a small knob of butter into a heavy saucepan, I laid the grounding, so to speak, for the work that on this bad day of all bad days, was to prove one of stratagema, shifts and subterfuges to overcome the poorest kind of rarebit husbandry.

The butter melted, I added what seemed a proper quantity of grated, rasped, slivered, diced or cubed cheddar cheese to give an adequate covering to her toast.

Speaking of which, said toast was put in hand under the gas-fired grill. Making perfect toast on such an appliance is not easy. Anyone, given bread and heat in that order, can turn out what might be charitably described as a charred ruin, to be scraped surreptitiously over the sink to remove the worst of the black patches. But p. t., recognised by husbanded regions of evenly distributed golden crispness, takes a bit of doing.

It took, on that day, half a loaf. Trial and error, that tenacious tutor of the most talentless, led me through a wasteland of scorched bits to the promised perfect toast.

The first development with which one has to contend is that the initial blast of heat causes the top side of the bread to curl upwards. This prevents an even browning, which undermines in this opening gambit the very concept of p. t. At the first sign of a brown rim to the bread slice, therefore, the alert chef turns it over, the application of heat to the nether side reversing the curl. In due course, rim browning will begin to occur on this other side. To secure an even sheen of the right tone of brown, the slice of bread being operated upon must here be rotated horizontally, the front section being taken to the rear of the grill, allowing the rear portion to arrive at the front. When the toast is de-curled and evenly browned, it must be turned over, back to its original top side uppermost, but with the original front at the back and, as follows naturally, vice versa. All clear so far?

By this method, I said, perfect rarebit toast is made. But I will not describe to you . . . .

'Good,' they said.

. . . . . the alarums and excursions, the agonies and ecstasies, the high points and low points, that had to be endured before . . . .

'Get on with it,' they said. And somebody added: 'What about lunch?'

'I'm coming to that,' I said, patiently. For one must be patient.

By this time, I went on, the cheese has melted. In fact, because the p. t. making had held up operations somewhat, as if that first Pyramid stone simply would not slide smoothly into place, the cheese had been removed and restored to the stove so many times, melting, solidifying and re-melting in the process that it had begun to resemble the basic ingredient of a cheese coloured motor tyre. At such a moment, the alert chef, or to put it more simply in a single word, I, could not help but notice that from the cheese had departed most of the sharp, tangy flavour that is destined to bring a gentle salivation to her lips and is one of the principal reasons for creating the w. r. It must be restored in some way, and the chef, or to put it another way, me, clutching at straws, as the saying is, even if in the wrongly objective case, reaches out his hand blindly and finds in it when he, that is to say, I, have the courage to open my eyes, a tin of mustard powder. A half-teaspoon of this added to the melted and almost depraved cheese, achieves the required restoration of taste, and adds a little extra something in addition. Poor husbandry triumphs again!

But, even though we may seem to be approaching journey's end, this is a delusion. Like Poor Pilgrim, we must face yet another trial.

The perfect toast is lightly coated with butter, on which is knifed a goodish layer of the cheese mix. The dish is then returned to the grill to be given its final crispness.

Horror, tragedy and disaster stare one in the face. The heat of the grill melts the cheese which oozes petulantly off the toast leaving patches of naked bread exposed to the blast of heat.

The w. r. begins to look like a portion of dog afflicted with mange. What is required is something to hold the cheese in place on the toast while the final touch, to the degree of browness as laid down in the manuals, is being added. Bastions or bulwarks of steel spring to the mind and are rejected on the grounds that no such b's or b's are readily available in the ordinary kitchen.

Resort is then made to the ready solver of all problems, old trial and error himself, giving rise, some pound and a half of cheese later to the solution, or what might more properly be termed, because of a sensitivity to the liquid association in the word that by now amounts to a positive phobia, the resolution. This, to be blunt about it and come directly to the point, amounts to no more nor less than one ounce or heaped tablespoon of flour of either the plain or self-raising variety. Added to the cheese as soon as the melted state has been reached it adds a firmness to the mixture no matter what extremes of heat are applied.

With it comes a bonus. For there is now a surplus of capacity in the mopping-up-of-liquid department. So, in addition to the previously mentioned mustard, other flavourings can be considered as eligible for the w. r. mix, of which, high on the list must come the dark aroma of Worcester Sauce.

The home and dry situation is almost in sight. Now we have the perfect toast, melted cheese, added flour, mustard and w. s. The mix on the toast in this final stage now sits firmly in place, gathers an even tan like that of the Pyramid engineer under the grill of the Egyptian sun.

'Are we having welsh rarebit for lunch, then?' they wanted to know.

'The dish you are going to enjoy for lunch,' I said, 'I have in the last hour re-titled 'Mermaid Ham' after the celebrated statuette of that delightful subject to be found parked on a rock in Copenhagen Harbour.'

'Oh?' they said.

'It was to have been something else,' I told them, 'but I don't wish to bore you with the details.'

'Why not?' they said. 'You've bored us with everything else.'

That is part of the pleasure of entertaining old friends. There is no hiding of true feelings. One always knows where one is with them.

'Very well,' I said.

I had no trouble with the spinach, I began, apart from the fact of having bought a huge quantity, three pounds, in fact, and meticulously trimming every leaf of any blemish, this, now it has been boiled in the merest modicum of water (salted), has reduced to such a small quantity that I doubt whether any one of you will get more than a passing hint of its flavour.

Nor, I went on, did I have any more than my customary difficulty with the noodles in the largest saucepan I could find, they, despite the most rigid precautions, sticking resolutely to the bottom, and burning, although I have been able to scrape off enough to make up a decent portion of same per person.

There was no problem in dicing the tinned Danish ham, nor in putting together the ingredients of the sauce, incorporating the ham therein, arranging the noodles in a ring round the edge of a shallow casserole dish, laying down another ring inside this of spinach, piling the ham and cream sauce mix in the centre, dusting overall with paprika and returning briefly to the oven.

'So, lunch is ready at last,' they said, getting up stiffly out of their deckchairs.

'First, I said, 'there is something I should tell you.'

'Haven't you told us enough,' they said.

'The hazards of cooking in confined spaces,' I began, 'are amplified when the chef's spectacles are temporarily fogged by steam and the keenly attentive eye fails to pick up an essential point of detail . . . . . .'

'Don't tell us,' they said. 'We do not wish to know. Lead us to the groaning board. Bring on the vittals. Do not, in the meanwhile, waffle, procrastinate or deviate by the merest iota from the immediate task in hand.'

Wolves gathered round the dismantled components of a sheep could not have fallen to with greater relish. In the uping and downing of serving same, the backing and forthing with condiments, ingredients and utensils, I never did get around to telling them the shameful truth, that I had left out of the sauce the essential cheese.

'Very tasty,' they reported, afterwards. 'Very toothsome.'

They walked back soggily like wolves who see no need for further sheep for several days at least.

'Better than your usual,' they said, sinking back wearily into re-clining postures. 'We'll have that again next time we come.'

Thus it is that from poor husbandry, good husbandry emerges, triumphant at last, leaving containers of potential alcohol lying about the place, while forgotten milk transforms itself to cheese. All around us this experimental activity is going on all the time. In camp sites, fragments of this and that are fluttering accidentally down into pots of bubbling hot water. In laboratories, test tubes of one thing and another become inadvertantly mixed. In a wayside cafe, a hurtling assistant skids momentarily on a patch of grease and the contents of one sauce-pan pour into those of another, and in that flash, another item is added to the menu of life.

At dark moments, what strikes one, lending needed balm to the bruised soul, is this undimmed power of poor husbandry to surmount any obstacle. It is, one begins to realise, what really good cooking is all about.

MONEY

It is a curious trade, I said, that flourishes by contriving to arrange a shortage of that commodity for which ordinary citizens everywhere have the most urgent need.

It is a fact, I went on, that these citizens to whom I allude, cannot do without the stuff and yet cannot lay their hands on it. It eludes them, and is said to be in short supply, while organisations such as yours would seem to be geared up to dishing the stuff out in handfuls, as lavishly as required. That you fail to do so is a circumstance that leads one to the dark suspicion of the market in the stuff having been, in some way, cornered. Were one not reliably informed otherwise, I hastened to add, as there appeared on him what one can only describe as the beginning of a bridle, and one likes to keep on the right side of these chaps when one is trying to negotiate one's way out of a temporary shortage.

'Its the way things are,' he said.

Should it have happened, I continued, that you earned your crust by the vending of baked beans, broken biscuits or brown boots, it could be safely assumed that every baked bean, broken biscuit or brown boot (pairs of) listed on the company's manifest would be matched by an actual b. b., b. b. or b. b. somewhere about the premises. Such is not the case with you, I said. Although the stuff is catalogued in your books as being stored in such abundance that one wonders why no visible signs exist about your establishment of a bursting of seams, this failure of said seams to burst is explained by there only being a miserly few token samples to be found in your stores, the remainder having been scattered every which way throughout the commercial purlieus, if that is the term I want, resulting in a short fall of supplies when the previously mentioned ordinary citizen comes knocking at your door with a request for same.

'Its not quite like that,' he said.

At this point the astute reader, keeping an alert finger on the unfolding of events will, doubtless, have come to the conclusion that he has no idea what is going on here. 'What the hell is going on here?' is how he might express it. And the proposition will be put about that the author has finally gone off his rocker. The opinion will be vouchsafed that in this matter of rockers being gone off, no previous rocker has been gone off more substantially than this one.

Let us, therefore, allay these doubts of the author's sanity and state categorically that the occasion being described is that which can be indicated by the phrase 'having lunch with the bank manager'. In eight words I am having lunch with my bank manager. And in this general area of bank manager/lunching with, I have a curious circumstance to report.

In my green years, when the first thoughts of opening a bank account came to the surface, the bank chosen was one of that minority of small financial concerns in which a family atmosphere prevailed, and in which the manager occupied a position of 'in loco parentis' to his clients. References were required on joining, and when one of these proved to be that of my father-in-law who had utilised the facilities of another branch of the same concern for more than three decades, this stood me in good favour when my name came up for votes at the next meeting of the membership committee. Funds were accepted, a cheque book issued, and business of a financial nature – the paying in and the drawing out – was briskly got down to.

Over the years, one thing led to another, and one of the things it led to was a series of invitations to have lunch with this self-same manager at which a portion of the bank's substance was expended on providing a generous supply of the traditional baked meats and two veg to my plate. These invitations occasioned no deep stirrings in my bosom until the day when the thought came to my mind, in that spontaneous way thoughts have, and having come was checked up on and found to be generally correct, that each of these invitations coincided with a peak point in the performance of my overdraft.

What, from this, one asked oneself, there being no one else about at the time, might one infer? Was the manager, with these critical figures emblazoned on his mind, availing himself of an opportunity to check how his wilting patron was standing up to the strain? Or was he trying to ensure that the poor devil had at least one last decent meal before having the final bucket kicked from underneath his feet? Perhaps we shall never know.

When those green years of which I have already spoken began to turn yellow, curl at the edges and go crisp at the extremities there came what is known in the trade as a turn of events, said turn involving a crossing of oceans, plains and mighty mountains. The activities therein pursued in those distant places led to the drawing up, from time to time, of fiduciary instruments in my favour, such instruments to bestow upon the recipient any monetary benefit, having to be negotiated, as the term is, through the usual channels.

The most usual channels are banks, and banks being what banks are, the holder of a fiduciary instrument is inclined to place his business with a devil he knows rather than one he does not. The outcome of this philosophy was that f. i's came winging in to the aforementioned bank from distant quarters resulting in an accumulation of funds in the coffers. Man, as the poet reminds us, lives not by bread alone — 'This bank-note world' as Fitz-Greene Halleck puts it. To obtain the necessary money for the purchase of necessaries one must resort to a bank.

'Strictly speaking,' he said, 'what one obtains from a bank is only partly money.'

'Oh?' I said.

'Yes,' he said. 'If you will cast your mind back to the year 344 BC., or thereabouts, a certain Lucius Furius — some say it was a chap called Camillus — built a temple to Juno Moneta on the spot where the house of Manlius Capitolinus stood. To this temple was attached the first Roman Mint, and the coins issued by that establishment were called 'moneta' hence our word money.'

'I didn't know that,' I said.

'The coin in question,' he said, 'was made of bronze and named an 'as'. Originally it weighed about a pound, or 'libra', but what with inflation and devaluation, eventually it was reduced in size to weigh about half an ounce, making it about as portable as a credit card.'

'I didn't know that,' I said.

'Hence, as a consequence and because of this, money strictly speaking refers to coins. However, these days, few persons requiring to make use of a bank's facilities expect to receive payment in coins. They want notes which, for reasons I will not go into now as I see you are anxious to finish your lunch and your recital, are known as currency.'

As I was saying, I said, the situation in which I sometimes found myself to be was, of requiring funds, said funds being available but several thousand miles away, and no immediate way of hands being laid on them.

The obvious solution was to despatch a cable requiring a proportion of these funds to be remitted. But, banks are mightily reluctant to act on the instructions of cables. 'Who is this person?' they mutter, with an excess of distrust and misgiving in their faces, holding the offending communication up to the light. 'How do we know the person named herein is the person we know to be the account holder and thereby entitled to enjoy the benefits of the funds deposited with us, and to instruct us to remit one hundred pounds as directed?'

A knotty problem you will agree, cables being what they are. Anyone, as you will point out, can send a cable.

It happened, I went on before he could point this out, that on a visit to these parts, I was having lunch with the then manager, doubtless a professional ancestor of yours, when discussion turned to this particular problem. Somewhere between the soup and the nuts, with the encouragement of wine, a way round was found. On leaving the premises, we each took a copy of the day's menu, it being one of those establishments that posted a different menu for each day. My copy reposed for the next twelve months, until we should meet again, next to my heart. His went into his safe.

Subsequently requiring funds in some remote place, I requested him to forward same, by cable, adding as an addendum thereto, the first item on the menu. These tidings winging in to the bank's letter box, it occupied no more than ten minutes or so, to discover where the safe keys had last been put down, where they had now got to and how long it was going to take to get them back. This accomplished, the safe could be opened and the menu items compared.

Thus, it might turn out, that my first message would read: 'Please send one hundred pounds. Pea soup with ham.' To be followed by: 'Please send one hundred pounds. Lancashire Hot Pot.' And so on, through the restaurant's score card. An infallible system, you might think.

'You might,' he said.

The point I am trying to make, I said, is that that is the only experience I have of food being convertible into money. Or currency. Most of my experience runs entirely in the opposite direction.

'Ah,' he said. 'But then you aren't a farmer.'

Perhaps, I said, that is the very point I am trying to make here.

An early farmer of the kind that we have previously introduced on these pages, coming in from his fields at knocking off or tool downing

time, and fancying as he strides through the muck, a refreshing bowl of
onion soup will be unable to satisfy that expectation without having
gone through an extended list of activities prior to the knocking-
off time in question. These, as listed from the top downwards, are:

1. Some weeks or months previously there was a planting of
    onions in his top soil.
2. Said onions came up.
3. Said onions were gathered in, put in store, in which place they
    were not attacked by microbes, viruses or any one of a variety
    of creatures who have the taste for onions.
4. His wife, cook or other help-mate was in the mood for cooking.
5. Sufficient bones were to be found lying about the place to boil
    down to stock.
6. The early farmer had, at some convenient moment, done a deal
    with a passing merchant, for salt.

These requirements having been satisfactorily concluded, and no
subtle variations on the basic onion soup mix being desired, it was on
the cards for soup of that type to be dished up on demand.

A last minute switch to mushroom or carrot soup could not be
entertained without running a quick check through the list, as listed,
substituting in each case, mushrooms or carrots for onions, as appropriate. These limitations would put something of a brake on the drawing
up of imaginative menus. But the advantage would be gained of there
being liberal supplies of soup (onion, mushroom or carrot) without it
being necessary to cross any person's palm with coins of the realm.

It is not the same with us. I said. The taste for onion soup can be
quickly gratified by trotting to the nearest grocery or supermarket
store, there to exchange coins for onions (or mushrooms, or carrots).

'Or a tin or packet of the dried stuff,' he said.

Please! I rebuked him. We are speaking here of good husbandry. Go
wash your mouth.

Any early farmer, having planted onions and successfully lodged
these in his store room was likely to face a culinary situation that could
be described in the phrase: 'onions with everything.' The only way of
breaking free of its onion-laden atmosphere would be to scout around
the countryside in the hope of finding another e. f. whose position was
similar, but matching. In other words, one for whom the descriptive

phrase might be 'mushrooms (or even carrots) with everything'.

An exchange or barter could be worked out on the basis of so many onions for so many mushrooms (or carrots). Ah! But here we come to what is put down in the text that accompanies these manoeuvres as 'the rub'. How many onions should be exchanged for how many mushrooms (or carrots)?

The onion farmer, let us call him Farmer O, will be, let us say, of the opinion that one pound — or one kilo, for metric readers — of onions is equal to, and a fair exchange for, one pound (or kilo) of mushrooms (or carrots). All clear, thus far? When the onions under negotiation are weighed in the balance opposite the mushrooms that are party to the same agreement, it is seen that for this modest pile of onions, on the one hand, he is to receive this mushroom mountain on the other, it being that mushrooms weight lighter than onions.

Here, the mushroom farmer, let us call him Farmer M, slides away into that human contortion known as 'the bridle'. He bridles, remembering all those long hours crouched over damp peat, encouraging his infant mushrooms with soft cries of 'Come on, then!' and 'What ho!'

He expresses it as being his firm opinion that if, in the larger arena of human affairs it is thought that an eye is a fair bargain for an eye, a tooth for a tooth, blood for blood, etc., then he sees no reason why a formula cannot be worked out on the basis of a mushroom for an onion, and vice versa.

Farmer O, chewing this over in that ruminative way early farmers had, comes back at this with the thought that mushrooms (and onions) come in different sizes. 'There are large ones,' he says, perceptively, 'and small ones.' If a large enough mushroom can be found to match that of a similarly sized onion, fair enough. But how many small mushrooms should be exchanged for one large onion?

Furthermore, Farmer O continues, having ruminated some more, since he was the prime mover in these negotiations, having left his farm bearing with him a burden of onions, while all Farmer M has done so far is sit around and wait for something or somebody, viz., Farmer O, to turn up, he (Farmer O) should have something added to his side of the bargain to take care of travel and other out of pocket expenses.

At this point, the discussion is on the point of breaking down, and farmers O and M, respectively, are on the point of leaving the negotiating table to return to the growing and cooking of further supplies of onions and mushrooms, when Farmer C hoves into view bearing a burden of carrots, and the whole business starts up once more.

Eventually a formula was worked out, based — in the case of the wellknown Farmer O — on how much he developed a taste for mushrooms (and carrots) and to what degree he had become disenchanted with onions. Like attitudes of mind could be ascribed to Farmers M and C, relating to mushrooms, carrots and onions, but not necessarily in that order.

The system was clumsy. In a bad year, with onions in short supply, Farmer O never knew beforehand if there was to be a shortfall in his expectations of mushrooms and carrots, or whether he might persuade Farmers M and C to bump up the exchange rate. If there was a glut, he might wheel and deal like a mad thing, and still be left with surplus onions, on his hands, as the saying is.

Here the script requires a fanfare of brass, the swelling strings pick up the heroic theme, and against this background of stirring music, Trader X comes trundling along the dusty highways and byways that connect the establishments of Farmers O, M and C. Aboard his pack animal the said Trader has supplies of every kind, ranging from beer mats to bird baths and boot laces. He is not especially interested in the conversion of these items into equivalent quantities of onions, mushrooms and carrots, not having anything in which to carry these bulky comestibles. He requires something of a more handy, portable nature, suitable to slide down neatly into the leather container strapped about his waist and known by well-informed persons as a purse. What he wants is money.

Now a fresh system breaks out. Like the fire into which the infant Abraham was thrown, trade turned into a bed of roses (or, as in the case histories being here discussed — beds of onions, mushrooms and carrots respectively, with other beds of beer mats, bird baths and boot laces on the side). How it worked is, roughly, as follows.

Trader Y set himself up in business in some nearby town. To him, Farmers O, M and C went with their supplies of onions, mushrooms and carrots, holding back some for their own requirements. Trader Y. . .a word has to be invented here, something different from exchanging one load of items for another. . .let us call this word 'purchase'. . .Trader Y purchased the onions, mushrooms and carrots with something which, as we know, was going to become known as money later on, but at that early stage was nothing more than small heaps of coins. But, with these coins, Farmers O, M and C could — note the word — purchase bm's, bb's and bl's from Trader X, who with these coins could now go and 'purchase' onions, carrots and mushrooms from Trader Y, leaving all persons concerned satisfied and contented with the bargains that had been struck.

The culinary residuum, if you will pardon the expression, of this arrangement was that the previously limited diets of Farmers O, M and C were now augmented by supplies of mushrooms, carrots and onions respectively, and cookery books with recipes featuring these commodities could now be consulted with advantage. Furthermore — if that is the word I want — Trader X now had supplies of o's, m's and c's to consume. While Trader Y could sell his c's, m's and o's to other interested parties, thus generally spreading what is known as sweetness and light.

The introduction of money to the food scene had a deeply-felt effect, as can be gauged from a swift survey of the Greek scene that was to follow on some time after the early farmer scene with which we have just been involved.

Let us begin with pots. The Greek form of money — although, as you will remember, not yet known by that term for which we have to await the arrival of the Roman scene some time afterwards — was called a drachma. Records show that secondhand panathenaic amphorae, or pots, sold in the Greek markets for a ½ drachma. A larger hydria has been found with the price of 3 drachma scratched on its bottom. The artist Euphronius was said to earn about 5000 drachma in a good year, which would go a goodish way towards providing supplies of onions, mushrooms, carrots or whatever else nourishes the artistic person. Poor men, however, clubbed together to buy an animal to sacrifice, the prices for sacrificial animals coming high in those times. And having sacrificed same, divided up the remains among the club members and so provided themselves with the Sunday joint.

All this took place in the Agora, or market place, and was supervised by Astynomoi, or town officials, whose other responsibilities included:

preventing dustmen depositing rubbish within 10 stades of the walls;
preventing householders blocking roads,

or

building out balconies,

or

having gutters that poured water into the road,
>   or
allowing windows to open on the road;
controlling the prices of flute-girls and harpists, so that they charged
no more than 2 drachma for an evening.

In Greek society, as this brief run through indicates, artists of the
Euphronius calibre were somewhere at the top of the heap, while flute-
girls found themselves somewhere towards the bottom. These status grad-
ings were reflecting in the quantities of provender each of them brought
into the pantry or larder, during the course of each week. Euphronius
type persons rolled in it, while flute-girls rubbed along on scraps.

What has significantly changed here since the time of the early
farmers, as the alert reader will have already spotted, is that neither
artists nor flute-girls poke their grubby little fingers in the soil anymore
for the purpose of raising crops. When they go to market, they go
bereft — if that is the word I want, of any supplies of onions, mushrooms or carrots. All they have is drachma which, although in itself,
doubtless a fine enough article, is useless in the kitchen as a comestible.
Drachma cannot be eaten; and in that simple truth we lay bare many of
the ills of our present world.

It is a truth about which men's minds are almost equally divided, if
one can judge from the utterances of poets and sages over the years.

Among those of the Money-is-a-Good-Thing school of thinking can
be included:

Cervantes — 'The best foundation in the world is money'
Thomas Fuller — 'A man without money is a bow without an arrow'
Sir Roger L'Estrange — 'Money makes the pot boil'

In that last regard, most writers have in their time, penned snazzy
little numbers for the ready market that come under the general heading
of 'pot-boilers'. The first use of that term, in that sense, by a writer is
generally credited to John Wolcot, an English lad. Sir Roger L'Estrange's
line in his reworked version of Aesop's Fables is dated 1692, but in the
true sense of the phrase does not quite hit the target.

John Wolcot (c. 1790) is much more on the button. In a little
offering entitled *The Bard Complimenteth Mr West on His 'Lord
Nelson'* he presents the opinion that the Lord Nelson piece in question
'will help to boil thy pot'. One likes to get these matters straight and
award credit where it is due.

On the Money-is-a-Bad-Thing side of the argument a galaxy of talent is to be found, standing up to be counted.

Shakespeare — 'Who steals my purse steals trash'

Chaucer — 'But one thing is, ye know it well enow,
    Of chapmen, that their money is their plogh.'

Anon — 'If you want to know what God thinks of money, look at the people he gives it to.'

A third category of 'mots justes' appear as general observatons that are repeated by one writer after another, on the grounds, no doubt, that you cannot have too much of a good 'mot juste'.

'Love of money is the root of all evil'.

'Money makes the man'.

'A fool and his money are soon parted'.

And for closers, we have:

Richard Cumberland — 'He that wants money wants everything.'

Benjamin Franklyn — 'If you would know the value of money, go and try to borrow some.'

Plautus — 'We purchase on Greek credit. . .cash.'

Racine — 'No money, no Swiss.'

Rowland Watkins — 'Who in his pocket hath no money,
    In his mouth he must have honey.'

Unknown — 'Why is the form of money round?
    Because it runs away from every man.'

Samuel Johnson — 'No man but a blockhead ever wrote except for money.'

'Quite right,' he said, speaking like a true banker.

Conjuring up, as that statement does, I replied, visions of money earnt, money spent and money to be accounted for to the tax authorities, may I quote to you the words of Robert Frost?

'If you must,' he said.

'I will, then' I said. And I did.

> 'Never ask of money spent
> Where the spender thinks it went
> Nobody was ever meant
> To remember or invent
> What he did with every cent.'

'Talking of money spent. . .' he said, looking round for the bill.

The rise of the banking system can be equated with the increased demand for cookery books, I said.

'How's that again?' he asked.

It works this way, I told him. Let us scamper through the Roman era with its porgy orgies, and cut right through to the heart of the husbandarial theme like the celebrated Accius Naevius.

Who, as you know, I went on before he could ask, was a celebrated augur in the reign of Tarquin the Elder. When the said Tarquin consulted the said A. N. on the subject of military estimates, A. N. advised that to increase the number of centuries, which was how divisions of armies were known in those times, would be injudicious and unwise. In a word, he said the auguries were against it.

This put the said Tarquin in a bit of a spot, he having already rather set his heart on having a few more centuries about the place. In order, therefore, to test out the rightfulness of the auguries, to see that they were in full working order, he asked the said A. N. to enquire of them if the thought then uppermost in his, the said Tarquin's, mind was feasible as a working idea, or not.

This in turn rather put the said A. N. on the spot. But, drawing his augurial robes about him as impressively as he might, he went through his routines and came up with the opinion that the feasibility of the aforenoted idea was confirmed.

'Splendid,' said the said Tarquin. 'The thought that I have in mind is that with the small hand knife you have in your hand you could cut through this solid whetstone.'

Accius took a deep breath, stepped forward, and with his pocket knife gave what is described as a bold cut, and the block fell in two, as reported by Livy, a parttime journalist of those days.

In like mannner, I said, let us now cut through to the heart of this husbandry issue.

Had you been extant in the 13th century, I told him, you would not have been able to fulfill your role of banker unless you had happened, at the same time, to be a priest. In the ordinary purlieus of this land persons of humble descent lived in rude huts. And rude huts being what rude huts were, such persons felt that these were not proper places to keep such small amounts of cash as came their way. The proper place, to their way of thinking, was the most solidly constructed establishment to which they had access, viz., the local church. Here they went, then, to deposit their coins for safe keeping. And, because it was handy, any village business transactions that needed to be transacted were transacted there, with the village curate looking on with a kindly smile.

Among the commodities that did not feature in these transactions, if I may use that word, were onions, mushrooms and carrots, it being the habit or custom of the rude persons inhabiting the aforementioned huts, to raise such supplies of o's, m's and c's as might be required in the rude soil surrounding these huts. Should it happen that none of these were immediately available as articles of diet, they would turn their attention to whatever veg might be on tap, viz., beans, tur or pars — neeps, or similar.

The point I am trying to make is that, as with the early farmer system of things, there was no hie-ing and ho-ing to the local super store for the requirements of life.

These rude persons made their livings by working for the local Lord, who in return, gave each chap a patch of land in which to raise veg and other provender for his own consumption. In addition, the local Lord would supply other items, such as building materials for the building of cottages or rude huts, materials for the making of rude furniture with which to furnish huts of the like description, and wool for the spinning and weaving of cloth to make rude clothes.

There were some things these rude persons, no matter how nifty with their crafts, could not produce for themselves, like salt, knives, spices, tar, rope and iron. To begin with the local Lord would finance these purchases by flogging the surplus to his requirements in market towns, buying the above with the proceeds of same, and making a distribution to the rude persons under his command.

All this, however, was time consuming, and the local Lord began to think of ways of getting out from under. Suppose, he reasoned to himself, instead of doing all this time-consuming marketing and distributing, one gave out to the rude peasantry something that could be exchanged for such requirements in the markets to which reference has been made, the middle man aspect of the business could be entirely done away with.

And, local Lords, being educated and not at all rude, would chat around with other local Lords of like mind and disposition, and having ferreted among old tomes at the local library, one of them eventually came up with the idea of money. Instead of giving out to the rude persons things, why not just simply give them spots of cash money.

This was a pretty simple thing for local Lords to get under way. All that was necessary was for the l. L. to get hold of a bar of silver weighing a pound, chop it into 240 pieces, call each of these a penny, and to show the stuff was the genuine article, to stamp on it a star or 'steorra' from which the present term 'sterling' derives. All clear thus far?

By these means, it came about that rude persons had pence in the pocket, same to be deposited for safe keeping with the local curate.

'What about the cook books?' he asked.

'I'm coming to that,' I told him. Bankers, used to the merry hum of commerce, are such impatient people.

Part of the contract which rude persons had with their local Lord, was to do a certain quantity of work in his fields, or on his premises in exchange for a rent free rude hut and messuages. With the tempo of life hotting up apace — rude persons being actively engaged in agriculture, banking and marketing — it was not always convenient for there to be a downing of tools and a trouping off to the l. L's establishment. So, with money in the bank or church, rude persons felt themselves to be in a position to negotiate a waiver of clause one, paying the l. L. a few pence in exchange for a release from working for same. Thus, there began the idea of rent.

'The cook books,' he said, drumming his fingers on the table top.

We shall come to that now, I said. Let us examine the accounts of one such rude person, or tenant farmer, as he now prefers to be called, as befits a man who pays rent, runs a business, is self-employed and has a bank account.

'Only at the local church,' he said, as if cheques drawn on the Church of England are of less worth than those requiring a joint stock bank to pay certain sums on demand.

All the same, I said, a man who has made his mark on the world. Such a man might be making £3 10s profit a year in the 13th century. From this he would pay out 10s for rent and other dues. In turn he would charge other persons for the use of his pasture and common rights. His wife and child brought in a bit on the side, bringing up the total to somewhere about £4 a year, enough to provide quite a fair supply of extras to the ordinary rude requirements of life.

As a for instance, I told him, four quarters of wheat to provide the family's bread would cost £1 3s. 6d. Two quarters of second class malt for brewing, sufficient to give about four gallons of ale each week — enough to drown quite a modicum of sorrows, would run to 7s. 7d. To these basic items we must add 800 pounds of meat a year at a quarter penny or farthing a pound, bringing the total budget to £2 7s. 9d. A further 12s. 3d. would take care of clothes, boots and similar necessaries leaving a whole £1 to be splurged on luxuries, or for depositing with the church's saving scheme, provision being made for rainy days.

Noticing the happy connection between curates and money supply, the son of such a chap might decide to take up a religious career, or to make his money building churches, or to open his own bank – one merely sketches in here a multitude of possibilities, you understand – so that by the fourteenth and fifteenth century, so much of this kind of thing had been going on that money was all about the place.

'Yes, but what about the. . .' he began.

I ignored him.

To begin with, the only foods the poorest people bought were probably fish, salt and a few of the cheaper spices. Later, as money got about, chaps were spending their days galloping hither and yon, tracking down salt herrings, eggs, sturgeon, pears, wine, pepper, cloves, mace, ginger, cinnamon, rice, almonds, saffron, raisins, sugar loaves, treacle, dates, and oranges, to name but a few.

When it was just a question of the 'roast meat on Sundays and Thursdays at night' as Thomas Tusser puts it, with, for the rest of the week, pease and bacon, pies of meat or fruit, brawn, pudding and souse, the occasional goose, turkey or chicken, the ordinary house person had no great difficulty in coping with the culinary tasks required. But, faced suddenly with cascades of salt herrings, almonds, treacle and oranges and the like the ordinary house person felt more inclined to bury her head in her house apron and resign herself to what has been described as anticipations of doom and foreboding.

She needed help. Or, to put it more succinctly, if that is the word I want, she needed a cook book.

But, how was this to be provided? you will ask. Cook books do not grow on trees. They must be written by cook persons with the gift of the pen, able to clutch that instrument firmly in their hands and make the required brisk strokes legibly on the scroll in question.

Even before this, I went on, said cook persons must somehow find the time and wherewithal for making purchases of essential ingredients with which recipes are to be tried out before being included in the tome. How was this difficulty to be overcome?

I will tell you, I said. In a word, the budding cook booker needed a bank.

Is it to be imagined, I said, that there could ever have been created openings for the more enterprising of the penners of cookery tomes and the publishers thereof without the intervention of banks? How does one imagine Mrs Beeton would have fared, Mr B being tied up all the time with his own matters of moment, had she not had the broad shoulder of her neighbourhood, friendly banker to whom she could pour out her troubles when the onion sauce boiled over, and on which shoulder she could rest her head for a refreshing weep when the going got rough in the matter of her mushroom soufflé? Who else could she touch for the necessary advance against the next royalty cheque for the third edition?

And is this not right and proper justice? I asked.

'A speculative investiment,' he murmured. 'High interest rates.'

Is there not some moral law, I asked, that requires banks to share the burden of responsibility in the same way that other portions of the citizenry are required to do? How does one imagine this situation to have arisen? Would the urgent and desperate need for cook books ever have come about without the involvement of banks in the expansions of the food supply trade? Could shippers have shipped the stuff in, merchants merchanted same, shoppers shopped it − if that is what shoppers do, and consumers consumed ditto without the intervention of busy bankers busily banking away in the background like billy-oh, tiding each chap in the long chain of commerce, over until the next linking chap came along to cough up the necessary?

'What has all this to do with husbandry?' he asked, showing signs of becoming restive, so far as bankers of whatever ilk show signs at all.

It has been said, I said, not by me, although I echo the sentiments, naturally, that the central defect of the medieval way of doing things in the food and culinary lines, was that there existed no system of storing the surplus of a good year against the advent of a bad one.

'A point of view with which no right thinking banker would disagree,' he said.

Don't interrupt, I said.

Today, I went on, what with mountains of various kinds − butter and beef and whatever else, including for all I know, onion, mushroom and carrot developments of the same kind − we give so much of our time and attention to working out how best to store the stuff, that we have almost begun to lose sight of the fact that some person somewhere in the husbandry field has to poke their green little fingers (or large gnarled ones) in the good earth or soil, or do whatever else may be necessary to produce the stuff in the first place. The result is that the ordinary cook person in the average cooking room or kitchen has become confused.

'There are all those mountains of cookery books to advise, direct and guide them,' he said.

Undoubtedly, cook books are a sound investment. The demand for them never flags. Their production, sale and use, provides an interesting illustration of that paradox advanced by Zeno in the matter of Achilles and the tortoise, with which we will not here bother as it is not relevant to what we are trying to say.

'What are you trying to say?' he asked.

Let us imagine that the production of cookery books is always twice the demand. In the formula put forward by the previously mentioned Greek philosopher and founder of the Stoic school, it is argued that if the demand for cook books is fifty, a hundred are produced. When production shrinks to fifty, there is still a demand for twenty-five. Production goes down to twenty, but there is still a demand for ten. And even when only two cookery books are in the production pipe-line, a position likely to be regarded as minimal by any publisher no matter how humble, there still remains a demand for one. Production, in fact, can never quite keep up with demand.

'I shall have to think about that,' he said, thoughtfully thinking about it.

The storage philosophy has entirely taken over in the mind of the ordinary cook person, I said. Kitchens are no longer places where food is cooked, but where it is stored. The rot set in, one supposes, with the making of jam, an activity innocent enough in itself, but leading to darker things like preserves and pickles. The kitchen has become a space occupied by mountains of tinned, frozen and freeze-dried goods together with other manifestations of the squirrel complex. The original theory that this was the place where food got the culinary heave-ho and the chef's one-two, has been lost sight of.

It has become instead, the room assigned for the heating of industrial gunge.

Now, let it not be said that I am against gunge. Gunge in its place is doubtless very good, as gunge goes. Gunge fans the world over will leap to its support and who would deny them this enjoyment.

Yet, the suspicion remains that gungery has got out of hand. There has been a gunge explosion. On every hand, gunge flourishes. Restaurants such as this, I told him, in which culinary heave-ho-ing might be thought to be the idea uppermost in the mind of the proprietors, prove on detailed examination to be gunge ships sailing under gunge flags of convenience.

The menu is composed, not so much of the ingredients listed therein, as slabs of prefabricated material designated in the catalogue from which they can be ordered, payment with same, as Gunge A, B or C for the main courses – Gunge D being the special Gunge-of-the-month, with Gunges 1, 2 and 3 as side orders. Slices of ditto are cut from these slabs as orders from the clientel out front come rolling in and are given the quick warm-up treatment before being served up with the Head Waiter's blessing.

Gungery has invaded the kitchen. . .

'What's wrong with that?' he asked.

What is missing, I told him, is the backing and filling, the edging forward and the drawing back, the tossing in of a dash of this, a handful of that which is so much a part of the exploratory, creative, adaptive – if that is the word I want, life of the true cook.

'Can't have waste,' he said. 'Bad economics.'

It has long been a preoccupation of mine, I told him, that for every guy and gal living south of the menagerie lion. . .

'The what?' he asked.

Ah, I said, I see there must be some defining of terms. In the days of my youth, as the poet has it, the Equator was commonly described by teachers flourishing in that period, as an imaginary line running round the centre of the earth. A contemporary, receiving the message in garbled form, mis-read it as a menagerie lion committed to this self-same running round, a concept which I have always found more acceptable than that offered previously.

'I see,' he said. 'We are speaking of the Equator.'

And the guys and gals living to the south of same, I went on, for every one of whom there must be guys and gals to the number ten, a hundred, a thousandfold, living to the north of ditto. This is a fact of life by which I have long been preoccupied.

'True,' he said, inferring that this was an odd aspect of the human condition about which to have a preoccupation.

By-passing the gunge syndrome, I said, and reverting to cooking of the more traditional kind, what one wants is not so much storage and more of a touch of rhythm in the system.

'Rhythm?' he queried.

What will be seen to dominate the food arena, by any competant, unbiased observer, by which I mean one specially hired for the occasion, is the flow of the seasons, the rhythmical unfolding of the deckchairs and picnic hampers in the summertime, as the song writer has it, when the living is easy, and the folding up and putting away of same in the outhouse, shed, conservatory, garage or utility room, when what is known by Russian authors as the bleak frosts of winter, draw nigh.

Summer is when nature comes to the boil. It is the season for all men. The time when fruits and veg come rolling off Mother N's production lines creating that commercial situation neatly identified by the poet Pope when he wrote: 'A glutted market makes provisions cheap.'

What farmers and other producing-type persons want is to sell everything they produce at the highest possible price. What ordinary consumer-type persons want to buy is everything produced at the lowest possible price. What gets in the way of these ambitions being satisfied, is winter. Farmers and other p-t p's, understand that while things grow in the summer they cease to do so in winter causing an unhealthy interruption of what you of the banking fraternity know as cash flow, arousing such thoughts in the minds of the aforesaid farmers and p-t p's as 'What next?' and 'Where do we go from here?' As a consequence, they hold back, reasoning that stuff which in the summer sells for the well known peanut will be up in the coconut class by the time winter's frosts have slammed the door on nature's bounty − if that is the phrase I want.

'There are tinning and freezing contracts,' he murmured.

Go wash your mouth, I said.

It is a fact well known to devotees of the cricketing game that one person's summer is another's winter, and, one supposes without going into the thing too deeply, vice versa. While chaps in one half of the globe are togging up with bat and pads preparatory to a brisk stroll out to the wicket, others in the other half are honing away at the skis and shaking out resident beetles from the fur-lined anoraks.

This being the case, even the most ordinary or average commercial mind should not find the matter beyond its resources to devise a scheme whereby the summer largesse of the cricketing crowd should be globally distributed to include the ski mob, with the expectation that there will be a turn round in the order of play at half time.

Only one detail stands in the way of the fulfilment of this noble scheme, I said, a point which has already been raised on the agenda, to wit, namely and viz., the imbalance in the number of persons resident north of the menagerie lion and those south of same.

The commercial mind wrestling with the fine print of this scheme is driven eventually to the conclusion that there are too few guys and gals in the bottom or southern half to be able to do much in the way of mopping up the north's surplus. And when half time comes, the self-same paucity of g's and g's results in nature's bounty being less bountiful than necessary to fill what the poet Cowper has termed 'the aching void' of the northern horde. An impasse, as some kind of foreign negotiator might have put it.

'Isn't that what happens now,' he said.

At this very moment, I said, gracing my stores are onions, fruits of a Chilean autumn or fall, come to bless my English spring. But the facts remain as stated. Too many of the one, too few of the other.

'If you say so,' he said.

I said I did say so and we both let the matter rest.

The result is, I went on when I had got my breath back, the ordinary food-eating-type person, spends as much time peering into his purse or wallet, as his larder or refrigumrator. His taste buds and stomach hardly get a word in edgewise.

What happens? I asked. The f-e-t p goes off to market, super, hyper or street, with the said stomach sending up signals that what would be most acceptable in the regions over which the said stomach had jurisdiction would be something in the onion line, as it would be an onion tart.

On arrival at the precincts of the market selected, the discovery is made that internatonal consortia who operate in this field have cornered the market in onions and are holding out for a bigger whack all round. Onions are to be compared with diamonds, rubies and pearls, not absolutely beyond price, but heading generally in that direction and not the sort of purchase to be lightly considered by an ordinary f-e-t p without a deep study of the runes, the FT Index or Dow Jones Average and the current rates applicable to substantial bank loans.

As a result carrots are substituted for onions and there is nought but wailing and a boiling of juices down in those nether regions that had been anticipating onions and for which veg the green lights had been laid out in readiness. This is a situation which leads to the spreading of darkness and gloom, and a resort to gunge, which expedient explains much of the unrest currently to be found among food-eating-type persons.

It might be thought that things had changed since medieval times, but the order of change can be indicated by the two words: 'not much'. G's and g's, otherwise known as f-e-t p's, of the thirteenth century, expecting no more than a daily ration of coarse bread or maslin, ale, pottage, cheese, eggs and oat-cake were not often going to be disappointed. Bored, yes — you would have answered on the questionnaire. Disappointed, no. Part two of the same q relating to present times might be truthfully answered the other way round: Bored, no. Disappointed, yes. And there in a nutshell, as someone once said, you have it.

The intervention of money to food matters, while no doubt spreading sweetness and light in many quarters, casts a shadow across the field of play that the aforesaid s and l does not find it easy to remove. Like the blot on the shirt that the Brand X biological detergent will not remove, the stain remains. Sometimes, like Aholibamah, it makes us feel we would like to be transported away to a brighter world than this.

But the dinner gong continues to sound at regular intervals and if we are going to answer its call, only stratagems and tactics of a forthright and devious character will permit us to do so. The fact has to be recognised that, despite the soft music, subdued lights and general suggestion of 'rest-your-weary-head-on-our bosom', the ordinary place of food business is a battlefield, every price tag a bullet, every special offer an exploding shell, and the turnstile through which you pass to reach the cash desk a mine field. Only skills of deployment equal to the combined resources of Rommel, Montgomery and Eisenhower will see you through.

'You paint a bleak picture,' he said.

Not at all, I said. One tries to look at things as they are. Attila the H., that well known man-about-wars might have found that his tactics of pillage and plunder would still work well enough to earn the Good Husbandry Seal of Approval. Those of us less gifted in the arts of p and p must adopt more the attitude, approach and posture of fifth, sixth and even seventh columns, winnowing our way into establishments of the kind under discussion, and filleting out the bare bones of bottom prices.

Successful practitioners in the business of war winning are generally agreed that the first requirement of practitioners (successful) is what is known as intelligence, this being a commodity not to be confused with that like-named commodity that most of us think we have but psychologists the world over prove conclusively that we have not. The intelligence to which reference is made herein is that quiet word about the doings and goings-on of the other side without which no practitioner (successful) can map out his strategy (successful). If the enemy plans to make a swoop towards the right flank it is essential to know about this beforehand so that, (a) the right flank can be removed elsewhere, and (b) a counter swoop can be organised towards a direction where the enemy is not, having by then removed himself to where our right flank is supposed to be, but isn't. All clear thus far?

Intelligence in the food war comes from many sources. (Alert and attentive readers will recall that some aspects of this plan of campaign have already been exposed to the public gaze on earlier pages). In my own case the first pointers on the state of play come from an event that occurs at lunchtime each Thursday. This is the BBC Shopping Basket in which a standard collection of items are priced for various regions of the country. Persons hiding their identity under veils and dark glasses enter commercial food premises of every kind, noting prices, bargains and special offers, concealing note pads, pencils and digital calculators in their fur tippets. These Mata Haris of the supermarkets — if I may call them that, wing their data back to BBC premises where other persons grind it up finely, compounding it into a kind of broadcasting pill, one to be taken each week before shopping, preferably with liquid refreshment.

Having thus noted down the first slings and arrows of outrageous shopping, one turns the quick ear to the local commercial radio station on the Friday morning, in the commercial intervals of which between records, sometimes now known, one understands as discs, there comes further market information of a more detailed kind. The Slap-happy Food Stores, we gather, is offering tinned prunes at a knockdown, unrepeatable price. Consulting the records housed ordinarily in a disused soup toureen on the third shelf counting from the top down, one discovers that this price is 2p higher than the ordinary price for t.p.'s quoted elsewhere. As a result the Slap-happy merchants are scratched from the fixture list.

After a day's hard study of this kind, guidelines for operation 'Grab-bag' can be laid down.

But, there is one further preliminary. Rising from that condition which according to the playwright Shakespeare knits up ravelled sleeves of care, we tune in at six-thirty on the Saturday morning to the programme broadcast for farmers, in which hard-headed, horny-handed sons of toil present their agricultural soundings in the markets. There is a glut, we learn of sprouts of very poor quality, and we scrub sprouts from our list. There is a good deal of rubbish in the carrot world, we hear, and carrots too get a quick flash of the blue pencil. After another ten minutes or more of this pretty punchy stuff, we stagger away from the radio wondering if shopping will ever again be worth the effort and if, indeed, there is any basis for thinking that life as we have known it can continue to go on.

But, even on the bleakest day the sap somehow rises and fore-warned to the eyebrows with intelligence we get down to cases. A quick run round the available super or other markets is made to check that we have more or less got our facts straight. This will reveal that, as between two different establishments, one will be up on this and down on that. Or, the position might equally be reversed, one being up on that and down on this. One never knows what to expect.

This is followed by a jostle through the open-air market. Surveying the produce on the stalls one becomes aware of a cosmetic factor that can only be described as — The Cosmetic Factor. Carrots will be found in supermarkets, neatly packaged and of a slender, tapering elegance suggesting that refined persons have carefully selected these as much for their aesthetic as their carroty qualities. Elsewhere, on stalls, retailing for considerably less will be found carrots of such monstrously uncarrot-like shapes that only the colour gives a clue to their true identity.

However, as Miss Stein herself might have said, and may well have done for all I know, 'a carrot is a carrot is a carrot'. Sliced into a casserole, daube or stew, it goes about its carroty business just as well as any of its more elegant and stylish relatives. Mongrel carrots, it has to be said in these egalitarian days, are all right.

Then begins a process known in sailing circles as tacking, in which the shopping person, seeking to make headway against the force eight commercial winds that bear down on him, goes this way and that way, picking up a bargain here, a special offer there, a best buy wherever.

En route a shop is found displaying an announcement that an aggre-gation of their prices results in the firm conclusion that the result is 30p below the BBC's Shopping Basket price. A line of the kind attri-buted to bees is made in this direction.

At the end of the day, results having lived up to expectations, the weary shopper wends his way homeward o'er the lea, leaving the world to darkness and unsold remainders, warmed by the knowledge that,

looking at the situation in the round, taking into consideration all aspects, he has come out once more ahead of the game.

This is the very foundation of Good Husbandry, I said.

'Interesting,' he said, rising to his feet, having obtained a revised version of the bill from which the errors present in the first edition resulting in a degree of over-charging, had been removed.

'Before you go,' I said, 'There is something.'

'Yes?' he asked.

'I am just on my way to do the shopping, as it happens,' I said. 'And things being what they are, what with one thing and another, postal delays and the advance from the publisher not yet having managed to filter through the tribes of hostile natives that clearly infest the communications networks of the nation. . .'

'Yes?' he asked, again.

I wonder if you could see your way clear to cashing me a small cheque, I asked. Just for the wherewithal, you understand.

And he did.

WEIGHT

Life had delivered what the celebrated Wodehouse describes as the sleeve across the windpipe.

I had required a pound and a half of onions. I had asked for a pound and a half of onions. Bearing these preliminaries in mind, I had the not unreasonable expectation on returning home to find reposing among the various purchases made during the course of a busy morning a pound and a half of the self-same vegetable.

Now, reposing on my scales was something less than a pound and a half.

One does not expect when opening negotiations for a pound and a half of the edible bulb of the liliaceous Asiatic plant to receive at the termination thereof an alderman in the gullet. (An alderman, I hasten to explain to readers not versed in these matters is a term used by the criminal fraternity for the type of burglar's crowbar used in forcing safes. A heavier jemmy is known as a Lord Mayor — this information I toss into the pool for free and without obligation.)

The quantity required had been asked for in a firm, clear voice, to be supplied as per the terms stated on the cardboard wedged into the mound of onions on display with a small wood peg. From that instant of time, contractual obligations could be deemed to exist on both sides, I — the purchaser — to cough up the necessary coins of the realm, he — the stallholder — to supply onions in the quantity asked for, viz., a pound and a half.

'Try the other scales,' she said.

It was salt in an old wound, a term used to convey the sharp feeling of statements of that kind and deriving from the practice, apparently once common, of rubbing salt in old wounds. Quite how humankind got onto this business of salt wound-rubbing escapes me. I mean, what is the point? Salt, as everyone knows, is thrown into coffins because Satan — that celebrated fiend-about-hell — hates salt. In Scotland, salt is shovelled into the mash when brewing is in progress because witches can't bear the stuff and will avoid it at all costs. Both, straight-forward, sensible ways of using the commodity. But, salt in wounds? Sometimes one wonders where humankind gets its ideas.

But, to revert to the wound under discussion, we have on our premises, two scales. The first in chronological order, reading from left to right, is a beam scale of a delicate and sensitive nature. The impression is conveyed that it was assembled in a factory staffed with maiden aunts. Any ontoward thing upsets it. Utter a harsh word, or direct a stern glance in its direction and this is enough to set up such a flutter in its system that all thoughts of rendering judgments in the matter of weight fly from its mind. It needs a rest, a quiet day by the sea, enjoying the caress of sea breezes and the plaintive cries of swooping gulls to set it to rights. Should this remedy not be available, some alleviation — if that is the word I want, of the unnerved state into which the beam scale has got itself, can be secured by easing a small screw and sliding a weight up and down a bar, this soothing motion having the effect of calming the disordered fulcrum, as would the cool hand of a gently nurtured maiden upon the heated brow of a similarly disordered person.

Such a scale, in full nick, is simplicity itself to operate. The desired weight is pre-set by sliding other weights than the one previously re-ferred to, back and forth along other bars. The goods to be weighed, in this case — onions, are unloaded into the pan or hopper. When the beam from which the scale takes its name, rises to a horizontal position, confidence can be felt that goods — still onions, of the required quantity repose in the aforesaid hopper. All clear thus far?

Such a scale suffers from what I feel obliged to name as a psycho-logical weakness. This can be illustrated by what psychologists know as a case history — in this instance, one having to do with a pound and a half of onions, the quantity called for, when peeled, by the recipe currently in production. A pound and a half is set on the beam. Onion peeling begins. The keen-edged knife flashes round the bulbs. One by one they are deposited in the hopper. The task is arduous requiring prodigies of exertion and concentration.

At this point the onion-peeler person passes a weary hand across the beaded brow and asks the question: 'How much more?', the answer to said question supplying a modicum of encouragement, indicating, on the one hand, quantity completed (large), and on the other, quantity to be completed (small). A word, even a hint from the beam scale, one feels, would work wonders.

But, does the beam scale cooperate? Does it weigh in with a cheery word? Does it salute the dedication of the onion-peeler in question and urge him on with gentle cries of: 'What ho!'

It does not. Not a nudge, hint, wink or suggestion escapes it as to how matters stand. With what amounts to a callous indifference it stands aside and lets the embattled onion-peeler struggle through to the bitter end, or fall by the wayside in the attempt.

'What I want,' I had said, when the matter came up, linked to a discussion of hypothetical birthday presents, 'is a scale with a dial.'

A scale with a dial is precisely what I got. What had not been anticipated was that the dial was composed of thin card and held in place by a press-fitting, transparent plastic face which caused said dial to bend, pressing it against the rotating needle preventing same from rotating. This rather got in the way of the scale doing its job of indicating the weight of goods contained in its hopper. Removal of the plastic face allowed the needle to rotate. It also permitted the dial to fall out.

The chances of said scale playing its part in the weight measuring game are slim; they are what members of the horse betting fraternity might judge to be odds of around 100:1 against. It is not an issue on which gambling men with funds at their disposal would be prepared to lay out said funds. The scale, as a scale, is pretty well a dead duck.

It can be brought to life again, uttering a faint quack, by some person standing by with a thumb at the ready to push the dial back into place, thus allowing the needle to rotate and go about its business of indicating weight. But, the same person could just as well be using the same thumb to slide beam scale weights up and down their beam and so measure the progress of onion peeling in hand. In any case, the beam scale is probably more accurate than the scale with a dial.

Thus, a tension in the weights and measures department grew up. Forces pulled this way and that. On the one hand a need was felt to show appreciation of the gift of a scale with a dial by using same with or without the dial falling out. On the other, one needed to know with some certainty how many onions had been peeled.

At last, by a subtle diplomatic move, on the grounds that, as Latin-speaking persons have it — 'Pertusum quicquid infunditur in dolium perit' — or to put it another way — 'all is lost that is put in a riven dish' — the riven dish of this instance the dial falling scale, was quietly nominated for the Chiltern Hundreds. The beam scale was returned from retirement, and a glister restored to the business of weighing peeled onions.

But, like Althaea's brand, the matter smoulders on, flaring a few sparks whenever the question of determining weight crops up.

'Try the other scales,' she said — this being by way of a flashback to the first occasion when a report of that utterance appeared on these pages — and when smouldering matters flare up, one knows that the correct thing is to divert the attention with torrents, cascades and fountains of words, this being the remedy most immediately available.

'One cannot have weight without length,' I said.

'Why are you trying to change the subject,' she said.

'What gave you the idea that I was changing the subject,' I replied, changing the subject.

It was merely my intention of pointing out that once one begins to get down to the basics of the business of evaluating the weight of peeled onions one enters the realm of deep waters, than which none run deeper.

Wise men have laid it down, I said, that weight is the gravitational force exerted on matter by the earth. In the matter of these onions, it is the attraction the same have for the earth, or it may be the other way about, one never knows with these affairs how and where they start.

It may interest you to know that these peeled onions would, if transported about complete with measuring devices of a suitable sensitivity, be shown to weigh different amounts at different places on earth and at different heights above sea-level. So that, should it happen that one wished to purchase a pound and a half of onions, as it might be, the pound and a half purchased at the South Pole would be either more or less than the pound and a half of which delivery was taken forty thousand feet up in a Jumbo jet.

'They don't sell onions at the South Pole. Or in jets,' she added.

But I could see she had grasped the theory of the thing.

Now, I said, let us change hats for the moment. Let us move away, as that seems to be the way things are going these days what with the Common Market and international agreements of every kind, from the pound and a half of onions to a mode — if that is the word I want, that is more in the line of a kilogram of onions.

What, I asked her, is a kilogram? A thousand grams, you will reply, as the name of the weight-measuring unit in question suggests. In that case, I continued, pressing on while I had her full attention, she being inclined when I am speaking to remember other engagements, and wander off, what is a gram?

Wise men have laid it down ('The same wise men', she asked? 'Possibly', I told her. 'You know how it is with wise men. They never know when to stop.') that a gram is the mass of one millionth of a cube metre of water at its maximum density.

What, alert and attentive persons will wish to ask at this point, do wise men have to say on the subject of a metre? — this being, it would seem, germane to the subject under discussion.

The w.m. to whom reference has already been made have given it as their firm opinion that a metre is one ten-millionth part of the distance along a meridian from the north pole to the equator. The w.m. in particular who uttered this utterance in the first place with any measure of authority were those then occupying the pews of the National Assembly of France in the years 1791 and 1795.

Over the years other w.m. of a French persuasion looked over this work of these early w.m. and found it good, as a consequence the system which by then had come to be known as the metric system because alert persons had noted that metres seemed to be at the heart of it, was made compulsory for all commercial transactions in France as from, and by decree dated, July 4, 1837. If after that date you stepped up to the nearest stallholder dealing in the appropriate commodities and asked for a pound and a half of onions, he would be entitled with a gay 'Oo-la-la!' to waggle his index digit in your face and request that you rephrase the demand in terms of grams, or kilos thereof.

Every now and then, the French being as a nation passionately attached to the idea of accuracy, although not being terribly accurate at being accurate, came to the conclusion that it was too complicated and not terribly accurate to have chaps laying out measuring tapes along a meridian from the equator to the north pole, particularly as the chaps at one end were not absolutely certain where the equator might be, one chap having the idea it was here by this large tree and another chap being equally convinced that it was more over there near the bushes at the foot of that hill, while the chaps at the other end were running round in circles trying to find where the north pole had got to.

An International Commission of the Metre was set up in 1872 and after a good deal of moustache-blowing and fingers-under-the-collaring it was agreed to cut a long story short and to accept the bar of metal lodged in the Archives of Paris as being, for all practical purposes, a metre, regardless of whether it was exactly a ten-millionth part of the distance from the equator to the north pole, or not. 'Ya-boo!' and 'Sucks to you!' – or the French equivalents thereof, liberally translated, were the opinions the most frequently heard to be launched against opponents of this scheme. And, in order to complete a good job before lunch, they agreed to take the same view of the standard platinum-iridium kilogram lodged in the same Archives.

'Have you finished?' she asked.

Not quite, I said. Thus it can be seen that to define weight one has to be able to define length as well. Hence my opening remark.

The words that next spring to the lips are those suggesting that events then moved apace. Of course, those of us who dabble in historical matters, when we use the word 'apace' we do not intend to convey the same sense of 'apace' as might come from the pen of your motoring correspondent. Spherical objects when given the urge to move down a smooth, inclined plane, as the textbooks have it, continue on the downward path with the same gathering of speed as one who slides away from the pinnacles to the potholes of society. Historical matters have the same inevitability, but less pace. So that, when one uses the word 'apace', it is to be understood that something of the order of three years was to pass before the subject next came up under the hammer.

Nations from far and wide – well, at least, not whole nations but just one or two chaps from each one – came to a General Conference of Weights and Measures, signing treaties as if treaties had only just been thought of and everyone wanted to have one to take home as a souvenir. An International Bureau of Weights and Measures was set up at Sèvres in the suburbs of Paris, behind the closed doors of which much sleeve-rolling-up, and getting-down-to-things resulted in quantities of replicas of the previously agreed standard metre and kilogram being made for export to all those nations who had filled up order forms saying they would like to have one to put on the President's mantle-piece.

One of the nations to fill in the order blank, subject to the terms and conditions laid down, copies of which can be had on application in triplicate to the IBWM, as above, allowing three months for delivery, postage and packing extra, was the US of A. In due course, delivery was taken of prototype metre No. 27 and prototype kilogram No. 20, which were lodged in the custody of the National Bureau Standards at

Washington, D. of C., where, in the bowels of which they might, like Amaranths, have eternally reposed, everlasting and fadeless, had there not been further dark moves in the wings.

Ben Harrison, then the incumbent President, did what Presidents should never do, and involved himself in a rash deed, the rashness of which was to become apparent later on. With a rush of the red stuff to the head, what with the New Year celebrations and everything, he put his name to a paper accepting the above prototypes as standards of all matters relating to the lengths of metres, on the one hand, and the weights of kilograms on the other, on January 2, 1890.

Having done so he began to kick himself under the table for having been such a headstrong, rash, impetuous President, and regretting that he had not insisted on an escape clause in fine print at the bottom of page two.

For what happened next, and here we have another of these historical nexts, not the next of everyday life where ordinary persons can understand the term 'next' as meaning, what for the want of a better word I can only describe as next, but an historical next which in this case happened to come seventy years later.

Chaps in the Weights and Measures trade had for years been perturbed at the slithery nature of the commodity in which they dealt, to wit, the standard metre (with which is to be associated the standard kilogram). In warm weather, it seemed to them, this metre expanded and became more of itself. While, when winter's frosts lay all about, it contracted to a shorter shift than seemed justified in the circumstances. 'Now you see it, now you don't' was just about how chaps in the Weights and Measures trade expressed it. Something of a more reliable and trustworthy nature, they felt was called for. A standard metre you could trust.

It seemed to them a situation undermining the very foundation stones of the W and M industry that persons purchasing, let us say, a metre of bread, spaghetti or sausage during the months November to March inclusive, in the northern or upper hemisphere, might get less than they bargained for. Persons concluding the same transaction during the period June to August might be so burdened down with lengths of bread, spaghetti and sausage that they hardly knew how to put the next foot forward.

Chaps of the W and M trade looked upon the standard metre (with which is to be associated the standard Kilogram) and like the Ancient

Mariner when he looked upon the albatross, did not like what they saw.

Matters were put in hand. Events proceeded afoot. For the historically minded, 'afoot' is by a hair's breadth slower than 'apace', whereas, 'in hand' hardly represents movement at all. It can be gauged as the speed with which the statue of the Venus de Milo turns its head to look out of the window to see what is happening to the weather.

After a good deal of this-ing and that-ing, W and M chaps agreed that the standard metre which had caused them so much disquiet over the years, could be tossed out on its ear, and generally given the proverbial 'Heave-ho'. What should come into its place was a standard metre to be equal to 1,650,763.73 wavelengths of radiation from the krypton-86 atom, this being in a vacuum and corresponding to the transition between the levels $2p_{10}$ and $5d_5$ of the said atom.

This, however, did not as expected instantly spread sweetness and light to all sectors where W and M matters hold sway. Persons engaged in the purchasing of bread, spaghetti and sausage found themselves suddenly in deep water.

If it should happen that on a day, as it might be in October or April, a doubt enters their minds that the length of bread, spaghetti or sausage, which has just come into their possession at the conclusion of some monetary exchange, is at variance with that standard length of one metre as recommended in all the official literature on the subject, how shall they now check whether their metre of b. s. or s. is true or false?

Chaps with supplies of the krypton-86 atom are not to be found on every street corner. One does not see them strolling about with quantities about their person. Faced with the request: 'May I borrow your krypton-86 atoms for half a tick — the ones I have in mind being those corresponding to the transition between the levels $2p_{10}$ and $5d_5$ together with the vacuum that goes with them,' such persons can be expected to give something that looks and sounds like a frosty reply. 'Go and get your own krypton-86 atoms' just about sums up their attitude.

But you will be wondering in what way this change of technique is of such a profound rashness as to disturb the slumbers of Benjy Harrison. I will tell you.

On the fateful day in 1890 when he set pen to paper as outlined above, the distance between the Washington, D of C, where said pen was located, and San Francisco where, doubtless, subsequent events made him wish he was, was calculated in miles and yards, said miles and yards being based on the relationship it was then thought these units had with the standard metre.

The rising of the krypton-86 era above the W and M horizon led to a re-appraisal — if that is the word I want, of this relationship. A falseness was detected. Something was not quite right. Directors of national standardizing laboratories from the US of A, UK, Australia, Canada, New Zealand, and South Africa got together for a W and M wing-ding, at the end of which, downing great draughts of warm milk and raw egg and brushing what remained of the crumbs of the previous night's feast from their waistcoats, they announced to the agog world that henceforth and for all time, the yard was to be 0.9144 of a metre exactly. As a result, the distance between the said Washington and the said San Francisco was found to be 26 yards longer than previously.

Washington and San Francisco had moved further apart — a circumstance calculated to shatter the tranquility of the Presidential post-prandial zizz a little more than somewhat as Damon Runyon might have put it.

Worse was to come. The pound, it was declared at the same time, was now to be 0.45359237 of a kilogram exactly. (In passing, it can be noted that this unit of mass is called a 'slug' — this information I toss into the hat for free.)

The consternation of consumers everywhere can be imagined.

'No it can't,' she said.

As in the present instance, I went on, of a person requiring a certain quantity of onions (to wit, a pound and a half), now finds himself faced with the task of putting in an order for 0.68038855 of a kilogram thereof, and not knowing — it being that 0.45359237 is not divisible by 2, whether the greater accuracy is secured by upping the demand to 0.68038856, or cutting back to 0.68038854.

'Does it matter?' she asked.

At this very instant, I told her, eagle-eyed officials — direct descendants, in an administrative sense, of those sharp-faced Astynomoi who prowled the purlieus of the Agora keeping a watchful check on the rates being charged by flute-girls, are pacing our own streets with very much the same concerns in mind, although it has to be admitted that the present demand for flute-girls in England is not what it was.

'What is all this about flute girls?' she asked.

Our subject is good husbandry, I said. The good husbandry person is one who has the quality known as 'follow through'. Such a person, by study, investigation and attention at the 'qui vive' level at all times, knows what are the best goods on offer, what are the best prices to pay, what are the signs of best quality, what are the trade fiddles operating in this arena of the commercial punch-up, and how best to pull off a satisfactory coup, as it might be in onions, to complete the transaction in question. In other words, the good husbandry person knows where to get his (or hers).

The question that springs to all lips is: 'Ah, but where is his (or hers) available?'

When time was so young that it barely knew enough to be able to count itself from one tick to the next, his (and hers) was customarily brought round by pedlars. The name derives, not, as ignorant persons might think, from the Latin, pedes, or feet, but from the ped, a hamper without a lid in which were stored fish or other articles to hawk about the streets, as the good Brewer puts it.

The same excellent person goes on to report that at Norwich there is a Ped-market in which there are exposed for sale eggs, butter and cheese. But, we get ahead of ourselves.

Pedlars, as we have said, got about from place to place conducting their business on what is known as the door-to-door basis. This was especially the case in country districts where, doors being in short supply, every door got its full share of attention.

'See you next June,' the pedlar might say, in his gruff way, as he left. And if it should turn out that the time was somewhere about half-past July before the lady waiting behind the door heard the gruff old pedlar's gruff boots come gruffing up to her door, why, that was perfectly all right. Time, being so young and ticking itself off so slowly and carefully, there seemed to be more of it to go round.

Pretty soon, time got better and better at the ticking game, counting itself off with nimbler ticks. To keep up, pedlars had to hop to it. Now, it was not so much of your easy-going half-past July, but a brisker 'half-past this week and where the hell has he got to' kind of attitude, by which time, the said pedlar still not having turned up, the lady waiting behind the door, gave up waiting, came out and put her pedes to appropriate use by taking herself to the nearest village or town in order to secure hers (or it might be his, especially if she were married, if you see what I mean).

If there is one thing that sorts out the country person from those dwelling in towns it is re the matter of doors. Country persons see no

need for great numbers of doors cluttering up the terrain. 'A door here and a door there,' about sums up their attitude.

The town person does not feel comfortable without a good quantity of doors about the place Wherever he sees a gap, he plugs it with a door. 'You show me a hole,' he says, 'and I'll show you a door to go in it.' This question of doors expresses the essential difference between town and country, and if you happen to be in the door-to-door business it is a distinction of some consequence. The country pedlar finding himself plunged in the door-filled world of the town does not know which one to knock on next. While he is trying to make up his mind, hanging about in the street, his mind in a whirl − you get the picture − the town person lurking behind the doors mentioned loses patience and comes out to knock, as it were, on the pedlar's ped.

When this has happened several times in quick succession, the thought comes to the pedlar caught up in this hectic experience of door-bound life, that if Muhammed hangs about long enough, the mountain will indeed come.

An associated functionary also earning his crust in this sector of the

commercial arena is the hawker, or huckster, so named from a variety
of more ancient words of various origins, meaning to stoop or bend. A
hawker, or huckster, is one who stoops or bends under his burden, as
it might be, a ped.

Hawkers and pedlars quickly cottoned on to this hanging about
concept of marketing strategy. Picking out nice draught free squares at
the centre of towns, with plenty of tall well-built habitations all about
to fend off the swirling breezes that are so much a blot on the
pedlar's (and hawker's) life, these places came to be called markets.
Firmly putting the door-to-door aspect of commerce behind them,
pedlars (with which are to be coupled hawkers) became stall-holders
and to them came persons of every description to get theirs.

No doubt, such being human nature, there were those who bewailed
the passing of the door-to-door, and others who persisted in this line
of business, complaining that stall-holding in a market place or square
was unfair competition.

But, persons seeking to get theirs, tend to get it, such being the ways
of traders, in that form in which they are most prepared to receive it.
Or, to put it more crisply, stalls were in, door-to-doors out.

When a chap, or chapess, for the peddling and hawking life had no
sex bar, has been standing for some time, long years in some cases,
buffeted by those unkind elements that despite the most rigid precautions creep past the protection afforded by the well-built premises
surrounding the squares in which the hawking and peddling is being
conducted, it occurs to those so engaged how much better things would
be all round if they also could be accommodated in well-built premises.

Peddling and hawking having supplied the where-withal, or moola,
premises are commissioned from builders. Looking round for a name
by which these shall be known, recourse is had to the Anglo-Saxon
'sceoppa' — a stall or booth, allied to 'scypen', a pen for cattle, not
forgetting the Low German 'schupp' a shed, and the keen mind arrives
at the word 'shop', meaning a shop.

This placed these scypen, schupp or shop keepers behind doors
where they began to await the arrival of those energetic door-to-doorers
of the modern world, the commercial travellers. But that, as somebody
once said to somebody else, is another story.

The result of all this medieval sleeve-rolling and girding of traders'
loins was that a goodly number of them gathered to themselves what
we now know as riches, this being a commodity described by a word

which has the distinction of puzzling word scholars all over the place, some claiming that the word has no singular, and others that it has no plural. (The other word in this class or category is 'alms', the protagonists in that case being, on the one hand, Dr. Johnson (no singular) and Dr. Murray on the other hand (no plural)).

It is a fact of life that a poor man, never having had more than a passing contact with the folding stuff remains remarkably unimpressed with the stuff's usefulness. 'Does it bring ease of heart, a song to the voice and a merry smile to one and all?' he asks himself, as he hews this and draws that in the cheerful way poor persons have.

'It does not,' he replies to himself, hawking under his burden.

Should it happen, and it does happen sometimes, that riches come to him beyond the dreams of Avis (his life's mate), the question of the usefulness of riches is brought forcefully to his attention. As he surveys the pile of the spendable stuff now reposing in his coffer – as he is not all that rich, he has only the one, as yet – the thought comes to him with some force: 'Is this enough?'

His attitude towards it is much like that of Althaea towards her brand. You know the story, of course. Her son, Meleager, was to live so long as a log of wood, then on her fire, remained unconsumed. With a gentle poke here, and another there, Althaea managed to make it last for many years. Then one day, in the way these things suddenly blow up between mothers and sons, an exchange of words blew up between these two, resulting in the emotional circumstance now described by psychologists and other practitioners of that ilk as 'the blowing of the top'. Althaea blew her top, and kicked the log at the centre of this story, into the centre of the fire, where it was consumed in a few minutes, Melaeger cashing in his dinner pail as per the arrangement outlined above.

The ex-poor, newly rich person views his riches in much these same terms. A sudden kick, to his mind, could send the fatal log crashing to the heart of the fire resulting in the swift elimination of the said riches, and his return to the previous status of poor person.

'This is not a good thing,' he says to himself, forgetting for what was then known as the nonce, the question of heart easement, voice singing and merry smiling.

He takes what seems to him the only sensible course of action, viz., to open up another scypen, schupp or shop, on the grounds that if one of same equals one filled coffer, two will result in two coffers, three filling three coffers, and so forth, the formula repeating itself until, as it is said, 'the cows come home,' it being understood that cows, being silly, never come home. Pretty soon he has branches everywhere and is so busy pulling in the spendable stuff and packing it away, with gangs of artisans — if that is the word I want — hard at it, knocking up coffers, that all thoughts of hearts getting eased, voices being used for singing and merry smiles having a stab at smiling, slide right down to the bottom of the list.

Among the world's persons for whom the easing of hearts, raising of voices in song and squeezing of faces into merry smiles has little appeal, are to be numbered the Chinese. Inscrutable, is the word that comes the most readily to the mind when thinking of a way to describe the nation of persons mentioned above. Smiling — no. Heart-easing — no. Voice singing — no. Inscrutable — yes.

As has already been noted on these pages, the Chinese have always been a busy race of persons, actively engaged in getting in on the ground floor of the tea trade, securing a toe-hold at bargain basement level in the vegetable business, and making an early start on the pro-duction of roast pork. Neither did they omit to get the retail chain store business under way, several chains of which could be discovered clanking vigorously in China two or more thousand years ago, when the years were measured in BC's, and not the later AD's.

Equally low down on the easing-singing-smiling scale are the Germans whose natural inclinations have generally tended towards the filling of coffers. 'If one has coffers,' they can be heard to mutter, 'and it is the purpose of coffers to be filled, then it behoves all right-thinking persons to set about the business of filling them as rapidly as possible.' Among the most stalwart champions of the coffer-filling philosophy were the Fugger family who, in the 15th century, capitalising on the Chinese experience, as it were, started up what the encyclopaedia, with its encyclopaedic knowledge of such things, describes as 'mercan-tile operations of a chain-store character.'

In 1643 a chain of pharmacies was founded in Japan. And, following its charter in 1670, the Hudson's Bay Company developed a chain of outposts in Canada. Passing Eskimoes were encouraged, should they happen to require a little of this or that, to make a bear-line for their nearest, friendly, neighbourhood outpost.

Yet, the fact remains, that as one passes along the freeways, motor-ways, autoroutes and autobahnen of life, no beckoning neon signs

direct us toward chain stores of a Chinese, German, Japanese or Canadian
life style. What predominates — if that is not too strong a word, is something American in character and recognised as such. There is a reason.

In the world today, the chain store as it is now known, is generally
believed to stem from the founding of the Great Atlantic and Pacific
Tea Company in New York City in 1859.

'All hail, the A & P!' cry devotees of the chain-store game who if
asked to sum up the activities of the said enterprise, might be heard to
describe it, after a bit of thought while toeing and heeling the boot
into the soil, as 'The Apollo' of the chain-store world.

Critics of this and business empires deriving from it, who attempt
to attribute to the growth of such stores the characteristics reported of
Apollodorus by Plato, namely, to wit and viz., 'envied by all for his
enormous wealth, yet nourishing in his heart the scorpions of a guilty
conscience', are rebutted by the previously mentioned devotees who
by this time have given up toeing and heeling the soil in case passing
scorpions might be disturbed by same. These said devotees argue right
back that in the business of providing the facilities whereby persons
get theirs, the said facilities would wither as trees in the desert if the
said persons did not find that these offered a convenient way of securing theirs, it being acknowledged that theirs was to be found at the
premises in question waiting to be secured. This, cry devotees, is why
chain stores flourished when they did, A & P being followed by others,
like minded.

'Ah!' reply the critics. 'Is this not another case of Antimony?'

'Antimony?' she asked.

'Antimony, indeed,' I said.

The tale is told in Ben Jonson's dictionary of how a prior served up
a supply of this mineral to his pigs, said pigs waxing remarkably fat as
a result, this often being the way with pigs who get theirs in abundance.
Putting two together with another two, experience showing that this
is a useful thing to do when twos abound, the prior of the convent
at the centre of the drama reasoned that what is good for pigs might
equally be good for monks. It was his ambition, as prior, to have
nought but fat monks about him in much the same way that the noted
Roman leader, Caesar, J., expressed the view that he only cared to have
well built chaps in his immediate vicinity. Musing in this fashion, the
goodly prior slipped antimony into the monks' dinner pails, whereupon, as a monk, they all cashed in same and retired from life.

The point I am trying to make, I went on before she could interrupt, is that what suits some does not suit others. To some, the day
when the A & P first opened its doors, proved to be, like the Pickwick
pen, a boon and a blessing to men. Others just turned up their toes
and checked out.

'According to you,' she said, 'the A & P got rich on the patronage of
pigs. Not a nice thing to say.'

It is true, I replied, that I would have wished the old prior might
have chosen some other mammal, as it might have been okapi, gazelles
or wildebeestes, for his dietary experiments. But as every pig person,
from Lord Emsworth onwards, knows, pigs are admirable creatures,
high minded and moral to a fault.

A & P having pioneered the chain store idea, other chaps came
along, muttering to themselves that chain stores might be all very well
in their own way, but there were other lines of approach to the business
of satisfying the public re the matter of seeing that as many of them as
could be crammed into the premises, got theirs. What about, they said,
casting around for some new idea in which their unfulfilled longings
could be. . .what is the word I am looking for? Fulfilled, that's it.

Word had come to them of enterprises of a particular type that had
been started in Japan as early as the 17th century, Japan being a place
where the commercial spirit flourishes and where one imagines that
even the ancient samurai as they wandered about looking for persons to
carve into ribbons were not averse to including the gift of a few trading
stamps as part of the service they offered.

Moving on a couple of hundred years, what do we find? Horse buses,
I said, is exactly and precisely the articles in question that we discover.
Buses of the horse-drawn variety that brought people from the edges
or suburbs of towns, into the centres of same, and having brought
them there, took them home again. Of course, if that had been all that
was involved the horse-bus business would soon have faded away as the
joy of giving a gift fades when the bill, subsequently, comes to hand.

Few persons would have been willing to cough up the necessary
coinage, sufficient to provide hay for the horses and vittles for the
personnel or crew of the vehicles to sustain them during the voyage or
journey, if said voyage or journey only resulted in a passage from, on
the one hand – the suburb, to, on the other hand – the town centre
with no pleasurable interregnum between before being transported
back to the one hand, or suburb. All clear thus far?

Once this difficulty had been pointed out in Paris – a city much dedicated to the joys of the commercial life – there was much balding of skulls by scratching and wearing of brains thin by racking, before solutions were forthcoming. Among those scratching and racking like billy-oh, were the proprietors of a large speciality store in the capital city mentioned above, called the 'Au Bon Marché'.

'Why don't we,' they argued around about the year 1860, 'turn ourselves into a Department Store?'

At this, champions of the chain store idea groaned aloud. But, there was no – as they say – gainsaying the idea. It had to come. Suburban persons of every description flocked through the doors convinced that if there was one place on earth – or, as in this case, Paris – where theirs was to be obtained, this was it.

Pretty soon, the owners and occupiers of suitable premises in the U S of A – who are all pretty smart chaps, quick on the uptake, if you know what I mean – took note of these developments and swiftly got down to a bit of sleeve-rolling-up, to convert the said suitable premises, suitably. By what has become known in the trade as World War One department stores modelled on the original 'Au Bon Marché' could be found in countries throughout the world, including the Argentine, Mexico and Egypt, to name but a few.

Although the owners of such enterprises have been busy all these years trousering the hard stuff as rapidly as it came rolling in, the public have, it seems, not cast all their pebbles in the one barrel. According to that repository of commercial knowledge, the U S Census of Business, scanning the figures for 1967, of the 1,577,302 whose doors were open for trade in that year, 97% of these were single-establishment companies. They accounted, according to the same source, for 60% of total sales. Which still means, however, that the remaining 3% of enterprises raked in 40% of the moola.

Public sentiment has often been hostile to chain stores, probably indicating a passion – if passion is the right word, for horse, and other kinds of, buses. The pro-bus lobby managed to get under the ribs of the executive branch with chain-store tax laws in 29 of the States subscribing to membership of the U. thereof. In Denmark there was a law prohibiting retail merchants from owning more than one store in each municipality. The Poujadist movement in France in the late 1950s and early 60s brought what is known as political pressure – a process which in France involves cobble-stone heaving, car burning accompanied by high-pressure jets of water from high pressure hoses – to bear in favour of small businesses and against the retail chains.

Thus we enter the second quarter of the twentieth century – count them, one, two – with the public uncertain where next to go to get its – if its is the word I want, confused between the conflicting claims of the small business brigade, the chain store gang and the pro-horse bus or department store squad. The word went round the commercial enclaves that what was needed was some new way in which the public could be persuaded to part with the ready in exchange for theirs. Skull scratching and brain thinning of a very concentrated order then ensued.

The first to emerge from this condition with what one can only describe as the light of inspiration alight in his eyes was a certain Michael Cullin – this happened in the neighbourhood of Chicago, a pleasant lakeside resort to be found, rumour has it, on the shores of the pastoral Lake Michigan, and much given over, it is confirmed by the same rumours, to the pursuit of the pastoral life and bucolic living. In a sentence, an ideal location, one would think, for the origination of what can only be described as a pioneer concept. For it was here that the said Cullin, M., Esquire, opened the first unit of what was to become the chain of King Kullen – and here is the vital word you have all been waiting for – supermarkets.

'Yes, friends,' the said Cullin could be heard to announce with justifiable pride from the forecourt of his newly operational premises. 'This is where its all at.'

It was soon at plenty of other places, supermarkets popping up like mushrooms on a warm night. And those with a yearning to get theirs, tried out this new way of getting same, and found it good.

But hark! Do we hear a distant shuffling of feet, a rising murmur of voices as of dispossessed persons lamenting their dispossession and feeling themselves to be in a mood to do something about it? Yes, we do. For there in the wings, so to speak, are the hordes of little shopkeepers wanting nothing more of life than to keep right on with their little shopkeeping (or scypen-keeping, not forgetting schupp-keeping).

Doing what men everywhere do when a crisis threatens, they formed a committee, appointed a chairman, ran swiftly through the preliminaries and got down as rapidly as possible to the Other Business item on the agenda, none of them at that stage having much of an optimistic view that any other business would be coming their way in the future. But a Ways and Means group had some thoughts about ways and means from which came up the notion that they needed to band together. 'United we stand,' as the leader of that group put it. 'Divided we don't do so good.'

They formed what wiser pens than mine have dubbed — retail cooperatives. And, sooner than pretty, little men all over the place were seeing that the future need not be so dark as they had supposed. Other men, neither more nor less little than the first lot, put their shoulders behind the idea of voluntary chains of small retailers sponsored by large wholesalers. 'Our idea,' one of them explained somewhere in Europe of the 1960s, 'is for large wholesalers to sponsor voluntary chains of small retailers', putting the idea into a nutshell. As a result, at least four huge wholesaler sponsored chains of small voluntary retailers sprang up — if springing up conveys the proper idea to you, each of them including 15,000 small voluntary retail stores, or more. The 30,000 'Spar' small v. r. s. were to be found, if you looked, in ten countries, each s. v. r. s. using the same name and, as a rule, offering the same brands of products.

One thing led to another, as Newton might well have confirmed, as he shifted his deck chair indoors, complaining that there was no chance for a man to get some serious work done with all these damned apples dropping down all over the place. Then, before he, or you, could say 'Pippin' there he was having all these good ideas about gravity. Similarly, it would be convenient to be able to report how a commercial philosopher of the type prone to park himself in a deck chair in order to mull over the commercial prospects prevailing, parked himself in a deck chair, and how a large block of hail struck him forcibly about the head, thus putting into his mind the idea of bulk buying freezer centres. One simply does not know how these ideas crop up, and the commercial philosphers involved are either too bone idle to report the facts to us, or too busy getting on with more lucrative commercial philosophising.

The implications for the good husbandry person do not need to be spelled out.

'Yes, they do,' she said.

Oh well, if you insist. . .

Faced with the routine task of securing his (and/or, as it may be, hers) on the most advantageous terms, the good husbandry person seeks guidance as to which way he should turn next.

It will not be forgotten that mention has already been made of certain eagle-eyed officials, pacing our own streets, keeping an eagle eye on the trends of commerce, and in particular conducting checks on those matters that are uncheckable by the ordinary g. h. p. with the resources ordinarily available to him as he stands at Heaven's Gate, the Portals of Hell, or, as in most instances, the other side of the stall or counter from which the business in hand is being conducted.

Such checks are many and various, or it may be the other way about. They focus on quality, quantity and price, with the third eye which all Astynomoi descendants have, on service. The attentive glance of such a functionary might light upon a tinned goods counter on which are displayed tinned goods, each labelled according to the contents supposedly therein. Some inner instinct prompts the e-e. o to open the can. What does he find? Or, to put it another way — what does he not find? He does not find the ingredients listed on the label.

Such phonus-bolonus of the tin-labelling fraternity takes two forms. Things are to be found in the tin which should not be in the tin. Things are to be found on the label that are not in the tin. Phonus-bolonuses of this kind are not readily detectable by the g. h. p., he or she not having access to the interior of the tin under consideration prior to purchase, and not much opportunity of identifying the strange contents thereof afterwards. If the manufacturer, if we can call him that, of the tin claims on the label that he has included lashings of something called mono-galliwallium, the g. h. p. cannot check up on this not knowing what mono-galliwallium looks or tastes like, and whether it is a good thing to have anyway. All he knows is that meals like mother made, or would have liked to be able to make, got along pretty well without m-g.

Moving away from tinned goods, the e-e. o. bends his attention towards milk. Is it up to scratch, he asked himself, in the matter of fatty content, or does the quantity of water swilling about in it give rise to the suspicion that the stuff has been left out in the rain overnight? On the basis that what goes in has a lot to do with what comes out, the e-e. o. shuffles off to cowsville and makes a check on the commodities being stuffed into the cow at the front end and what effect this may be having on the stuff coming out of the cow at the lower end, if one may put it that way without giving cause for complaints from cows on the grounds of indelicacy. Cows, it should be recognised, do have their feelings, after all.

Other phonus-bolonuses, or possibly phonus-bolonusi, relate to what an inventive and imaginative person, such as one explaining about

same, might term 'verbal labels'. These v.l.'s might be statements, on
the one hand, made by a sales person selling a car, and on the other
hand, the car itself, the span between these two hands being considered too wide for the person in the middle, to wit, or it might be,
viz., the sales person, to get away with it. Similar divergencies from the
straight and narrow path crop up when persons with cash money in
hand advance along it (ie., the said path) in the general direction of
clothes, furnishings and appliances. A 'new and unused' leather coat is
found to be so well worn that there are even cigarette ends in the
pockets. A shirt washed strictly according to the printed instructions
on the label, shrinks and looses its bloom of colour. What is worse,
even the label shrinks and fades so that the instructions can no longer
be read. Fruit and veg on display at the front of the fruit and veg stall
have all the airs and graces of rich relations with only a distant nodding
acquaintance with the poor relations at the rear of the stall with which
the cash customers are served. Reductions from recommended list
prices are proclaimed with a brave 'Hurrah!' for goods which e-e. o's
know for a fact do not have recommended list prices, and are selling
elsewhere for ordinary prices that are notably lower than those to
which these reduced prices have been reduced to.

All these case histories are the kinds of tales of woe that bring e-e
o's and g. h. p's together on the same platform, addressing the multitude with one voice. Will the multitude listen? 'Will it, heck!' – as the
poet rather neatly puts it.

'Caveat emptor!' cry these self-same e-e. o's and g. h. p's with the
self-same one voice. The multitude, thinking this to be a three-year-old
running in the two-thirty at Kempton Park puts its money on the
nose at 20:1, thereby losing its shirt and any opportunity of bewaring
like billy-oh when the matter of making purchases comes up.

Meanwhile, divergers from the s. and n. path flourish as the green
bay tree, rolling the stuff in as hard as they can go and putting it away
where it will do the most good.

The great advantage of the metric system, now taking over in grand
style, and something of benefit to those persons wishing to keep
under sharp scrutiny the strategems of pedlars engaged in the divergencies of trade, is that it removes from common circulation all those
confusing bushels, butts, pipes, pottles, tuns, barley grains, wheat
grains, drams, duck weights, quadrans, stones and wool weights by
which ordinary persons have been confused for so long. Confusion,

as a wise man once said, is not a sound basis for eagle-eyed scrutiny.

'What is all this?' she asked. 'Onions, flute-girls, duck weights — aren't we getting a little out of our depth?'

The point I am trying to make, I told her, is a simple series of directives as to where ordinary persons can best expect to lay their hands on theirs.

We start with the modern pedlar, a person who crams the confusion of a shop into the confinement of a van, driving same from place to place, operating on the age-old door-to-door basis. Next in line is the stall operative, followed by the shop-keeper, followed by the chain-store chap, followed by the department store nabob, followed by the supermarket tycoon, followed by other hordes of hypermarketeers, discounteers, freezereers — if that is the word I want. You name them, I said, they are out there somewhere — catalogue houses, mail order firms, vending machine controllers. . .

One simple fact has to be realised. Each of these practitioners of the commercial game seeks to work in isolation from all the others.

The door-to-door merchant standing on your door-step sees himself well on the way to conducting you, your heirs and successors to the cleaners if no alternative establishment is to be seen on the horizon. If the door — your door, as it happens, is located next to a chain, department or supermarket store, his room to manoeuvre you into his corner is somewhat diminished.

The door-to-door chap will lower his sights if there are stall-holders just down the road. Stall-holders will cut things more finely if shop-keepers are to be found round the corner. Shop-keepers will trim their demands nearer the bone if chain stores set up across the street. Chain stores will hold their price tags at half-mast if department stores are in the offing. The opening of super, hyper, discount and freezer markets has much the same effect. Each bewails the arrival of the next in line as the death knell of civilisation as we have known it. Yet, in the end, some of each category survive because g. h. p's find them suitable places for the practice of g. h. This is on the basis that they are all alternatives to each other, places where the this of one store can be compared with the that of another, or vice versa.

'Suppose they get together?' she asked. 'Suppose these commercial types get together, as one hears they do from time to time, agreeing prices among them and so forth?'

It is true, I agreed, that this is tried. The weakness of such an arrangement is that the ordinary merchanting practitioner of whatever size — be it large, medium or small — is so conditioned by the traditions of trade to diverge from the s. and n. at every opportunity, that if it should happen agreement is reached that onions, as it might be, should toe the line at 20p a kilo, it will not be long before one practitioner, whose premises might chance to be in the shade, sees the sun beaming and trade bustling about a competitor, attempts instantly to get in amongst the g. h. p's with a price of 19p. Seeing this, and a corresponding swing in the trade balance as word spreads through the ranks of the g. h. p's present with a consequent thinning of same about his onions, the second operative slides a swift 18p price ticket in amongst the front ranks. As with dams, once one brick goes, the whole tumbles.

Strategy is no alternative to vigilance. Any g. h. p. supposing otherwise is likely to find himself in the position of Arcite; the prize (in my case onions, in his case the lovely Emily) almost in his hands is snatched therefrom at the last moment.

'Thumbs?' she queried, with that look on her face.

It can be calculated, I told her, that inch for inch and gram for gram, the thumb is the most weighty and costly organ of the human body, this circumstance arising from its use in a sleight-of-hand manoeuvre dating from the dawn of trade, and known as the 'thumb-on-the-scale' technique.

A pound and a half of onions having been commanded, the trader ladles onions onto the scales. At the critical moment the thumb of the said person is dexterously introduced to the weighing area where it makes its presence felt in the form of a gentle pressure, this suggesting to the prospective customer that onions to the weight of a pound and a half are being supplied, whereas the goods in question consist more of an onion and thumb mixture, the thumb not being included in the transaction, there being little demand for thumbs in the average household.

This is the explanation, I went on, for the present shortage of supplies in the onion department, as indicated.

'There is another,' she said.

'Oh?' I said right back at her. Then my keenly tuned brain made a lightning scan of the message being presented, and additional reply material was added to the first. 'What?' I asked.

'This,' she said, tipping out my shopping bag. A largish onion rolled from it. When added to those previously placed on the scales, the beam weight had to be advanced beyond the pound and a half mark before equilibrium occurred.

It just shows, I said, there is sometimes a natural justice. Even when no one is looking.

THE AMERICAN

Good husbandry is not a term much bandied about in California. Local persons, if accosted and asked about same, would doubtless advance the opinion that husbandry (good or bad) has some reference to property laws, divorce and the payment, or non-payment, of alimony.

The newly arrived person, newly arriving in those parts to take up residence, finds that the opportunities for practising good husbandry are limited, if not non-existent. But, to begin at the beginning. . .

The scenario runs in something of this fashion: the plane, train, bus, ship, car or other form of transportation sets down the newly arrived person at the heart of, or somewhere toward the perimeter of, let us say, Los Angeles.

A close-up shows the n. a. person facing his new future with head raised and nostrils flared. What noble thoughts race through his noble mind? I will tell you.

The head-putting-down aspect of life is the one that strikes him as having the highest priority. Where, he asks himself, is one to put down one's head?

We cut to the automatic newspaper vending machine conveniently positioned on the corner of the street. The n. a. person approaches with firm tread. By inserting coins he can secure two and a half pounds dead weight of newsprint, it being a Sunday and this being the local rag. Turning to the classified ad section, of which the paper seems to consist of little else but, he finds listed therein columns of habitations, all of the utmost desirability and immediately available on the most generous terms. He has only to present himself at the portals thereof, with cash money or its equivalent in his hand, to be welcomed with open arms, in one of which he is pretty sure to spot a wallet, money pouch or purse.

Having got the head-putting-down situation firmly under control, the next item in the order of business is the food-in-the-tum position, food-in-the-tumery being something with which n. a. persons have regular contact. Hardly more than a few hours at a time pass by before this food-in-the-tum item crops up.

This is something the g. h. p. likes to keep under personal control, arguing that, since he supplies the tum concerned, he might as well go the whole hog and supply the food that completes the equation. Food, he knows, starts with soil, and to the end of putting himself in touch with some of the same, he looks from the window of his habitation to see what supplies are about.

Soil, he finds, is thin on the ground. Californians do not much care for the stuff and get by on the barest minimum. Gardens, as gardens, are not a part of the Californian life-style, the ordinary household finding that it can get along quite well with a few square yards or metres of a friable substance distantly related to soil. One imagines there are factories somewhere churning out the stuff and that Los Angeleans, being a touch on the tight-wad side, purchase as little as possible, spreading it thinly.

According to official statistics supplied by the impartial Californian All-The-Year-Round organisation, it never rains in Los Angeles except between two and three o'clock on one of the Wednesday afternoons in February. Residents believe this no less readily than the members of the A-T-Y-R org., and plan accordingly, equipping their gardens with sub-soil buttresses of water sprinklers at one yard intervals. The water that sprinkles from these has to be paid for by the gallon (how old-fashioned California is! Yards and gallons, egad!) which results in the sprinklers being turned down to the lowest level of sprinkling compatible with anything that could be called irrigation. In these circs. only a scrubby grass can grow and all thoughts of nature's bounty in the form of fruit and veg must fly from the mind.

Fruit and veg do grow in California, it is true. There are prison camps of them subsisting in conditions that would make the tyrants of old appear as pace-makers or front-runners in the field of social advancement. Guards with raw-hide whips stride between the serried ranks of cowering vegs, cracking same and uttering harsh and raucous cries.

'Grow, damn you!' cry the guards, and the vegs have no option but to comply, or to suffer one of those fates with which death compares favourably. And when the chaps from the Geneva Convention come round to see how things are running along under martial law, the miserable vegs are pumped full of horrible drugs, called hormones, which plump out their flesh with water, making the Geneva Convention chaps think that things are going along swimmingly.

'What happy vegs!' they murmur to themselves as they drive away in their cars with the windows wound tightly up and the radio playing full blast.

Faced with this situation the g. h. p. casts around for supplies of the essential fruits, vegs and other commodities by which life as we know it is kept going. The door-to-door merchant, he discovers, no longer has a place in the Los Angelean scale of things. Citizens of that metropolis have a deeply-rooted suspicion of all persons who arrive unheralded at their doors and give expression to this hostility by seeking to gain an entry into the body of the said unheralded person standing on their doorstep with any suitable instrument or appliance that might happen to be handy, as it might be, a shot-gun, revolver, or a carving knife into the ribs. Door-to-door merchants conclude that this method of doing business does not indicate prosperity to be just around the corner.

Types of market exist at which types of stall are present with types of stall-holder trading thereat. But these markets have the elan of country clubs, the stalls appear as small pearls of prosperity in a sea of affluence, and the stall-holders look like barons of the more baroque class, bettering themselves. G. h. p's turn away from such places, bracing themselves for the impact as their hearts dive into their boots with a Bat-man type 'Thunk'. (Or, it might be 'Zunk', 'Brunk' or 'Crunk' — it is so difficult to get these things absolutely right.)

Shops, as shops, have, by and large, fled the fruit and veg domain. While department stores will have no truck with fruit-and-vegery. Thus is the g. h. p. driven into the arms of the supermarket proprietor, who plies his wares in the modern manner, occupying some part of the space available regularly in the two and a half pounds of newsprint that masquerades as the local newspaper, presenting his commercial message as often as money will allow on one or more of the seventy radio stations that keep things on the hop for twenty-four hours of the average twenty-four hour day, and getting in amongst the lads at the eight or nine (at the last count) television stations whose transmissions are enough to persuade the local citizenry what a good idea it is to roll down the blinds and pretend the sun is not out there sunning itself on their scorched patch.

The exception to this arrangement occurs, quite frequently, when the scorched patch is converted into a swimming pool, henceforth to be known as 'the pool' and not to be confused with that game enjoyed by billiards-type persons. When this happens, the television set is placed beside the 'pool' with a filter across its screen allowing it to be viewed in sunlight. By these means do the s-m. ops get their message across. Cajoled by these advances the newly arrived g.h.p. steps up to the front entrance of his first Los Angelean supermarket.

At first glance he thinks himself to be an Ali Baba who has by chance stumbled across the place where the Forty Thieves stash theirs. At least thirty-nine of the said thieving operatives are manning cash registers and the fortieth of them is, no doubt, scurrying about the premises racking up fresh supplies of goods in exchange for which members of the cash-carrying public thronging the place are being eased away from their cash.

Somewhere in the background a band is playing. Balloons rise up. Streamers are being thrown. The scene is not so much Mardi Gras, as Vendredi or Samedi Gras. Sales persons dance among the produce on offer as if in the last stages of ecstasy. Each of the forty light-fingered persons to whom reference has previously been made has apparently just become the proud parent of new-born infants and is in the mood to hand out cigars to all, and even sundry, should they happen also to be present. Busby Berkeley, one feels, could not have made a better job of expressing the joys of the weekly shopping expedition.

The intention is, of course, to cast a gloss or sheen across matters in hand. All, as somebody once said, is not something that somethings, gold and glisters being the relevant words to be inserted. The newly arrived emptor starts caveating like billy-oh. Autolycus, he feels, is working well out front with Sisyphus doing his stuff behind. Nothing is to be allowed to hinder the spreading of sweetness and light. Blemishes on oranges, well known arousers of dark thoughts in the hearts of the c-c. p. are touched out with bright sprays of paint. Loaves of bread are inflated with air pumps. Make-up artists from the film studios and morticians' parlours are engaged to bring life to the complexions of dead cakes.

'Begone dull care!' cry the forty practitioners concerned, and in the begoning thereof, care is taken that no member of the c-c. p. passes out through the portals with more than a small fraction of his c. intact.

When the resources of the two and a half pound newspapers, seventy radio and eight/nine television stations flag, other remedies are called upon to keep the old commercial message zipping along two skips ahead of the cash-carrying public (members thereof). Batteries of searchlights are rolled into place at sundown. Parades and jamborees of every kind are laid on.

Watching from the wings as an unbiassed observer, the newly arrived g. h. p. (you hadn't forgotten him/her, surely?) comes to the conclusion that members of the c-c. p. could enjoy a pretty cheerful life were they not burdened with the thought that, caught up as they are in this non-stop commercial whirligig, somewhere along the line soup was the substance into which they could expect to find themselves falling. The net result of these merchanting hurricanes, trading typhoons and commercial tornadoes was, to their view (ie., the c-c. p's view), the creation of a Lake Avernus-type situation, the sulphurous and mephitic vapours from which caused passing birds to fall into its waters. Sulphurous and mephitic, they felt, just about described the nature of the emissions by which the humble shopping scene was obscured. If stopped, as they stumbled back across the supermarket car park with their weekly mountain of comestibles, and asked what stood between them and the simple enjoyment of the good life, 'sulphurous and mephitic vapours' was what they would be inclined to reply.

Being in this frame of mind those of the c-c. p. who aspired also to being g. h. p's have stood quietly in the background for a period of time denoted by the ancients as 'the while', and during that period have occupied themselves by grinding their teeth and clenching their fists and doing all the other things that frustrated persons do when frustrated.

'What can be done to put things right?' they asked themselves.

And they decided, as with one tooth and one fist, to cease this useless grinding and clenching and to come out of their corners ready to take up the good husbandry cause.

The slogan that formed in their minds was something to the effect that, to quote a phrase, all is not gold that. . .

'You've already glistered your gold once,' she said. 'You can't glister it all over again. The public would never stand for it.'

In the days of which I speak, I went on, there was an establishment in Los Angeles wherein gold glistering was notable by its absence. I refer to the old Grand Central Market, an impenetrable corner of the commercial jungle, in the view of ordinary Los Angeleans, whose impenetrability only the most intrepid of white men could penetrate. Here were to be found stallholders gifted as was the Athenian Bee. . .

'Athenian Bee?' she queried.

The allusion is to Plato, I told her, a native of that city who lay in his cradle one day when a passing host of bees decided that his lips would make a handy place to swarm, and did so.

'Nasty,' she said.

The interpretation placed upon this manoeuvre at the time, I said was that in later life words would flow from his lips with the sweetness of honey. What the latter-day Los Angelean citizenry would dub 'a sweet talking man'. (As a matter of interest the same circumstance is reported of Sophocles, Pindar, St. Chrysostom, St. Ambrose and others. This, to my mind, casts no reflection on the veracity of the tale, but merely gives a hint as to the strange habits of the bees of those times. No cradled babe was safe from having his lips occupied by passing bees.)

Being purveyed — if that is the word I want, by these sweet-talking stallholders were fruit on which blemishes winked with wanton vitality, meat that bled, and cheeses with enough tang to overthrow a waggon load of marines.

Having by guiles, stealths and stratagems laid hands on the ingredients of good living, the g. h. p. seeks to convert these into the cooked forms of nourishment to which he has grown accustomed. For this, a kitchen is required. Here, an obstacle arises. The obstacle in question can be named without fear or favour, whoever they are.

It is the typical Los Angeles kitchen.

To come to terms with this environment — if that is the word I want, a few helpful words should be offered on the subject of the occupants of the kitchen under advisement, to wit., the typical Los Angeles family.

In any self-respecting household of that city, the dawn chorus is the call to action. Being natural-born get-up-and-goers, members of such a household, hearing this sunrise twitter feel at once the urge to get-up-and-go. With a swoosh, the male member has got-up-and-gone before you can say Laurel and Hardy. The female member, being hardly more than a twitch behind, pauses at the door of the kitchen before getting-up-and-going. What gives her pause is the thought that on her return that evening, and that of her spouse, timed to occur within a whisker of her own, baked meats and the groaning board will be expected to be in evidence.

How is this to be done, you will ask. I will tell you.

Pre-cut frozen veg are popped into pans with measured quantities of water. Pre-somethinged meat is delivered to the oven, skillet or grill. The calculator — without which no house is a home — is set to work. Lightning calculations are calculated like lightning. Dials are set. Buttons pressed. Switches switched. And 'Hey ho!' murmurs the female member departing for her round of female activities confident that science will see her through. Somethingtronic devices will activate — if that is the word I want, themselves somethingtronically and every item will be switched on at the correct moment to be ready at the time agreed upon so that the only obligation bearing down upon the family members enumerated as above reading from left to right, to wit, the male member, the female member, is to arrange their affairs so as to arrive back at the house/home at the hour agreed upon before the above lightning calculations were entered into.

The point to be made is that such a kitchen is one not intended to be occupied by humans. Any occupying humans occupying these kitchenry premises are an encumbrance, hindrance and an embarrassment. 'What are these humans doing here?' the said kitchen mutters to itself. 'Haven't they got anywhere to go to?' Any humans present become aware of this and shuffle off shame-faced.

It cannot be denied that one of the most persevering characteristics of good husbandry persons is that, show them a kitchen and, at once, they want to occupy it. This is their view, their philosophy. 'Show me a kitchen,' they cry, 'and I will show you a place waiting to be occupied.' No other approach to the kitchen situation seems to them to be tenable. So that, if all the kitchens with which they are brought into contact by the ordinary routines of life are unoccupiable, this is going to be a considerable hindrance in the pursuit of their chosen life-style.

Los Angelean kitchens, it can be said, discriminate against the good husbandry person. G. h. is something with which the ordinary Los Angeles wishes to have no truck. 'G. h. is an alien philosophy!' cries the said kitchen, and slams its combined doors (oven, refrigerator and patio) in the g. h. p's face. A lobby has been set up in Washington seeking to persuade somebody to rewrite the Constitution to suggest that there should be no discrimination against any persons on the grounds of race, creed or husbandry, but hopes are not strong.

Meanwhile, there are ways out of the tangled web in the kitchen department of life. Not all kitchens are thus tainted. If g. h. p's are willing to accept a lowering of their standards and to occupy older kitchens then it is possible that among the more venerable properties in that region, those classifiable as antiques by which one refers to those more than ten — or even twelve — years old, kitchens of what can be described as the traditional, classical, occupiable type are to be found. In these, the said g. h. p's can throw themselves with whatever degrees of enthusiasm or abandon seem appropriate into the exercise of that craft which began all those thousands of years ago over a hot fire.

How, you will want to ask, has the Los Angelean kitchen come to this sorry pass? I will tell you.

It is generally agreed among medical men that being addicted to things is a bad thing. Accost any passing medical man as he makes his way along the highways and byways of life and quizz him on the subject. 'Show me an addict,' he will say, 'and I will show you a person who has got the wrong idea.' If, in the cause of spelling things out and getting things crystal clear (although, come to think of it, most crystals that one has come across in a long, crystal-filled life have tended toward the opaque) you press him as to what he means by 'being addicted' he will hum and ha a bit, hopping back and forth from one foot to the other, mutter 'hang on a moment', dive back to his premises, thumb through his medical dictionary, and come up with the snappy reply that 'an addict' is one who is addicted to a habit, especially the taking of drugs.

'Aha!' you come back at him, quick as a whippet, 'what, then, is a drug?'

Abandoning the safe haven of page twelve in the aforementioned medical d. he rifles on through to around page 308 and stumbles across a variety of answers (dictionaries have a neurotic fear of being wrong and when they are not quite sure what a word means they put down everything they can think of with the hope that one of them will turn out to be right). Among these is the suggestion that a drug is a narcotic substance.

'Is this leading anywhere?' she wanted to know.

Patience, I advised her. Sooner or later it is bound to lead somewhere.

Plunging deeper into the no-man's-land of page 661 — the medical dict. — we discover that a narcotic substance is one that induces mental lethargy, that soothes, relieves or lulls.

During the run-up to the average meal, the ordinary human person, or as a medical man would say, patient, exhibits symptoms of anxiety, tension and stress. Pain is felt in the lower region of the waistcoat. All of these adverse medical conditions can be eased by the intake of a narcotic substance we call food. The patient ceases to be anxious, tense, stressed and pained and becomes instead lulled, relieved, soothed and lethargic.

Pathological studies of the kind for which pathologists run up large grants from wealthy pathological institutes reveal that many such patients get hooked on food. They can't leave it alone. Every few hours they must have what is called in the trade, a food-fix. They become — and this is the pregnant term toward which I have been cautiously edging for the past two pages — food addicts.

The puritanical guidelines to life of the ordinary Los Angeles household are rigid, than which no other branches of puritanism are more so. 'If that's what food is,' they say to themselves (members of the household, not the guidelines which are, by and large, mute), looking food squarely in the eye, 'then we want no part of it. Food has to do with the nasty side of life. What happens in kitchens,' they go on, 'is just as bad as what happens in bathrooms. Both are equally nasty.' And they leave the house and go for a drive to get the taste of the stuff out of their mouths.

Ever since the twelfth or thirteenth century — one does not want to be pinned down to the nearest century or so — the idea has been slowly gathering among human persons that if one is going to have such a thing as a bathroom, the proper place for it is at the back of the house where no one will see it who does not need to see it. Barons building castles were so far removed from the bathroom philosophy of life that they frequently left them out altogether.

Now, with the benefit of modern insights, the Los Angelean family has started to work on the kitchen, edging it toward the more remote parts of the house in a position alongside the bathroom.

'You don't spend your day in the bathroom!' they cry. 'Why do so in the kitchen!' A quick in and out, in both cases, is their view of the correct m. o.

Some of the more advanced Los Angeles homesteads have made steady progress towards that distant millenium in which there shall be no kitchens, and thereby reducing the nasty side of life by half. In these dwellings the rooms can be ticked off from left to right — bedroom, bedroom, bedroom, bathroom — after which comes what the poet Cowper refers to as an Aching Void, or, as in this case, living area. Only alert and attentive persons will notice that in some part of this, heavily disguised by concealing flaps and other devices are certain primitive arrangements for dealing with — the word here should be uttered in a whisper to lessen the affront to sensitive senses — food.

After a long period of residence in the city under discussion, such as one extending for several years, it comes as something of a shock to persons of a traditionalist cast of mind where food is concerned, to realise that of a number of locally reared persons with whom one has developed a chummy rapport, not once has any one of them been seen —perhaps caught or surprised would be better words — in the act of eating.

The invitation 'What'll you have?' universally refers to offers of liquid intake, and in the households here under the microscope, as kitchens sink out of sight, domestic bars rise in the foreground, leading to the quaint reflection that as an activity which is the nurtured off-spring of generations of careful husbandry fades into a decline, another act that arose from carelessly leaving fruits about the place until they were on the turn slides into place and takes precedence.

For non-food persons, the weekly trip to the supermarket is an outing, an entertainment, the start to the weekend, a social occasion, a change to chinwag with the chums. In the midst of this vivid and vivacious concourse — if that is the word — suggestive of gatherings of nobles at the Palace of Versailles if it can be imagined that each noble is pushing along a small trolley — persons will, from time to time slip away, murmuring a discreet 'Pardon me', to deal with the nasty business of picking up some food.

Recognising what is going on in the minds of its patrons — just as did the sharp-eyed door-to-door chaps of the past — the supermarketeers do their best to make foods seem as unfoodlike as possible. Every opportunity is taken to put across the suggestion that the items on display are not so much food — what an ugly word that is! — as a kind of consumable bijouterie, decorative artifacts intended to bring joy and beauty to the home in about equal measures, to repose attractively in certain rooms of the house for brief periods, and then to be made to vanish by means that are not talked about or given any publicity whatever, to be replaced next week by other divertingly colourful pieces.

'Food!' says the average Los Angeles person if questioned on the subject. 'Go wash your mouth!'

The more scholarly and erudite of these families of whom I write look back at the culinary excesses of the past and are appalled by what they see.

The once proud and puissant empires of Egypt, Greece and Rome all inhabited by food-eating people, all humbled and in the dust. The citizens of Napoleonic France and Victorian Britain champed their choppers with the best of them. 'And look what happened to them,' whisper the scholarly and erudite persons of Los Angeles in horrified awe. If what it takes to avoid decay and decline of the civilisation of which one is a part is the simple avoidance of food, then they are the chaps to do it, they resolve among themselves. (It is held to the favour of the French that, as they gave up the use of bathrooms some-where about the twelfth or thirteenth century — one does not wish to be tied down to the nearest century or so — they are, in contrast to the Romans and the British who spent, and spend, a good deal of their time therein, only half damned). 'If that is what food eating leads to,' the same whisper continues, 'then food eating is not for us.'

What gets in the way of this heroic resolve is the large number of persons of non-Los Angeles origin resident in that city. If only locals were involved food could be held down to what is called 'a pretty low profile'. Indeed, persons who do not eat food can hardly be said to have much of a profile at all. Because of these strangers in their midst, there flourishes an extensive network of underground and undercover (plain) food suppliers. News spreads by word of mouth. Jewish bagels, it is said, can be had by interested parties from such-and-such an establish-ment at a certain hour on a designated day. 'Knock twice and ask for Sam,' is the instruction interested persons are given.

Elsewhere English sausages are to be had, French bread flown in from Paris at vast expense, suet for making suet puddings, the said suet being an item of such extreme illegality that to any alert and attentive customs official the apprehension of a suet-runner is worth an additional thousand a year on his pension. Despite the most power-ful vigilance and penalties, the Los Angeles authorities, with the full backing of the indigenous citizenry, have never been able to stamp out the reprehensible food trade.

Foodwise, Los Angeles was the sort of place T. S. Eliot had in mind when he wrote 'The Wasteland'. Nothing much there of juice and succulence, if you know what I mean.

Yet, even in the desert there are oases, even on the Moon faint traces of moisture. A national dish exists in those parts, the mastery

of which is something to which every g. h. p. should set the hand.

Here we come to the field of the historical conundrum. Those of us who have dabbled therein from time to time know from experience that whenever two or three historians are gathered together to sort out the facts of any such c. the only statement to which all of them are likely to be willing to pen their signatures is something to the effect that something somewhere happened. As to what the something was, where the somewhere was and what exactly happened, no common ground is to be found. In these circs. those of us of a more imaginative cast of mind are inclined to leap in with both feet and fill in some of the blanks.

Fields of historical conundrums (or conundri), as do fields elsewhere, contain thistles and nettles. In dealing with these, anti-thistlers are taught to root out, while anti-nettle chaps are shown the grasping technique. 'Root out your thistles,' they are told. 'Grasp nettles.'

The distinction is an important one to be clear about. No good can come from grasping thistles and rooting out nettles. So, just to keep the slate clear, let us repeat: Thistles – rooting out – yes, Nettles – grasping – yes.

Rooters up and graspers have the problem that it is often not until the final moment that the identity of the weed to be (a) rooted out, or (b) grasped, becomes clear. If a person is misled into rooting out nettles and grasping thistles, a sudden change is seen in their attitude to life. They turn into more serious, silent, thoughtful persons, their dreams pervaded by the tangled roots of nettles, their hands perforated by thistle pricks.

A person who happens to be knee-deep in historians as they grapple with an historical conundrum, and who attempts to fill in the blanks, finds himself thinking very much along the lines of nettle rooter-outers and thistle graspers. He wishes he had not done it.

But, I am going to, anyway.

Four thousand miles away from the previous location is a part of the North-west corner of Germany that in the thirteenth century combined with its neighbour Lubeck to join the Hanseatic League. Having said that, you have said just about everything that can be said without arousing the ire of one or other brand of historians. Readers are advised that from hereon, they, in company with the author, are on their own.

It was the custom of citizens of the city of which I am writing. . .

'Which city?' she asked. 'You haven't said which city.'

Patience, I advised. The reason for this clear omission will become apparent shortly. In any case, the clues liberally scattered throughout the first sentence with which this matter has been introduced to the readership will point the nose of any reasonably well-informed historian, or other person, toward the city in question. Anyone else can either go and look it up, pack it in, or await my pleasure, I said.

'If that's the way you feel,' she said, 'there's no more to be said.'

A good deal more remains to be said, I said, and having put her in the picture on the saying score, I got on with the above mentioned saying.

It was the custom in this city, as I was saying, I said, to consume Keftedes the recipe for which had come to them from Austro-Hungary.

'I see,' she said. 'They ate these Keftedes whenever they felt Hungary.'

The recipe for these consumable items to which reference has been made, I went on, is a simple one requiring the mincing of beefsteak. To this is added chopped bacon, crustless bread soaked in milk and then squeezed out, salt, pepper and grated nutmeg. Brisk mixing will result in an homogenous squashy agglomeration that, at first glance, looks so inedible that few persons have the strength of will necessary to turn the head back for a second look. Culinary-minded persons, however, are made of stronger stuff and press on, dividing the agglomeration into hand-sized handfuls, the same to be dusted with flour and placed in fat or butter for the necessary browning. As an optional extra, chopped fried onions can be put on top at the last moment. When the browning operation is completed, the browned item is dipped in concentrated meat stock and served with mashed potatoes and/or other vegetables. All clear thus far?

Citizens of the as yet unnamed city that occupies the heart and core of my story, I said, going about their daily raking in of marks often found themselves, around the stoking up and refurbishing hour of lunchtime, far from home and the domestic Keftedes, as described. Other citizens, therefore, found it a profitable, one might almost say — lucrative activity to leap into the breach, as it were, to open premises and supply the required Keftedes in situ, as required.

Keftedes-supplying establishments sprang up here and there, and it may have been, there and here as well. The citizens responsible found that the mark-raking side of the business ran in a pretty satisfactory way, marks getting themselves raked in at a high rate of rakes. Jack pots were filled as soon as brought into service, fresh supplies of pots (jack) having to be rushed in to cope with the flow. As happens whenever jack-pot hitting takes place, other citizens noticed this inflow of moola (Deutsch) and decided that this was too good an opportunity to pass up. They moved in, opening up further or additional establishments until the citizens of the unnamed city could be said to have Keftedes running out of their ears.

Inevitably, some Keftedes merchants found the going somewhat on the warm side resulting in them making that short journey described as 'going to the wall'. Wall-going became a way of life, the said wall becoming so much in demand you couldn't keep chaps away from it. 'Nothing like a decent wall to go to,' was their view of the position.

Having gone thereto, and the unnamed city having what are termed 'maritime connections', these largely taking the form of supplies of sea water with attached ships, some, or for the purpose of this story, at least one, having got as far as the wall thought that having got that far one might as well carry on in roughly the same direction to see what turned up. What turned up was them (him) on a ship moving steadily in a westerly direction, this continuing until an obstruction bobbed up to block any further progress in that direction (namely, west), the said obstruction taking the form of New York where the Keftedes merchant on whom we are now focussing our attention, got off.

Converting his ideas from mark-raking to dollar-gathering he set about considering ways and means to gather dollars. The first thing he noticed was the remarkable absence of Keftedes-palaces. There was nothing, he thought, more likely to result in a great gathering in of dollars than that New Yorkers should enjoy a ready supply of Keftedes. Setting up the old Keftedes stand, he felt, was pretty sure to result in dollar-gathering of a great order, with subsequent jack-pot hitting.

But, there were snags. A Keftedes merchant newly arrived in New York, having dipped into his depleted pot (jack) to the extent of the fare, meals en route and other necessaries finds himself standing on the quayside at New York somewhat short of the scratch, this scratch shortage obliging anyone considering the possibility of starting a Keftedes empire to set their sights low.

Not for them a plush palace with gay lights, with musicians and music to match, but more something on the lines of a wooden box on two wheels. Coins of the republic must be found for the purchase of the essential beefsteak (minced). But, how are the Keftedes clients to consume same? They can hardly walk about the streets clutching dittoes, dipped in concentrated meat stock and served with mashed potatoes or other vegetables, in their hands. A remedy must be found.

The Keftedes merchant wanders about the commercial purlieus of the city (to wit, New York), turning over in his mind, as do persons with things thereon, this idea and that. The true Keftedes requires quantities of bread, soaked in milk. One thing leads to another and pretty soon he finds himself on the premises of a bread-maker talking up the possibility of laying his hands on supplies of cheap bread.

'Cheap bread?' queries the bread maker.

'Cheap,' confirms the Keftedes chap. Adding, to make the position quite clear. 'Very.'

Every bread maker has his off days and this happened to be one of this bread maker's offiest. With his wife up half the night with the croup — an affection of the larynx or trachea marked by a hoarse, ringing cough and difficult breathing — than which, in his view, none could be hoarser or ringier, his fire had gone out and one batch of buns ended up only half-baked.

'Half-baked buns!' thought the Keftedes merchant.

'What an innovation! What an idea!'

For, in one of those flashes that come every now and then to persons caught up in a things-on-the-mind situation, there had come another thing on his mind that, as it were, cancelled out all the other things, to wit, a solution. Taking down this other thing or new idea verbatim, or roughly notion by notion as it sprung to his mind, the terms now read: instead of crumbing the bread and mixing it in with the beefsteak (minced) why not fry the bs (m) on its own and enclose it in half-baked buns thus supplying the Keftedes-eating public with a handy eatable container in which to consume the said Keftedes, as per specification. Thinking on these new lines fresh notions leapt to his mind which was now pretty empty of things, the original things occupying it having been scrubbed out. To save additional cooking facilities, always a sore point for scratchless persons, why not serve the chopped onion raw?

By now the notion-generating equipment was going great guns, notions flashing out of the machinery like sparks from a knife-grinders wheel. Forget the bacon, said one notion, and bacon was instantly forgotten. Scrub the mashed potatoes, and pots (mashed) were scrubbed in double quick time.

'Any other veg?' queried a thin voice from that rounded bit of the brain that sticks out at the back.

The Keftedes merchant, happening to glance down, saw that his legs, passing through an area recently occupied by market stalls and barrows who from the scene had flown, were knee-deep in discarded produce such as greeny lettuce leaves and semi-squashed tomatoes.

'Lettuce and tomatoes!' piped up another notion from somewhere down the lefthand side of his brain that had not been doing too much during all this mental turmoil.

More things led to other more things and it was not too long before the citizens of New York found on offer in their streets from a wooden box mounted on two wheels, samples of this modified Keftedes.

'Not bad,' they murmured, munching. Or, as anyone knows who has tried to combine murmuring and munching, what came out more resembled '. . .o. . .a. . .' than anything else.

'What's these called, buddy?' one of the more intellectually alert of them asked.

This question posed a problem for the Keftedes merchant. Not because he did not know the answer. What he did not know was the question. Being a n. a. person from a part of Germany more than four thousand miles away his command of the New York argot was defective on about five of the six available cylinders. What, he asked himself, was this New York-type person munching his Keftedes trying to get across to him with words that slid out of the corner of his mouth?

When, many years later than these events under advisement, a President Kennedy of the US of A, finding himself confronted with a large gathering of non-US-of-A-type persons, the place concerned being listed as Berlin (West) on the itinerary in his coat pocket, and desiring to find some form of address these Berlin persons would enjoy and understand, unburdened himself of the interesting statement: 'Ich bin ein Berliner'.

Pre-empting that mode by about a century and a half, give or take, this Keftedes merchant translated the question directed at him as an enquiry into his place of origin. Unbending himself to his full height, but leaving out the sinews-stiffening and the summoning up of the blood, he proudly declared: 'Ich bin ein Hamburger!'

'Well, well,' said the American persons present. 'So, they're called Hamburgers.' and the name has stuck.

When in the ultimate culinary Olympiad American cuisine is required

to show what it can do, it is not by the hominy grit, clam chowder
or cheese-cake that the gongs will be gained. Alone on that isolated
plinth — if plinth is the word — like a five minute miler who unexpectedly finds himself past the post in 3:53, the humble hamburger
will take the gold.

Good husbandry persons wishing to scramble aboard this bun wagon
can follow the classic recipe as outlined here with advantage, needing
to add for the final perfection some modern relish, as it might be, the
Thousand Island or Blue Roquefort Dressing.

But, Americans have grown careless of their heritage. Newly arrived
persons newly arriving thereat find it increasingly difficult to track
down h's cooked in the haute cuisine mould, those currently on offer
being more the concern of persons previously engaged in the boot-
repairing trade.

Citizens of A (US of) wishing to enjoy again that unique blend of
flavours which touching the taste buds releases memories of youthful
days, must return to Europe to do so, where hamburgers of the original
quality are now to be found, some of them even in Hamburg itself.

'What ever happened to that newly arrived person with which you
began?' she enquired.

'In the circs,' I replied, 'need you ask. He's newly left.'

THE FRENCH

It is well known by people who know about these things that the English do not understand the French, nor the other way about. This has partly to do with the fact that those English persons who pride themselves on speaking French use a form of that language that has not yet reached France. Similarly, that branch of the English tongue known only to French speakers thereof would, if introduced to England under that title — to wit., English as English persons speak it — give rise to the accusation that malfeasances were being perpetrated, not to mention torts.

Being English myself, I said, I suffer the double handicap of knowing the language and, therefore, knowing that, in company with pretty well all other English persons, I am less able to understand the English than the merest French person. To balance this incomprehensible incomprehension — if those are the words, I am able to offer an explanation of the French. Not that I understand the French. Who does? But as an outsider one sees things.

Of course, one suffers from the disability of having been to France and actually having spoken to, or attempted to speak to, French persons. To anyone putting together an explanation of France and the French, this is a burden. It is well known that film critics do their stuff best when their minds are not clouded and clogged by having actually seen the beastly film. Equally, only persons who have never slipped across the Channel on a cheap day excursion (and that is another thing one does not understand: why are excursions cheaper by the day? Elsewhere in commerce if one buys in bulk there is a reduction in price. Only with travel does one pay more for buying more, if you see what I mean. Where was I? Oh, yes. . .) can pronounce pronouncements on France and the French as if these were final judgments to stand for all time.

The trouble with pronouncements is that they are invariably

commissioned. They do not spring readily and fully formed to the mind while bath wallowing is in progress, or as the fragile body deck-chairs beneath a blazing sun with liquid refreshment close to hand.

What happens is that Person A — as it might be an editor or publisher, approaches Person B — as it might be and usually is, a writer, journalist or author, with a request for 1200 words on France and the French. The pay for producing same is pitifully meagre, in the view of the said writer, journalist or author (improvidently generous in the view of the editor or publisher) and can only be bumped up to a reasonable level by the claiming of expenses, these expenses having to be justified by the fiction of a trip to France for the purposes of research when everyone knows that the writer, journalist or author in question has travelled no further than to the shelves of his local public library there to consult the works of previous writers, journalists and authors similarly commissioned to pronounce on France and the French, knowing as he does so that the lavish expense claim he will subsequently submit can only be made claimable by the production of 1200 words of a quality known in the trade as 'hot and strong'.

'Pitch in,' the said writer, journalist or author hears from a spectral voice somewhere in the back of his mind, usually the bulbous bit that sticks out at the back. 'Make it hot and strong.' Dutifully, for one cannot ignore spectral voices from whatever source, he pitches in. 'Hot and strong' is the only way to describe the resulting 1200 words.

'Hot and strong' is almost, but not quite, the opposite of what, in similar circs, would be produced by any French écrivain, journaliste or auteur, writing about England and the English. 'Hot' — yes, he might easily go along with that. 'Strong' — perhaps that also. But — 'hot and strong'? Never. It is too much.

This pinpoints the essential single-mindedness of French persons. 'The essential ingredients of life,' declare French thinkers who have thought about the problem, 'like pills to be taken three times a day after meals, can only be taken one at a time.'

'One thing at a time,' echoes the ordinary French person, except that, being a French person, this sentiment comes out sounding rather more like 'une chose à la fois'.

The French person goes to the cinema and there flickers before him the images of Laurel and Hardy.

'What is this?' he mutters to himself in his French way.

'Laurel *and* Hardy?' He does not know where to look.

If he focusses on Laurel, the person Hardy gets up to some high jinks in the other corner of the screen that he misses. He transfers his attention to the person Hardy, and Laurel starts to whoop it up, and he misses that. Eventually, he stumps out to the box-office demanding his francs back. 'Laurel — oui' is his view of the situation. 'Hardy — oui.' But 'Laurel *and* Hardy'? Jamais — or never. 'Une chose à la fois' to his mind just about puts it in a nutshell.

So that when it comes to the question of food — you did realise that we were eventually going to get round to the question of food? Oh, good! — the French homme-dans-la-rue brings to that question the same attitude outlined above. 'Une chose à la fois' is the proper approach to his way of thinking, foodwise.

Take the matter of quality, French personnes-dans-la-rue are of the opinion that quality is quality and cannot be tampered with. The only way that fruit and veg can be purchased with a proper considera-tion being given to the quality thereof, is that every last fruit and veg under the hammer shall be pinched and turned over by the person making the purchase regardless of the full-throated opposition to this technique being put up in a non-stop barrage of French words by the proprietor of the stall, shop or other establishment being the other party to the transaction.

'Pinch your fruit and spare your purse,' would be the French way of putting it if they understood English.

The slanging matches to be observed in any French fruit and veg emporium centre on this confrontation.

The party of the first part does not see why his fruit and veg should be pinched and turned over until the purchase has been completed, this transferring ownership of the said fruit and veg to the party of the second part who can then pinch and turn over same to his/her heart's content.

Meanwhile, the party of the second part does not think it right that he/she should be expected to plonk down good francs for fruits and vegs whose pinching and turning over qualities remain untried and untested.

A disinterested observer of this French scene might see no possi-bility of any agreement being arrived at by these two parties. 'An impasse (from the French 'impasse')' is just about how the observer might describe it.

But the fruit and veg do get their due pinching and turning over.

The francs are plonked down. Business is done. Fruit and veg change hands.

The scenario by which this log jam of attitudes is broken runs roughly in this fashion. The veg pincher and turner over does the required pinching and turning over while the proprietor thereof is deeply engaged in negotiations with other pre or post pinching/turning over operatives. This pinching and turning over leads him to the selection of those fruits and vegs that are considered to be of the topmost quality.

From the corner of his eye, the said proprietor has seen this pinching and turning over in progress and has mentally added a few centimes to the asking price for each pinch and turning over observed. Haggling then begins, the dialogue running as follows:

Party of the first part: M'sieur will you cease to damage my fruits and veg by bruising them with your hands, which are doubtless contaminated by every kind of unmentionable disease...

Party of the second part: M'sieur, is it my fault that you choose to occupy your stall with fly-blown and cankerous produce of such a deplorable low quality that hard-working persons such as myself, for whom every franc counts with nothing left over for even the humblest luxury, must search with time-wasting toil to discover a few samples that may, perhaps, be barely edible...

P. of the 1st p: Is it to be tolerated that impoverished and honest traders who occupy the long hours of endless days with their labour in order to support the loyal wife, numerous children, grandparents of advanced feebleness and infirmity together with aunts, uncles and other more distant relatives...should be flagrantly humiliated and insulted by persons of low breeding and inferior social status...

P. of the 2nd p: How much?

P. of the 1st p: Twenty-three francs.

P. of the 2nd p: Eh, voila!

The P. of the 2nd p. then produces the required quantity of francs and makes his getaway satisfied that the better part of the deal is his, while the P of the 1st p. offers up a silent prayer to his patron saint for allowing him to charge double the going top rate, and get away with it.

But, the P. of the 1st p. does not have a monopoly of the eye-cornering business. The eye-corner has himself been eye-cornered, this eye-cornering alighting upon the latest model of the most expensive car parked just to the rear of the P. of the 1st p's stall. Mentally, he calculates — something all French persons are good at — the volume of fruit and veg trading necessary to finance such a vehicle. And one of those inner spectral voices that has previously informed these pages informs him that in any trading transaction the prices asked are as much a reflection of the quality of the trader as of his produce.

Trader A, the theory goes, has a much larger and more expensive car than Trader B. Along with this tribute to his quality Trader A has a larger house, larger wife and more children. This must be, the argument carries on, because Trader A does more business than Trader B. More people deal with Trader A, because of which he charges higher prices, not that his produce is better than that of Trader B, but because he, Trader A, is a better type of person to do business with. The key word is — 'type'.

'Ce type, la,' say French persons, and once your 'type' has been assessed, your role in life is cast for all time.

'On doit faire le snob,' says another of the spectral voices that have played such a large part in this diatribe, translating itself for the benefit of English persons tuned in to the spectral circuit as 'one must play the snob.'

'Le snobbisme' as all French persons know, is the cornerstone of life. Double snobbisme is even better. Trader B can only afford to run an old 'paneur', or banger. Trader A runs a deluxe car *and* a 'paneur' which he keeps exclusively for his annual trip to the tax man to explain how poor business has been, how little he has earnt, and how small a tax contribution he should make, if any.

Trader A, in the brief intervals between making his first and second fortunes, travels abroad. Travel, he has been told, broadens the mind and mind broadening, he feels, is just what he needs. He has a large car, a large house, a large wife (Oo-la-la!), a large number of children — why not a large mind?

'The mind,' he tells his tax man during the interview in which he submits his travel expenses as deductable business costs, 'should be broad.'

In the broadening thereof he visits in those foreign — what was the term? Ah, yes — mind-broadening places, mind-broadening establishments called supermarkets.

'C'est une chose ca, hein?' he says, thus showing himself to be well up with the big boys when it comes to placing the finger on the nub of a new idea. And yet, all the same — you know how it is, one has these feelings — and he has the feeling that something, some vital part of the package has escaped him. There is something in this supermarket business (or supermarché, as he calls it in his French way) of which he has not secured a proper grasp.

When he returns to France he erects 'un supermarché,' strictly in accord with the original blueprints. 'Voila,' he says to himself, there being no one else to listen. 'Doors this end. Car park that end. Shelves all filled. Trolleys at the ready. Lights switched on. Cash registers open for business. Where is the business?'

The business was still back at the old stall where the P. of the 2nd p. continued steadily pinching and turning over. He had seen the super-marché. He had even been inside. But it confused him. All those shelves, packets, boxes, cartons, bins, baskets, trays, trolleys — where would it all end?

'Where will it all end?' he asked himself, there being no one else willing to listen.

How could business be conducted in such a fashion, he wanted to know? How was one to pinch and turn over produce encased in plastic containers?

And where was the deluxe car now parked? He did not see it any-where about the premises. Did its absence suggest the proprietor was not so prestigiously profitable as previously? A stall, after all, was just a stall. It cost nothing. But this supermarché was clearly somebody's overdraft.

The whole thing made the P. of the 2nd p deeply suspicious and uneasy, and he stayed away.

The P. of the 1st p — now called Trader A — was greatly puzzled by all this. In theory franc-carrying persons should be flocking through his doors with their francs at the ready. Why was this not happening?

Somewhere, he suspected, in one of his cylinders the sparking plug was failing to come up with the vital spark. To uncover the guilty s.p. he financed another tax-deductible trip back to the fountainhead of supermarketeering where the pundits put his wise.

'Supermarkets mean low prices,' they told him.

'Low prices?' he queried.

'Low,' they nodded.

'Not high?'

'The opposite — low.'

'Resulting in low profits?'

'High profits,' they corrected.

'Low prices – high profits?'

'You've got it.'

He thought about this for a few days. Then he raised the question that lay at the heart of his entire commercial understanding.

'High prices – low profits?'

'You betcha,' they said.

So, he returned to France and lowered all his prices.

This distracted the P. of the 2nd p. Pinching and turning over were all very well in their way, he thought. Key stones in the French way of life. But low prices were something else.

And then the old 'une chose a la fois' popped up again. It was Laurel and Hardy time once more.

In offering low prices to the P's of his 2nd p, Trader A decided to spread the sweetness and light down the line to the chaps from whom he obtained his goods.

'If I pay you low prices this will result in high profits,' he told them, paying them low prices.

They, however, stuck to the traditional view that the high profits in question would be his and not theirs.

Working on the Marie Antoinette principle – or it may have been someone else – that cakes command cake prices and bread bread dittoes, the chaps from whom he obtained his goods began to supply goods that matched the prices being paid to them.

Which brings us right back to the bemused P. of the 2nd p wheeling his trolley in a lack lustre way about the premises. For, no sooner did he focus his attention on the prices department, juggling in his mind – something the French do constantly – with this low price against that high one, focussing, as you might say on the Laurel aspect, then things began to hop about in the quality, or Hardy, area. When he turned his attention to the Hardy/quality thing, the Laurel/price boys got up to tricks that he missed.

The poor P. of the 2nd p. tottered from the sm feeling that what he suffered from more than anything was a surfeit of 'choses'. One 'chose' at a time was the way he liked to conduct affairs, and not to have 'choses' leaping out at him from all corners like Mexican beans.

The next item on the agenda, it seemed, was very likely to be something in the nature of a head bursting, his head appearing to be rather much in that condition. The remedy, he knew from previous outbreaks of the head-bursting syndrome, whereby head-bursting had been prevented, was to take the said head to the bistro down the road where his napkin had reposed for many long years in its own napkin ring on the shelf among the naperies of the other regulars. A little napkin un-rolling across the lap, he thought, to be followed by the arrival at table of those traditional comestibles the spilling of which on trousers the napkin was neatly designed to prevent, would reduce the head at the centre of this situation to its normal non-bursting condition.

But, even there, solace was no longer to be found.

'Accentuate the positive,' sings the song writer, mentioning in almost the same breath that the elimination of the negative is also a pretty good idea. And another of life's gentle philosophers has come up with the suggestion that in the furtherance of any particular line of endeavour the best policy is the one indicated by the phrase, para-phrased into French terminology — 'in for a centime in for a franc.'

The bistro, being run, if run is the word when the action in question is more of a shuffle, by one of the indigent relatives of Trader A, as listed above, the accentuation of the positive took the form of centime and franc putting in.

The shelf on which reposed the napkins and rings of the regular clients was torn down and sent away to the local waste disposal unit to be wastefully disposed.

'Regular clients!' bellowed Trader A when questioned on this new policy. 'Tchah!' (Or it may have been 'Pshah!', 'Fchah!' or Kshah!' — it is not easy to get these facts exactly right.)

Then, he added in a French undertone, which is a tone louder than most other undertones: 'High prices! Low profits!' And a sigh escaped him for the dear days that were gone, and he regretted the slack way in which he had conducted his business all those years. Never mind — and a hard gleam came in his eye, like an octopus who has just spotted an unexpectedly large food supply and noticed that about his person have appeared two spare tentacles, this promoting him from the ranks to the status of decapus. Now he was making up for lost time. 'Le monde,' he felt, had definitely become his 'huitre' (or oyster).

A self-service counter was installed with arrangements for clients, regular or non, to serve themselves. Napkin unrolling across the laps was to be abolished, as were laps. Henceforward clients, both non and regular, would be expected to stand at tables to consume the food with which they had self-served themselves, this getting them off the premises more speedily and increasing the through-put.

To Trader A's way of looking at the revised m. o., clients should consider themselves fortunate in being provided with knives, forks, cups, plates and saucers, all absolutely free of charge. 'Chairs, also? — they should be so lucky!' was his view of the position.

It can be imagined that when the P. of the 2nd p, who it is to be hoped you have not forgotten and consigned to those remote crevices of the mind to which recollection seldom penetrates, arrived on the doorstep with his bursting head, its burstability was made even more explosive by being faced on arrival with a curt request to remove his napkin and attendant ring, these having become a drug on the market. When, the force of habit as acquired over the years being temporarily more potent than common sense itself, he took himself to the self-service counter and self-served himself, inwardly mourning the departure of the napkin unrolling elegance of yester-days he was not immediately aware of the Laurel and Hardy aspects of the new regimen.

The first bite-sized portion of what was announced above the counter as 'Fastfood' to reach his mouth gave him the clue. In making his selection he had in a bemused way kept his eye on the Laurel or low price corner, not realising that Hardy, for his part, was going great guns in the quality sector.

'Swings and arrows' was how he put it to himself, not so much bothered that it should be 'slings and arrows', but trying to get across the idea that in the upswings and downswings on the see-saw of life, the dermis, epidermis, Malpighian and other outer layers of the person become exposed to hard pricks.

'Deux choses à la fois,' in his view were just 'une chose' too much.

What was he to do? Should he transfer his custom to an establishment concentrating on the quality side of things, his head bursting condition was likely to be rapidly replaced by one of head shrinkage.

'Quality', say the chaps who run quality places (to be absolutely honest, 'qualité' is the word they use, but I did not think in this instance you would notice the difference) 'is Quality'.

And, they go on to point out that if quality is what you want, quality is what you will get, they being in the business of supplying persons on the lookout for same.

But, quality — being quality, if you see what I mean — has to be paid for and anyone whose inclinations lead in that direction should not expect to be enquiring what quality costs.

'Persons of quality,' declare the chaps who run quality places, 'do not enquire what quality costs. Any person making that enquiry debars himself from being a quality person.'

'How much does this cost?' asks the P. of the 2nd p his head now rapidly debursting, and is, as a consequence of making that enquiry eliminated from the select category of persons allowed to take on board quality meals. Flunkeys give him the elbow. They know how to recognise and deal with non-quality persons.

It may happen that the person at their gate is a Prince of some Realm, pledging the twinkling diamonds and dull gleam of gold in his coronet, against the cost of entry to such a place. 'Take it,' he urges, tears filling his eyes, 'just for a sight, a brief glance, the merest glimpse at the menu.'

The flunkeys examine the said coronet with cold care, its twinkling diamonds and dull gleam of gold impressing them no more than had these items been dross. All is not gold that glisters, they know, but to their view of things, a decent piece of gold should be able to manage a bit more in the way of a glow than this feeble gleam. While as to diamonds, twinkles are no doubt attractive enough in their way, but what they had in mind was something more akin to a sunburst.

Sadly, the Prince turns away. Quality has its price.

At the other end of the scale price cannot afford quality. Here, we must return again to Trader B, who all this while has languished through the pages of our narrative in the shadow of Trader A, whose footsteps he dogs, doing what he does, but never as well, by which one means to convey something so excruciatingly less well as to verge on the abysmal.

Trader B's stall, we remember, was parked at the back end of beyond. When Trader A opened his supermarket, Trader B matched the spaciousness, sweetness and lightedness with something dark, dank and crabby. Persons entering had the distinct impression of vast hordes of malignant spiders held at bay, but only just, waiting to enclose intruders in vast webs.

The 'Fastfood' by which Trader A's self-service launched its attack on the napkin-deprived public had at least the merits of showing some ressemblance to those forms by which food had previously been identifiable. A sandwich still had the outward form of a sandwich. Chips could be seen to be chips. Eggs − if one is prepared to stretch a point − more or less looked like eggs.

Round the corner in that nether world which is Trader B's natural resting place, his self-service offers the franc-carrying public something in the nature of an intriguing puzzle.

Self-service is what the sign says on the door, to be repeated in flickering and faded lights above the facade, and again, as if to make trebly sure the f-c p get the message, above the counter inside. 'But,' the f-c p asks itself, 'self-service of what?'

The impression gained by setting foot inside the premises is that one has entered some kind of macabre wool shop in which skeins of this commodity in a heavily matted condition are being offered for sale for an unspecified purpose.

If a team of little old ladies of advanced years and imperfect vision had been set the task of knitting a replica of a sandwich, basing their design on a fuzzy drawing without ever having actually seen a sandwich, nor had explained to them the theory and practice of sandwich construction, the item to come from their flickering needles would have been quite close to that currently on offer in Trader B's display cabinet, and known to be a sandwich by the plastic sign inserted in it, that said it was.

And, if the same devoted team of little old ladies had been awarded further commissions to exercise their skills in the creation of eggs by embroidery, crocheted chips, tatted toast and brocaded buns, all these would have satisfactorily conformed to the 'motif' of the establishment as already demonstrated by the products on display.

To complete the atmospheric ensemble it is only necessary — a touch of sheer genius this on the part of Trader B — to engage in the running of the place persons with no knowledge of French or any other identifiable language.

So that a person requiring the use of a sandwich and disbelieving the evidence of the plastic sticker declaring that the item on display in the sandwich case is, in fact, a sandwich, within the meaning of the Act, the said person is unable to obtain from the indigent staff any confirmation or denial as to the sandwichness of the sandwich in question.

The would-be sandwich user has to take the sandwich on trust. 'After all,' he muses, philosophically, 'what is a sandwich? What is its essential nature? Are bread and butter necessary to the concept of a sandwich? Are fillings of this sort or that a part of the intrinsic core around which the idea or notion of what a sandwich is, is built?'

After some deliberation, and three sandwiches, he reaches the conclusion that a sandwich is pretty much what a sandwich maker likes to think a sandwich is. If the views of the sandwich maker and the sandwich user happen to coincide, as with the meeting of great minds, there is a fusion, a coming together as it were, around a great central theme. But, if there is no such coming together, no fusion, no meeting of minds as described, who is to say that this person's vision of the sandwich is the correct one, in contradistinction to the other?

'Let each sandwich person enjoy his own vision of what a sandwich is,' muses the sandwich user in question, consoling himself with the thought that this, at least, is the cheapest vision available.

These are the two extremities — if that is the word — of the French good husbandry scene, the pricelessness of quality and the quality-lessness of price. Never, as somebody once said, shall the twain meet, speaking, of course, not of these twain, but two other twain, but the point still holds good, I think. Good husbandry persons (or 'personnes de la bonne économie rurale' — a term which loses a little something in the translation, but conveying the general idea, all the same) seeking to exercise their good husbandry find that the limits to their doing so are these two great forces of quality and price. 'Une chose à la fois,' is just about how French persons sum up the situation. One cannot have both.

While we have been sorting out this vexed question which, having now been sorted out, ceases to vex any further, goings on have been going on back at the supermarché with all the explosive quality associated with great guns, but conveying, in this instance, something more in the way of machine guns, that weapon being suggested to the alert and attentive ear — as it may be, that of Trader A — as he listens to the ceaseless clack of the cash registering. The registerers of cash who accompany the said cash registers keep going like 'chauve-souris' out of 'enfer', bats and hell being the translatable words. In his view, and it is a view confirmed by events, he has out-supermarketed those super-marketeers at whose knees he learnt his supermarketeering lo! those many moons ago.

What now? he asks himself. Has the watershed of the supermarket life been attained? Or, are there further peaks to conquer?

Musing in this fashion, this being a more dynamic variety of musing than the philosophic musing referred to above, he finds the trend of his thoughts leading toward the posing of a question.

'Is a supermarket good?' he asks himself.

'How's that again?' he queries.

'What I mean is,' replies to himself, 'is the idea of the supermarket a good idea?'

'Yes it is,' he confirms.

'If a supermarket is good, must not a super-supermarket be better?'

'Probably,' he answers. Then a thought strikes. 'Except that it could not be called that.'

'Dear, oh dear,' he tells himself. 'Must call it something.'

If there is one thing that French persons are hot on it is euphony. 'Give us euphony or just chuck it in,' about sums up their attitude. And no branch of the euphonic business strikes them as being so much in need of euphonic experts as that brand that goes tooth and tongue with the speaking of the French language. 'If it doesn't sound nice,' French euphonic experts declare, 'it isn't French.' Just to get the thing down on a regular basis they have put together laws saying what is French and what isn't so that French speaking persons know pretty much where they are.

Supermarché, in the opinion of these experts, is just about French. Not great French, but French enough to get by. But, super-super-marché? Dear me, no! they declare, with one voice, as if one person, although, in fact, being lots of persons.

And with the utter logicality of French persons, they go on to ask: 'Can there be degrees of superness?' Is not a super thing already as super as it can be? Anything less than super is not super. Super things are no more nor less than super. For anything more than super some ultra-super word must be found.

Thus the French experts argued, coming — as is the way with experts — to no final conclusion and dropping the ball — if that is in fact what was dropped — back into Trader A's court.

'What,' Trader A asked himself, 'can be more super than super?'

Thumbing through his dictionary (French), something French persons do constantly, so that they can check that what they think is French is actually French and not something else inferior, nasty and undesirable, this attention to detail spreading understanding and comprehension, not to mention sweetness and light, among French speaking persons and those aspiring to be so, Trader A came across the revelation to end all revelations (not that revelations could ever end, they being a growth industry) that the prefix 'super' springs from Latin origins, than which few origins are more inferior (or less superior, if one is not skating a touch on thin ice there). The Romans, after all, were a pretty scruffy lot.

'What is wanted,' Trader A said to himself, there being no one else listening, 'is a nice, solid, decent, respectable Greek word, the Greeks, contrary to rumour and expectation, having a word for most things.

The Greek prefix for 'super', Trade A found out, was 'hyper'. 'Now there's a prefix,' he said admiringly. 'Super — out. Hyper — in,' just about expressed his view of the position.

Thus it was that Trader A's places of business became hypermarkets.

Miss Mitford, many years ago, outlined a way of life in which distinctions were drawn between u and non-u items, these representing, as it were, the credit and debit sides of life's many-paged ledger. The translation in French would read, as has been indicated, u equals 'snob' — non-u equals 'non-snob'.

Suddenly, hypermarkets were 'snob'. Everyone used them. Even, it was said, the President of France himself (you know the chap — can't think of his name for the moment), or if not actually the President, certainly his wife, or if not her, a personal friend of hers or somebody employed by the personal friend. Anyhow, one of those.

This narrative has now brought the alert and attentive reader to the point where large numbers of French persons are flexing their dedication to 'le snobbisme' by going to these hypermarkets, and the said a and a r will now require to know what a hypermarket is, or looks like. That requirement will now be satisfied.

A quick glimpse from a distance conveys the idea that a hypermarket looks like a Las Vegas gambling hell. A longer look from a shorter distance confirms that impression.

It is a square building pinpointed by bright lights. It is more active by
night than by day. Persons come there after the hours of darkness to experience a kind of entertainment. This takes the form of a type of gambling, the fixed rules of which, as laid down by the management stipulate: 'Heads, we win. Tails, you lose'. Music is heard about the premises as if its presence, in some way, contributed to the effectiveness of breathing. The clatter of single-armed bandits, students of these matters discover, is very similar to the clatter of cash-registers.

What, serious good husbandry persons will want to ask at this point, do hypermarkets contribute to the skills, arts, crafts and sciences of good husbandry. Do they breed a kind of hyperhusbandry?

The hypermarket represents a curious inversion of the traditional foot-in-the-door technique of the door-to-door trader. He, as will be recalled, seeks — or sought — to advance his trading position by inserting his foot in the victim's, or customer's, door. The hypermarketeer works the other way about, inviting the victim, or customer, to insert his (or her) foot in his (the hypermarketeer's) door. Just as when the door-to-doorer got a foothold it was difficult for the said foot to be removed, so in these modern times, once the client has got his foot into the hypermarket premises, it is difficult to get it out again.

The ordinary French hypermarket suffers the prevailing 'une chose à la fois' syndrome. Persons entering therein for the purpose of carrying on good husbandry find that 'une chose' is very much 'à la fois'.

'Give us liberty or give us death' was a stipulation laid down by other persons in other times that conformed to this classical 'une chose à la fois' philosophy. Liberty, they felt, was a nice thing to have. All right-minded chaps should be in favour of doses of liberty being distributed among the populace at large. But if, because of a shortage of the said commodity or ingredient, ie., and viz., liberty, there was not enough to go round, then death too was a tidy way of tidying up the untidiness of a libertyless life.

Good husbandry persons are given to laying down a similar stipulation with regard to those marketable comestibles that qualify under the general good husbandry banner. 'Give us quality or give us low prices' they stipulate. Quality, they feel, is a good thing to have. All right-minded chaps should be in favour of. . .etc., you see the point?

What do the hypermarketeers reply? Don't you bother your heads about quality, they answer. Don't you fret about low prices. You just thank your lucky stars that things are going as well as they are. Do you realise the dangerous nature of the commodity that we market for your ultimate benefit. 'Good heavens!' cry the hypermarketeers, raising their arms and voices both at the same time, 'we should get danger money just for handling the stuff.'

'Persons die of food,' they go on. 'Look at history,' they cry out. 'Look at the untold harm food has done' — and they then go on to tell it.

Anacreon was choken by a grape stone.

Bacon died of pneumonia contracted when stuffing a fowl with snow.

Fabius was choked by a single goat-hair in his milk.

Gabrielle (La) died from eating an orange.

Otway, the poet, when starving was given a guinea to buy bread and

choked on the first mouthful.
Philomenes died of laughter at seeing an ass eat his figs.
George, Duke of Clarence, drowned in a butt of malmsey.
Applus choked when supping up the white of an egg (under-boiled).

'Nasty stuff, food,' say the hypermarketeers.
G. h. p's removing their feet from the premises with difficulty trudge
back to square one to have another think.

*   *   *   *   *

The ultimate of good husbandry, good husbandry thinkers have concluded, is a food that costs nothing to produce, is universally available
in unlimited abundance, tastes delicious, can be cooked in numberless
ways for negligible cost, is utterly nutritious and produces no disagreeable effects on the digestion. All known husbandry falls somewhat
short of this ideal in one respect or another.

Manna came close, but even that had to be augmented with supplies
of quails.

The manna as then supplied would fail to conform to present food
regulations without the addition of preservatives, the said manna not
keeping overnight. Bright and cheery persons coming down to enjoy a
hearty breakfast of the said manna are likely to be somewhat put off by
the discovery that during the hours of darkness 'it bred worms and stank'.

Breeding worms and stinking are not qualities now commonly
listed as among the desirable qualities of breakfast foods. Manufacturers
do not list on the side of the package as encouragements to a quick sale,
the information that 'this manna if left overnight will breed multitudes
of worms and volumes of stinks'. Nor do they add that 'when the sun
waxes hot it melteth'.

Those persons seeking to build a manna mountain from any manna
supplies that prove to be surplus to current requirements would be
well advised to take the most serious precautions against melting, worm
breeding and the generation of stinks.

Even though a diet of manna and quails does not seem to be the
answer, good husbandry persons cannot help feeling that the ultimate
in good husbandry lies just around the corner, if one could only discover where the corner is. To which end, good husbandry thinkers
cannot do better than advise that good husbandry is something at
which persons of every kind should have a pop.

'Keep popping,' just about sums up their attitude.